FORMULAE

Mathematics

A COMPENDIUM OF FORMULAE, DEFINITIONS & EQUATIONS

USEFUL FOR

- School Curricula - I.C.S.E., C.B.S.E., State Boards, NTSE & Olympiads
- Engineering Entrance & other Competitive Examinations

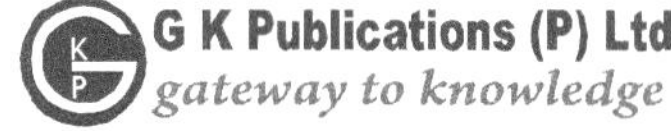

Title : Formulae Mathematics : A Compendium of Formulae, Definitions and Equations

Language : English

Editor's Name : Amit Singh

Copyright © : 2022 CLIP

Typeset & Published by :

Career Launcher Infrastructure (P) Ltd.

A-45, Mohan Cooperative Industrial Area, Near Mohan Estate Metro Station, New Delhi - 110044

Marketed by :

G.K. Publications (P) Ltd.

Plot No. 9A, Sector-27A, Mathura Road, Faridabad, Haryana-121003

ISBN : **978-93-92837-72-2**

Printer's Details : Printed in India, New Delhi.

For product information :

Visit ***www.gkpublications.com*** or email to ***gkp@gkpublications.com***

PREFACE

While appearing for exams with subject like Mathematics, it is very important that one is thorough with key points such as formulae, equations and definitions. This would help a student to solve any kind of problem without chaos or confusion during the exam. But it is not an easy task for a student to run through pages of huge books just to cover up the important points as this involves a lot of time. In such case, a handbook furnished with all important points can serve as a complete solution. Hence in this book the basic concepts with key points have been covered to give the reader the first hand information of each topic in the subject.

This book can be useful for various entrance exams such as:

- School Board Exam
- NTSE
- Olympiads
- Entrance Exam for Engineering & Medical
- Other Competitive Exams

In case of any suggestions for further development, you can share your feedback at gkp@gkpublications.com

All the Best!

G K Publications

CONTENTS

1. Mathematical Notations ---------- 1-4
2. Greek Alphabet ---------- 5-5
3. Table of Multiple & Sub-multiple Factors ---------- 6-6
4. Units of Measurements (Metric Systems) ---------- 7-11
5. Constants ---------- 12-13
6. Number System ---------- 14-20
7. Elementary Number Theory ---------- 21-22
8. Fractions ---------- 23-24
9. L.C.M. & G.C.D. ---------- 25-26
10. Ratio and Proportions ---------- 27-29
11. Time and Work ---------- 30-30
12. Trains ---------- 31-33
13. Clocks ---------- 34-38
14. Calendar ---------- 39-43
15. Rate and Speed ---------- 44-45
16. Percent & Profit and Loss ---------- 46-47
17. Discount ---------- 48-50
18. Savings Bank Account ---------- 51-51
19. Partnership ---------- 52-52
20. Simple and Compound Interest ---------- 53-55
21. Mensuration ---------- 56-66
22. Sets ---------- 67-74
23. Functions ---------- 75-89
24. Statements ---------- 90-94
25. Algebraic Multiplication & Divisibility Principles ---------- 95-96
26. Identities (General Formulae) ---------- 97-98

27. Polynomials -- 99-101
28. Principle of Mathematical Induction ------------------ 102-104
29. Square Roots -- 105-112
30. Linear Equations and Inequations ---------------------- 113-116
31. Surds --- 117-121
32. Real Numbers -- 122-124
33. Binomial Theorem -------------------------------------- 125-131
34. Decimals -- 132-134
35. Calculus -- 135-155
36. Matrices --- 156-170
37. Statistics --- 171-179
38. Permutations and Combinations ---------------------- 180-184
39. Progressions --- 185-188
40. Linear Programming ------------------------------------ 189-191
41. Probability --- 192-194
42. Trigonometry --- 195-216
43. Heights and Distance ------------------------------------- 217-219
44. Geometry -- 220-239
45. Analytical Geometry --------------------------------------- 240-256
46. Complex Numbers -- 257-262
47. Conic Section -- 263-267
48. Vector Algebra --- 268-277
49. Factorization -- 278-279
50. Paper Measure --- 280-280
51. Bodmas -- 281-282
52. Logarithms -- 283-287

chapter 1

MATHEMATICAL NOTATIONS

$=$	:	is equal to
$\neq$	:	is not equal to
$+$	:	plus
$-$	:	minus
$\times$	:	multiply
$\div$	:	divide
$:$	:	is to
$::$	:	is as
$\therefore$	:	therefore
$\because$	:	since
$\pm$	:	plus or minus
$\cong$	:	congruent to
$\equiv$	:	identically equal to
$\vert\vert\vert$	:	similar
$>$	:	greater than
$\ngtr$	:	not greater than
$<$	:	less than
$\nless$	:	not less than
∞	:	infinity
σ	:	sigma
Σ	:	sigma
α	:	is proportional to (or) varies as

$\in$	:	belongs to
$\notin$	:	does not belongs to
{ }	:	set
Θ (or) ϕ	:	empty set
$\subseteq$	:	subset
$\subset$	:	proper sub set
$\supset$	:	super set
$\cup$ or (μ)	:	universal set
$\cup$	:	union of sets
$\cap$	:	intersection of sets
$\wedge$	:	and (conjunction)
$\vee$	:	or (disjunction)
$\Rightarrow$	:	implies
$\Leftrightarrow$	:	implies and implied by
~	:	negation
%	:	percent
.	:	point
$\leftrightarrow$	:	equivalent
$\rightarrow$	:	ray
—	:	line segment
$\angle$	:	acute angle
$\perp$	:	is perpendicular to
//	:	is parallel to
__	:	obtuse angle
$\llcorner$	:	right angle
$\angle$	:	acute angle
Δ	:	triangle
$\square$	:	square

▭	:	rectangle
▱	:	parallelogram
$\odot^{ce}$	:	circumference
$^\circ$	:	degree
$'$	:	foot (or minute)
$''$	:	Inch (or) second
m	:	metre
mm	:	millimetre
cm	:	centimetre
km	:	kilometre
Rs.	:	rupees
π(pi)	:	$\frac{22}{7}$
$\sqrt{\ }$	:	square root
$\sqrt[n]{\ }$	:	nth root of
( )	:	small bracket
[ ]	:	square bracket
—	:	line bracket (or vinculum)
{ }	:	flower bracket (or braces)
$\forall$	:	for all
$\exists$	:	there exit atleast one (or) for some
N	:	set of positive integers or natural number
W	:	set of whole numbers
Z	:	set of integers
Z^-	:	set of negative integers
Z^+	:	set of positive integers
Z^*	:	set of non zero integers

Z_n	:	(0, 1, 2, 3..........n)
Q	:	set of rational numbers
Q^-	:	set of negative rational numbers
Q^+	:	set of positive rational numbers
Q*	:	set of non zero rational numbers
R	:	set of real numbers
R^-	:	set of negative real numbers
R^+	:	set of positive real numbers
R*	:	set of nonzero real numbers
C	:	set of complex numbers
!	:	factorial

chapter 2

GREEK ALPHABET

Α	α	ALPHA	Ν	ν	NU
Β	β	BETA	Ξ	ξ	XI
Γ	γ	GAMMA	Ο	ο	OMICRON
Δ	δ	DELTA	Π	π	PI
Ε	ε	EPSILON	Ρ	ρ	RHO
Ζ	ζ	ZETA	Σ	σ	SIGMA
Η	η	ETA	Τ	τ	TAU
Θ	θ	THETA	Υ	υ	UPSILON
Ι	ι	IOTA	Ω	ω	OMEGA
Κ	κ	KAPPA	Φ	ϕ	PHI
Λ	λ	LAMBDA	Ψ	ψ	PSI
Μ	μ	MU	Χ	χ	CHI

chapter

3

TABLE OF MULTIPLE & SUB-MULTIPLE FACTORS

Prefix	Symbol	Multiplying Factor
Exa	E	$1000000000000000000 = 10^{18}$
Peta	P	$1000000000000000 = 10^{15}$
Tera	T	$1000000000000 = 10^{12}$
Giga	G	$1000000000 = 10^{9}$
Mega	M	$1000000 = 10^{6}$
Kilo	K	$1000 = 10^{3}$
Hecto	h	$100 = 10^{2}$
Deca	da	$10 = 10^{1}$
Deci	d	$0.1 = 10^{-1}$
Centi	c	$0.01 = 10^{-2}$
Milli	m	$0.001 = 10^{-3}$
Micro	m	$0.000001 = 10^{-6}$
Nano	n	$0.000000001 = 10^{-9}$
Pico	p	$0.000000000001 = 10^{-12}$
Fento	f	$0.000000000000001 = 10^{-15}$
Atto	a	$0.000000000000000001 = 10^{-18}$

chapter

4

UNITS OF MEASUREMENTS (METRIC SYSTEMS)

MEASURE OF LENGTH

10 millimetres (mms)	=	1 centimetre (cm)
10 centimetres	=	1 decimetre (dm)
10 decimetres	=	1 metre (m)
10 metres	=	1 decametre (da.m)
10 decametres	=	1 hectometre (hm)
10 hectometres	=	1 kilometre (km)

MEASURE OF AREA

100 square millimetres	=	1 square centimetres
100 square centimetres	=	1 square decimetres
100 square decimetres	=	1 square metre
100 square metres	=	1 square decametre
100 square decametres	=	1 square hectometre
100 square hectometres	=	1 square kilometre
1 hectare	=	10,000 square metres

MEASURE OF VOLUME (SOLIDS)

1000 cubic millimetres	=	1 cubic centimetre
1000 cubic centimetres	=	1 cubic decimetre
1000 cubic decimetres	=	1 cubic metre

1000 cubic metres	=	1 cubic decametre
1000 cubic decametres	=	1 cubic hectometre
1000 cubic hectometres	=	1 cubic kilometre

MEASURE OF CAPACITY

10 millilitres	=	1 centilitre
10 centilitres	=	1 decilitre
10 decilitre	=	1 litre
10 litres	=	1 decalitre
10 decalitres	=	1 hectolitre
10 hectolitres	=	1 kilolitre

Measure of weight

10 milligrams	=	1 centigram
10 centigrams	=	1 decigram
10 decigrams	=	1 gram (gm)
10 grams	=	1 decagram
10 decagrams	=	1 hectogram
10 hectograms	=	1 kilogram (kg)
100 kilograms	=	1 quintal
10 quintals (or) 1000 kgs.	=	1 metric tonn.

REMEMBER	
deca for 10;	deci for $\frac{1}{10}$
hecto for 100;	centi for $\frac{1}{100}$
kilo for 1000;	milli for $\frac{1}{1000}$

LENGHT AND AREA

1 micron (μm)	=	10^{-6} metres
1 Aungstom (A)	=	10^{-10} metres
1 Fermi (Fm)	=	10^{-15} metres
Area (a)	=	100 $metre^2$
Barm (b)	=	10^{-28} $metre^2$
1 kilometre	=	10^3 metres
1 metre	=	10^2 centimetres.

MEASURE OF TIME

60 seconds	=	1 minute
60 minutes	=	1 hour
24 hours	=	1 day
7 days	=	1 week
15 days	=	1 fortnight
28, 29, 30 or 31 days	=	1 month
12 months	=	1 year
365 days	=	1 year
366 days	=	1 leap year
1 year	=	anniversary
10 years	=	decade
25 years	=	silver jubilee
50 years	=	golden jubilee
60 years	=	diamond jubilee
75 years	=	Radium jubilee or Platinum jubilee
100 years	=	century
1000 years	=	10 centuries or 1 Millenium

EQUIVALENTS

The following equivalents enable one to change measurements in one system to those in another.

UNITS OF LENGTHS

12 inches	= 1 foot (ft) = 0.348 metres
3 feet	= 1 yard ("d)
1 yard	= 0.9144 metres
22 yards	= 1 chain
1 kilo metre	= 0.621 miles
1 mile	= 1.6093 kilometres (or) = 1760 yards
1 inche	= 2.54 centimetres
1 hector	= 2.471 acres

UNIT OF AREA

1 square foot	= 144 square inches
	= 0.0929 square metres
1 square metre	= 1.196 square yards
1 square yard	= 0.836 square metres
1 square kilometre	= 0.3861 square miles
	= 1000 hectares
1 square miles	= 2.59 square kilometres
	= 640 acres
1 acre	= 4840 square yards
	= 4046.86 square metre
100 square metres	= 1 Acre
100 ares	= 1 hectare = 1000 sq. mtrs.

UNITS OF VOLUME

1 gallon	=	4.5461 litres = 8 pints
1 litre	=	0.220 gallons = 61 cubic inches
	=	1000 cubic centimetres
	=	17598 pints
1 cubic inch	=	16.38716 cubic centimetres
1 cubic foot	=	28.317 litres
	=	1728 cubic inches
	=	0.0283 cubic metre
1000 litres	=	1 cubic metre

WEIGHT (OR) UNIT OF MASS

1000 milligrams	=	1 gram
1000 grams	=	1 kilogram= 1.072 seer
	=	2.20462 Ibs.
100 kilograms	=	1 quintal
10 quintals	=	1 tonn
1 pound (lb)	=	16 ounces = 0.4536 kg
1 seer	=	0.93 kilogram (kg)

chapter 5

CONSTANTS

1. $\pi = \frac{22}{7} = 3.14159 = 3.1416$

2. $\frac{1}{\pi} = 0.3183$

3. $\pi^2 = 9.8696$

4. $\frac{1}{\pi^2} = 0.1013$

5. $\pi^e = 22.4592$

6. e = Natural base of the logarithms = 2.71828

7. $\log_{10} e = 0.434294$

8. $\log_e 10 = 2.30259$

9. $\log_e N = \log_{10} N \times 2.30259$

10. $\log_{10} N = \log_e N \times 0.434294$

11. $\log_{10} = 0.49715$

12. $\sqrt{e} = 1.64872$

13. $e^{\pi} = 23.14069$

14. $e^{-\pi} = 0.04321$

15. $\log_{10} 2 = 0.30102$

16. $1 \text{ radian} = \frac{180^\circ}{\pi} = 57\ 17'\ 45''$

17. $1^\circ = \dfrac{\pi}{\text{radians}} = 0.0175 \text{ radians}$

18. $\sqrt{2} = 1.41421$

19. $\sqrt{3} = 1.73205$

20. $\sqrt{5} = 2.236$

21. $\sqrt{7} = 2.646$

22. $\sqrt{11} = 3.316$

chapter

6

NUMBER SYSTEM

In the decimal system in use, we represent numbers, however large, by using the only digits 0,1, 2, 3, 4, 5, 6, 7, 8 and 9.

PLACE VALUE CHART OF THE NUMBERS

1. Hindu Number System

Ten Crores 10,00,00,000	Crore 1,00,00,000	Ten Lacks 10,00,000	Lack 1,00,000	Ten Thousands 10,000	Thousands 1,000	Hundreds 100	Tens 10	Units 1
10^8	10^7	10^6	10^5	10^4	10^3	10^2	10^1	1

Hindus are familiar with very big numbers like

(*i*) Mahasamudram = 10^{52} (1 followed by 52 zeroes)

(*ii*) The ancient said that the number of species of living being is 2^{96}.

This is very large number with 29 digits.

(*iii*) They used a unit of time called *Sheersha prahelika* with contain 194 digits.

(*iv*) 1 Thallakshanamu = 10^{53} (contain 54 digits)

(*v*) 1 Asankhaya = 10^{140} (contain 141 places)

2. English Number System

Hundred Millions 100000000	Ten Millions 1,0000000	Million 1000000	Hundred Thousands 100000	Ten Thousands 10000	Thousands 1000	Hundreds 100	Tens 10	Units 1
10^8	10^7	10^6	10^5	10^4	10^3	10^2	10^1	1

In the english system of numeration, an example of large number is a trillion which is equal to million-million.

1 Trillion = 10^{12} (contains 13 digits)

1 Googol = 10^{100} (contains 101 places)

1 Googole plex = $10^{Googol} = 10^{10^{100}}$

BINARY NUMBER SYSTEM (Base-2 Number System)

It represents numeric value using two digits usually '0' or '1'.

This system is used internally by all modern computers.

Sixty Four's Place 64	Thirty Two's Place 32	Sixteen's Place 16	Eight's Place 8	Four's Place 4	Two's Place 2	Unit's Place 1
2^6	2^5	2^4	2^3	2^2	2^1	1

This system is used in computers and electronics.

For Binary systems the number just to the left of the point is a whole number, as we move left, every number place gets 2 times bigger. And the number just to the right of the point is a negative integers, as we move further right, every number place gets 2-times smaller.

e.g. 1011.101

$\Rightarrow$ $1 \times 2^3 + 0 \times 2^2 + 1 \times 2^1 + 1 \times 2^0 + 1 \times 2^{-1} \times 0 \times 2^{-2} + 1 \times 2^{-3}$

= 11.625 in decimal

Decimal →	0	1	2	3	4	5
Binary Number →	0	1	10	11	100	101

Decimal →	6	7	8	9	10	11
Binary Number →	110	111	1000	1001	1010	1011

Decimal →	12	13	14	15	20	30
Binary Number →	1100	1101	1110	1111	10100	11110

Decimal →	40	50	100	200	500	1000
Binary Number →	101000	110010	1100100	11001000	1111101000	1111101000

HEXADECIMALS NUMBER SYSTEMS

A hexadecimal number is based on the number base 16. It look like the decimal numbers upto 9, but then there are the letters (A, B, C, D, E, F) in place of the decimal numbers 10 to 15.

Decimal →	0	1	2	3	4	5	6	7	8	9	10	11	12	13	14	15
Hexadecimal →	0	1	2	3	4	5	6	7	8	9	A	B	C	D	E	F

The number just to the left of the point is a whole number; as we move left, every number placed gets 16 times bigger.

The number just to the right of the point is negative integer; as we move further right, every number place gets 16 times smaller.

e.g. 2E6. A3 $= 2 \times 16^2 + 14 \times 16^1 + 6 \times 16^0 + 10 \times 16^{-1} + 3 \times 16^{-2}$

= 742.6367

ROMAN NUMBERS SYSTEMS

Roman numerals and their corresponding INDO-ARABIC numerals :

Roman Numerals	I	V	X	L	C	D	M
Indo-Arabic Numerals	1	5	10	50	100	500	1000

1. If a digit is repeated a number of times, then value of the digit is added as many times as it occurs.

   e.g. II = 1 + 1 = 2

   XX = 10 + 10 = 20

   CCC = 100 + 100 + 100 = 300

   MM = 1000 + 1000 = 2000

   Note : The symbols I, X, C and M are used upto only 3 times.

2. The symbols V, L and D are used only once in a number.

3. To write a number in which the smallest digit always comes to the right of the greater digit, we add the values of all the digits.

   e.g. VIII = 5 + 1 + 1 + 1 = 8

   XI = 10 + 1 = 11

   LXVI = 50 + 10 + 5 + 1 = 66

4. To write a number in which the smaller digit placed before the greater digit, we subtract the value of the small digit from that of the greater digit.

   e.g. IV = 5 – 1 = 4

   XL = 50 – 10 = 40

   LIX = 50 + (10 – 1) = 59

NATURAL NUMBERS

The numbers 1,2,3,4,5,...........are natural or counting numbers. The set of natural numbers is denoted by N.

Thus N = {1, 2, 3, 4, 5, 6,.......}

WHOLE NUMBERS

If '0' is in included in the natural numbers 1, 2, 3, 4, 5,......., it forms the set of whole numbers.

The set of whole numbers is denoted by W.

Thus $W = \{0,1,2, 3, 4, 5.........\}$

INTEGERS

The natural numbers 1,2,3....... together with '0' and their negatives –1, –2, –3.... are called *integers.*

The set of integers is denoted by Z (or) I

$\therefore$ $Z = \{......... -3, -2, 0, 1, 0\ 1, 2, 3,........\}$

REMEMBER
1. The set of negative integers is $Z = \{........-3, -2, -1\}$
2. The set of positive integers is $Z+ = \{ 1, 2, 3,...............\} = N$
3. The set of non-zero integers is $Z^* = Z - \{0\}$ hence 0' *is neither a negative nor a positive number.*
4. $Zn = \{........0, 1, 2...........n\}$

RATIONAL NUMBERS

A number which can be put in the form p/q, where p and q are both integers and $q \neq 0$ is called *rational numbers.*

The set of rational number is denoted by 'Q'.

Thus $$Q = \left\{x = \frac{p}{q}; p \in Z, q \in Z, q \neq 0\right\}$$

IRRATIONAL NUMBERS

A number which is not rational is called an *irrational number.*

The set of irrational number is denoted by Q′.

Thus $$Q = \left\{ x = \frac{p}{q};\ p = z,\ q = z,\ q \neq 0 \right\}$$

e.g. $\sqrt{2}, \sqrt{3.2} + \sqrt{5}$ ...... etc.

REAL NUMBERS

A number which is either rational or irrational is called a *real number.* The set of real numbers is denoted by R.

Thus R = {set of all rational and irrational numbers}

COMPLEX NUMBERS

If 'a' and 'b' are two real numbers, then the number (a+ib) is called complex number.

The set of complex numbers is denoted by C.

Thus $C = \{a + ib / a \in R, b \in R\}$

$\therefore$ $i = \sqrt{-1}$

Here 'a' is called real part and 'b' is called imaginary part.

SOME IMPORTANT LAW'S

1. *Commutative law of addition :*

$$a + b = b + a$$

2. *Associative law of addition :*

$$a + (b + c) = (a + b) + c$$

3. *Commutative law of multiplication :*

$$a . b = b . a$$

4. *Associative law of multiplication :*

$$a.(b.c) = (a.b).c$$

5. *Left distributive lawa :*

$$a.(b + c) = ab + ac$$

6. *Right distributive law :*

$$(b + c)\,a = ba + ca$$

CLASSIFICATION OF NATURAL NUMBERS

1 is the only unit in natural numbers.

(1) Odd Numbers

A number not divisible by 2 is called an odd number.

e.g. 1,3,5,7,9,11.......etc.

(2) Even Numbers

A number divisible by 2 is called an even number.
e.g. 2,4,6,8,10......etc.

(3) Prime Numbers

A number other than 1 is called a prime number, if it is divisible by 1 and itself only.

e.g. 2,3,5,7,11,13 .... etc.

(4) Composite Numbers

A number other than 1, which is not prime is called a composite number.

(5) Co-prime Numbers

If the Highest Common Factor (H.C. F) of any two numbers is 1 then the numbers is called co-prime numbers.

e.g. 18, 25

H.C.F of 18, 25 is 1

So 18 and 25 are co-primes.

PRIME TRIPLET

The set {3,5,7} of three consecutive primes is called prime triplet.

chapter 7

ELEMENTARY NUMBER THEORY

PRIME NUMBER

A number > 1 is called prime if it has no divisors except 1 and that number.

Twin Primes.

Twin prime numbers are primes differing by 2.

e.g. (3,5), (5,7)

PERFECT NUMBER

A number for which sum of all its factors is twice the number is called a *perfect number*.

e.g. 6 : (1 + 2 + 3 + 6)/2 = 6

28 : (1 + 2 + 4 + 7 + 14 + 28)/2 = 28

1. If 2^k-1 is a prime number, then $2^{k-1}(2^k-1)$ is a perfect number.
2. If a nautral number written as a product of prime factors is equal to $a^p. b^q. c^r$......., then the number of factors it has is

$$(p+1)(q+1)(r+1)\ ......$$

Greatest Common Divisors (G.C.D)

Two numbers are relative prime to each other if their Greatest Common Divisors (G.C.D.) is equal to 1.

Theorem of Gauss

If a, b, c are three natrual numbers such that c/ab and c and a are relatively prime to each other than c/b.

e.g. (*i*) $35 = 5 \times 7$

$21 = 3 \times 7$

$\therefore$ G.C.D.= 7

Hence 35 and 21 are not relatively prime to each other.

(*ii*) 24, 77

These have no common factor > 1

Hence they are relatively prime to each other

FIBONACCI NUMBER

Terms beginning with the third term are formed by adding the preceding terms (i.e. 0, 1, 1, 2, 3, 5, 8, 13...........)

i.e. $F_3 = F_1 + F_2$

chapter

8

FRACTIONS

FRACTIONS

A fraction is a quantity which expresses a part of the whole.

$\frac{1}{2}, \frac{1}{3}, \frac{1}{4}, \frac{1}{5}, \frac{1}{6}, \frac{1}{7}, \frac{1}{8}, \frac{1}{9}, \frac{1}{10}$ show a part of the total of an object.

$\frac{1}{2}, \frac{1}{3}, \frac{1}{4}$ are a new type of numbers. These are called *fraction.*

In fraction $\frac{1}{2}$, 1 is called the numerator and 2 is called *denominator.*

Proper Fraction

It is a fraction in which the denominator is greater than the numerator.

e.g. $\frac{1}{3}, \frac{3}{4}, \frac{8}{13}, \frac{11}{51}$ etc.

Improper Fraction

It is a fraction in which the numerator is greater than or equal to the denominator.

e.g. $\frac{2}{1}, \frac{4}{4}, \frac{5}{4}, \frac{5}{5}, \frac{6}{5}, \frac{17}{13}, \frac{19}{16}$ ...... etc.

Mixed Fraction

It is a fraction in which there is a whole number and a proper fraction.

e.g. $1\frac{1}{2} = 1 + \frac{1}{2} = \frac{3}{2}$

In $1\frac{1}{2}$, 1 is a whole number and $\frac{1}{2}$ is a proper fraction.

$$2\frac{1}{4} = 2+\frac{1}{4}=\frac{9}{4}$$

In $2\frac{1}{4}$, 2 is a whole number and $\frac{1}{4}$ is a proper fraction.

Like Fractions

These are the fractions having the same denominators..

e.g. $\frac{1}{4},\frac{2}{4},\frac{3}{4},\frac{5}{4}$ ...... etc.

Unlike Fractions

These are the fractions having different denominators.

e.g. $\frac{2}{3},\frac{4}{5},\frac{6}{7},\frac{8}{9}$ ...... etc.

Simple Fractions

It is a fraction both of whose terms are whole numbers

e.g. $\frac{3}{4},\frac{5}{7},\frac{11}{8}$ ...... etc.

Equivalent Fractions

Multiplying the numerators and denominator of a fraction by the same (non-zero) number, the results of the new fraction is said to be equivalent to the original fraction.

e.g. $\frac{1}{3},\frac{2}{6},\frac{3}{9},\ldots\frac{100}{300}$ are all equivalent fractions.

Complex Fractions

A complex (or compound) fraction is a fraction in which the numerator and denominator contains a fraction.

e.g. $\dfrac{\frac{1}{2}}{\frac{1}{3}} = \frac{1}{2}\times\frac{3}{1}=\frac{3}{2}$

chapter

9

L.C.M. & G.C.D.

FACTORS AND MULTIPLIES

If a number x divides another number y exactly, we say that

x is called factor of y.

y is called multiple of x.

Greatest Common Divisor (G.C.D).

The G.C.D. of two or more than two numbers is the greatest number that divides each one of them exactly.

The Greastest Common Divisor is also known as Highest Common Factor (H.C.F).

Example. Find G.C.D. of 32, 80, 208

Solution.

32	208	6	
	192		
	16	80	5
		80	
		0	

$\therefore$ Greatest Common divisor is 16.

Least Common Multiple (L.C.M.).

The least number which is exactly divisible by each one of the given number, is called the L.C.M.

Example. Find the L.C.M. of 15, 25, 45

Solution.

5	15,	25,	45,
3	3,	5,	9,
	1,	5,	3,

$\therefore$ L.C.M = 5 . 3 . 1 . 5 . 3 = 225

Formula.

Product of two numbers = L.C.M . G.C.D

$$\text{L.C.M.} = \frac{\text{Product of two numbers}}{\text{G.C.D.}}$$

$$\text{G.C.D} = \frac{\text{Product of two numbers}}{\text{L.C.M.}}$$

chapter 10

RATIO AND PROPORTIONS

RATIO

Ratio is the relation existing between any two quantities of the same kind.

1. Ratio of two quantities a and b of the same kind as $\frac{a}{b}$ or $a \div b$ and is denoted by a : b, and read as a is to b.
2. Order of the terms in the ratio is important. In general for $a \neq b$, the ratio a:b and b:a are different.
3. Ratio of two quantities is an absolute number if it has no unit.
4. In a partnership if investments are in the ratio a : b and the periods are in the ratio m : n, then they share profits in the ratio am : bn.

PROPORTION

An equality of two ratios is called proportion.

Thus a,b,c and d are in proportion if

$$a:b = c:d \text{ (or) } a:b :: c:d.$$

First and the fourth quantities are called *extremes* whereas second and third quantities are called *means*.

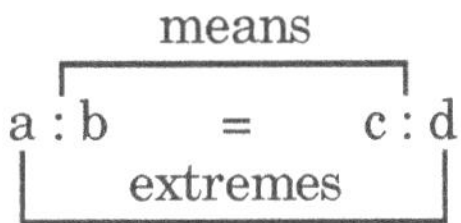

Some Important Points

1. Let a, b, c and d be in proportion, then

$$a:b = c:d$$

$$\Rightarrow \quad \frac{a}{b} = \frac{c}{d}$$

$$\Rightarrow \quad ad = bc$$

$\therefore$ Product of the extremes = Product of the means

2. If a:b = b:c, then b is called the mean proportional of 'a' and 'c'.

Also $\quad a : b = b:c$

$$\Rightarrow \quad \frac{a}{b} = \frac{b}{c}$$

$$\Rightarrow \quad b^2 = ac$$

$$\Rightarrow \quad b = \sqrt{ac}$$

Thus mean proportional of 'a' and 'c' = $\sqrt{ac}$

3. To divide n things between any two persons (say Siva and Ravi) in the ratio a : b, we have

$$\text{Siva's share} = \frac{a}{(a+b)} \times n$$

$$\text{Ravi's share} = \frac{b}{(a+b)} \times n$$

This process can be extended to any number of persons.

COMPOUND RATIO

Ratios are compounded by multiplying together the antecedents for a new antecedent, and the consequences for a new consequent.

Example. Find the ratio compounded for the four ratios :

$$4 : 3, 9 : 13, 26 : 5 \text{ and } 2 : 15$$

Solution.

$$\text{Required ratio} = \frac{4 \times 9 \times 26 \times 2}{3 \times 13 \times 5 \times 15} = \frac{16}{25}$$

NOTE
When the ratio 4 : 3 is compounded with itself, then resulting ratio is $4^2 : 3^2$. It is called duplicate ratio of 4 : 3. Similarly, $4^3 : 3^3$ is the *triplicate ratio* of 4 : 3. $\sqrt{4} : \sqrt{3}$: is called **subduplicate ratio** of 4 : 3. $a^{1/3} : b^{1/3}$ is called **subtriplicate ratio** of a and b

chapter

11

TIME AND WORK

1. If a man can do a piece of work in 25 days, then he will complete $\frac{1}{25}$ of the work in a day.

2. If a man does $\frac{1}{6}$ work in a day, then he will complete the work in 6 days.

3. If A does $\frac{1}{10}$ of the work in 'a' day and B does $\frac{1}{15}$ of the work in 'a' days, then A and B can do $\frac{1}{10}+\frac{1}{15}=\frac{1}{6}$ of the work in a days.
4. Time and work are always in direct proportion.
5. Men and work are also in direct proportion.
6. The number of men and number of days are inversily proportional to each other.
7. If a work is required to be completed in lesser days proportionally, then number of men will have to be increased and vice versa.
7. $N_1 \times R_1 \times D_1 = N_2 \times R_2 \times D_2 = W$

   where, N = Number of men

   D = Number of days

   W = Total work done

   R = Rate of work done per man per day (assumed constant if not given)

chapter

12

TRAINS

TRAINS PASSING A TELEGRAPH POST OR A STATIONARY MAN

Example 1. How many seconds will a train 100 metres long running at the rate of 36 km an hour take to pass a certain telegraph post?

Solution.

In passing the post, the train must travel its own length.

Now, $36 \text{ km/hr} = 36 \times \frac{5}{18}$

$= 10 \text{ m/sec.}$

$\therefore$ Required time $= \frac{100}{10}$

$= 10$ seconds.

TRAINS CROSSING A BRIDGE OR PASSING A RAILWAY STATION

Example 2. How long does a train 110 metres long running at the rate of 36 km/hr take to cross a bridge 132 metres in length ?

Solution.

In crossing the bridge the train must travel its oven length plus the length of the bridge.

Now, $36 \text{ km/hr} = 36 \times \frac{5}{18} = 10 \text{ m/sec.}$

$\therefore$ Required time $= \frac{240}{10} = 24.2$ seconds.

TRAINS RUNNING IN OPPOSITE DIRECTIONS.

Example 3. Two trains 121 metres and 99 metres in length respectively are running in opposite directions, one at the rate of 40 km an hour and the other at the rate of 32 km an hour. In what time will they be completely clear of each other from the moment they meet ?

Solution.

As the two trains are moving in opposite directions, their relative speed = 40 + 32 = 72km/hr,

i.e. they are approaching each other at 72 km/hr or 20 m/sec.

$$\therefore \quad \text{Required time} = \frac{\text{Total length}}{\text{Relative speed}}$$

$$= \frac{121+99}{20} = 11\text{secs.}$$

TRAINS RUNNING IN THE SAME DIRECTION.

Example 4. In example 3 above , if the trains were running in the same direction, in what time will they be clear of each other ?

Solution.

$$\text{Relative speed} = 40 - 32$$

$$= 8\text{km/hr} = \frac{20}{9}\text{ m/sec}$$

$$\text{Total length} = 121 + 99 = 220\text{m.}$$

$$\therefore \quad \text{Required time} = \frac{\text{Total length}}{\text{Relative speed}}$$

$$= \frac{220}{20} \times 9 = 99 \text{ sec.}$$

TRAIN PASSING A MAN WHO IS WALKING

Example 5. A train 110 metres in length travels at 60 km/hr. In what time will it pass a man who is walking at 6 km an hour

(*i*) against it

(*ii*) in the same direction?

Solution.

This question is to be solved like the above example 3 and 4; the only difference being that the length of the man is zero.

(*i*) Relative speed = 60 + 6 = 66 km/hr = $\frac{55}{3}$ m/sec

$\therefore$ Required time = $\frac{110}{55} \times 3 = 6$ seconds.

(*ii*) Relative speed = 60 – 6 = 54 km/hr = 15 m/sec.

$\therefore$ Required time = $\frac{110}{55} = 7\frac{1}{3}$ seconds.

Example 6. Two trains are moving in the same direction at 50 km/hr and 30km/hr. The faster train crosses a man in the slower train in 18 seconds. Find the length of the faster train.

Solution.

Relative speed = (50 – 30) km/hr = $\left(20 \times \frac{5}{18}\right)$ m/sec. = $\frac{50}{9}$ m/sec

Distance covered in 18 sec at this speed = $18 \times \frac{50}{9}$ = 100m.

Length of the faster train = 100 m

chapter

13

CLOCKS

The dial of a clock is a circle whose circumference is divided into 12 parts, called **hour spaces**. Each **hour space** is further divided into 5 parts called **minute spaces**. This way, the hole circumference divided into $12 \times 5 = 60$ minute spaces.

The time taken by the hour hand (smaller hand) to cover a distance of an hour space is equal to the time taken by the minute hand (longer hand) to cover a distance of the whole circumference .Thus, we may conclude that **in 60 minutes, the minute hand gains 55 minutes on the other hand.**

Note :

The above statement (given in bold) is very much useful in solving the problems in this chapter, so it should be remembered. The above statement wants to say that :

"In an hour, the hour-hand moves a distance of 5 minute spaces whereas the minute hand moves a distance of 60 minute spaces. Thus the minute hand remains $60 - 5 = 55$ minute spaces ahead of the hour-hand".

Some other facts.

1. In every hour, both the hands coincide once.
2. When the two hands are at right angle, they are 15 minute spaces apart. This happens twice in every hour.
3. When the hands are in opposite directions, they are 30 minute spaces apart. This happens once in every hour.
4. The hands are in the same straight line when they are coincident or opposite to each other.

TOO FAST AND TOO SLOW

If a watch indicates 9.20, when the correct time is 9.10, it is said to be 10 minutes too fast. And if it indicates 9.00, when the correct time is 9.10, it is said to be 10 minutes too slow.

SOLVED EXAMPLES

Example 1. At what time between 4 and 5 o'clock are the hands of the clock together?

Solution.

At 4 o'clock, the hour hand is at 4 and the minute hand is at 12. It means that they are 20 minute spaces apart. To be together, the minute hand must gain 20 minutes over the hour hand.

Now, we know that 55 minutes are gained in 60 minutes

$\therefore$ 20 minutes are gained in $\frac{66}{55} \times 20 = \frac{240}{11} = 21\frac{9}{11}$ minutes

Therefore, the hands will be together at $21\frac{9}{11}$ min past 4.

Direct Formula

Between x and (x + 1) o'clock, the two hands will be together at

$$5 \times x \times \left(\frac{12}{11}\right) \text{ min past x.}$$

In this case; $5 \times 4 \times \left(\frac{12}{11}\right) = 21\frac{9}{11}$ min past 4

Note : The direct formula is nothing special but a way to write the method in minimum time. If you remember it, you will get your answer faster.

Example 2. At what time between 4 and 5 o'clock will the hand of clock be at right angle?

Solution.

At 4 o'clock, there are 20 minutes spaces between hour and minute hands. To be at right angle, they should be 15 minutes spaces apart. So there are two cases:

Case I : *When minute hand is 15 min spaces behind the hour hand.*

To be in this position, the minute hand should have to gain $20 - 15 = 5$ minute spaces.

Now, we know that 55 min spaces are gained in 60 min.

$\therefore$ 5 minutes spaces are gained in $\frac{60}{55} \times 5 = 5\frac{5}{11}$ min.

Hence they are at right angle at $5\frac{5}{11}$ min past 4.

Case II : *When minute hand is 15 min spaces ahead of hour hand.*

To be in this position, the minute hand should have to gain $20 + 15 = 35$ min. spaces.

Now, we know that 55 minute spaces are gained in 60 min.

$\therefore$ 35 minute spaces will be gained in $\frac{60}{55} \times 35 = 38\frac{2}{11}$ min.

Hence they are at right angle at $38\frac{2}{11}$ min past 4.

Example 3. Find at what time between 7 and 8 o'clock will the hands of a clock be in the same straight line.

Solution. There are two cases:

Case I : *When they are in opposite directions, i.e. 30 min spaces apart.*

At 8 o'clock, they are 40 minute spaces apart.

Therefore, to be in opposite directions, minute hand will have to gain $40 - 30 = 10$ min spaces.

Now, 10 minute spaces will be gained in $\frac{60}{55} \times 10 = 10\frac{10}{11}$ min.

Hence hand will be in opposite directions at $10\frac{10}{11}$ min past 8.

Example 4. At what time between 4 and 5 are the hands 2 minute spaces apart?

Solution.

At 4 o'clock, the two hands are 20 minute spaces apart.

Case I : *When minute hand is 2 minute spaces behind hour hand.*

In this case, the minute hand will have to gain(20 – 2), i.e. 18 minute spaces. Now, we know that 18 minute spaces will be gained in

$$\frac{60}{55} \times 18 = \frac{216}{11} = 19\frac{7}{11} \text{ min.}$$

Hence they will be 2 minute part at $19\frac{7}{11}$ min past 4.

Case II : *When minute hand is 2 minute spaces ahead of the hour hand.*

In this case, minute-hand will have to gain (20 + 2), i.e. 22 minute spaces.

Now, 22 minute spaces will be gained in $\frac{60}{55} \times 22 = 24$ min.

Hence the hands will be 2 minute apart at 24 minute past 4.

Example 5. A clock is set right at 4 a.m. The clock loses 20 minute in 24 hours. What will be the true time when the clock indicates 3 a.m. on 4th day?

Solution.

Time from 4 a.m to 3 a.m on 3rd day = $24 \times 3 - 1 = 71$ hrs.

Now, 23 hours 40 minutes of this clock = 24 hours of correct clock.

or, $23\frac{2}{3} = \frac{71}{3}$ hours of this clock = 24 hours of correct clock.

$\therefore$ 71 hours of this clock = $\frac{24 \times 3 \times 71}{71}$ = 72 hours of correct clock.

$\therefore$ Correct time = 3 a.m. + (72 – 71) = 4 a.m.

Example 6. A clock is set right at 8 a.m. The clock gains 10 minute in 24 hours. What will be the true time when the clock indicates 1 p.m. on next day?

Solution.

Time from 8 a.m. to 1 p.m. on the following day is 29 hours.

Now, 24 hours 10 minutes of the clock = 24 hours of correct clock

or $\frac{145}{6}$ hours of this clock = 24 hours of correct clock.

$\therefore$ 29 hours of this clock $= \frac{24 \times 6 \times 29}{145}$ hours of correct clock

= 28 hours 48 minute of correct clock.

So, the correct time is 29 hours-28 hours 48 minutes before 1 p.m. or 12 minute before 1p.m. or 48 minute past 12.

> Note : The direct formula for the above two examples are found but they are complicated and confusing. So, you are suggested to understand the method clearly and apply the skip-steps rule to get the quick result.

chapter

14

CALENDAR

'Today is 15 August 1995', and you are asked to find the day of the week on 15 August 2001.

If you don't know the method, it will prove a tough job for you. This type of question is sometimes asked in competitive exams. The process of finding it lies in obtaining the number of odd days. So, we should be familiar with odd days.

The number of days more than the complete number of weeks in a given period, are called *odd days.*

e.g. (*i*) In an ordinary year (of 365 days), there are 52 weeks and one odd day.

(*ii*) In a leap year (of 366 days), there are 52 weeks and two odd days.

Leap and Ordinary Year

Every year which is exactly divisible by 4 such as 1988, 1992, 1996 etc. is called a leap year.

Also every 4th century is a leap year. The other centuries, though divisible by 4, are not leap years. Thus, for a century to be a leap year, it should be exactly divisible by 400.

e.g. (*i*) 400, 800, 1200, etc. are leap years since they are exactly divisible by 400.

(*ii*) 700, 600, 500 etc. are not leap years since they are not exactly divisible by 400.

Finding number of odd days.

An ordinary year has 365 days. If we divide 365 by 7, we get 52 as quotient and 1 as remainder. Thus, we may say that an ordinary year of 365 days has 52 weeks and 1 day. Since, the remainder day is left odd-out, we call it odd day.

Therefore, an ordinary year has 1 odd day.

A leap year has 366 days, i.e. 52 weeks and 2 days.

Therefore, a leap year has 2 odd days.

Century, i.e. 100 years has:

76 ordinary years and 24 leap years

$= [(76 \times 52) \text{ weeks} + 76 \text{ days}] + [(24 \times 52) \text{ weeks} + 24 \times 2 \text{ days}]$

$= 5200 \text{ weeks} + 124 \text{ days}$

$= 5200 \text{ weeks} + 17 \text{ weeks} + 5 \text{ days}$

$= 5217 \text{ weeks} + 5 \text{ days}.$

Therefore, 100 years contain 5 odd days.

Now (*i*) 200 years contains $5 \times 2 = 10$, i.e. 3 odd days.

(*ii*) 300 years contain $5 \times 3 = 15$ i.e. 1 odd day.

(*iii*) 400 years contain $5 \times 4 + 1 = 21$, i.e. no odd day.

Similarly 800, 1200 etc. contain no odd day.

Note : (*i*) $5 \times 2 = 10$ days = 1 week + 3 days, i.e. 3 odd days.

(*ii*) $5 \times 3 = 15$ days = 2 weeks +1 days, i.e. 1 odd day.

(*iii*) 400th year is a leap year, therefore one additional day is added.

How does the number of odd days help us in finding the day of a week

(*i*) **when reference day is given?**

Let a question like : January 1, 1992 was a Wednesday. What day of the week will it be on Jan1, 1993?

If you recall, 1992 being a leap year, it has 2 odd days. So, the required day will be two days beyond wednesday, i.e. it will be friday.

(*ii*) when no reference day is given?

In that case, we count days according to number of odd days.

Sunday for 0 odd day, Monday for 1 odd day and so on.

Let someone asks you to find the day of the week on 12th January 1979.

12th January, 1979 means 1978 years + 12 days.

Now, 1600 years have 0 odd day.

300 years have $5 \times 3 = 15$, i.e. 1 odd day

78 years have 59 ordinary years + 19 leap years

$= 59 + 2 \times 19 = 97$ days

$= 13$ weeks + 6 days = 6 odd days

Total number of odd days $= 0 + 1 + 6 + 12$

$= 19$ or 5 odd days.

So, the day was 'friday'.

SOLVED EXAMPLES

Example 1. January 5, 1991 was a Saturday. What day of the week was on March 3, 1992 ?

Solution.

1991 is an ordinary year, hence it has only 1 odd day. Thus January 5, 1992 was a day beyond Saturday, i.e Sunday.

Now, in January 1992 there are 26 days left, i.e. 5 odd days. In Feburary 1992 there are 29 days, i.e. 1 odd day.

In March 1992 there are 31 days, i.e. 3 odd days.

$\therefore$ Total number of odd days after January 5, 1992

$= 5 + 1 + 3$

$= 9$ days, i.e. 2 odd days.

Hence, 3 March 1992 will be 2 days beyond Sunday, i.e. Tuesday.

Example 2. Monday falls on 4th April 1988. What was the day on 3rd November 1987 ?

Solution.

Number of days between 3rd November 1987 and 4th April 1988

= 27 (November) + 31 (December) + 31 (January) + 29 (Feburary) + 31 (March) + 4 (April)

= 153 days = 21 weeks + 6 days

= 6 odd days.

Then, 3rd November 1987 was 7 – 6 = 1 day beyond the day on 4th April, 1988. So the day was Tuesday.

> Note : 3rd November 1987 lies before 4th April 1988, hence the required day will be 6 days before Monday or 7 – 6 = 1 day beyond Monday.

Example 3. Today is 21st August. The day of the week is Monday. This is a leap year. What will be the day of the week on this day after 3 years?

Solution.

Since this is a leap year, none of the next 3 years is a leap year.

So, the day of the week will be 3 days beyond Monday, i.e. it will be Thursday.

Example 4. It was Thursday on 2nd January 1993. What day of the week will be on 15th March 1993 ?

Solution.

Total number of days = 29 (January) + 28 (Feburary) + 15 (March)

= 72 days = 10 weeks + 2 days

= 2 odd days.

Thus, the given date will fall on two days beyond Thursday, i.e. Saturday.

Example 5. The first Republic Day of India was celebrated on 26th January 1950. What was the day of the week on that date ?

Solution.

Total number of odd days

= 1600 years have 0 odd day + 300 years have 1 odd day
+ 49 years (12 leap + 37 ordinary) have 5 odd odd days
+ 26 days of January have 5 odd days.

= 0 + 1 + 5 + 5

= 4 odd days.

So, the day was Thursday.

chapter

15

RATE AND SPEED

1. Distance = Time × Speed

2. Speed = $\frac{\text{Distance}}{\text{Time}}$

3. Time = $\frac{\text{Distance}}{\text{Speed}}$

4. 1 km/hour = $\frac{5}{18}$ m/sec.

5. 1 m/sec. = $\frac{18}{5}$ km/hour

6. If ratio of the speeds of A and B is a : b, then ratio of the times taken by them to cover the same distance is $\frac{1}{a} : \frac{1}{b}$ or b : a.

7. Let a man covers a certain distance at x kmph and an equal distance at y kmph, then

   average speed during the whole journey = $\frac{(2xy)}{(x+y)}$ kmph.

8. Time taken by a train to cross a telegraphic pole or a standing person

   $$= \frac{\text{Length of the train}}{\text{Speed of the train}}$$

9. Time taken by a train to cross a bridge

   $$= \frac{\text{Length of the train} + \text{Length of the bridge}}{\text{Speed of the train}}$$

10. Relative speed while moving in *opposite directions* is equal to the sum of the speeds.

    Relative speed while moving in the *same direction* is equal to the difference of the speeds.

11. Time taken by two moving objects to meet

$$= \frac{\text{Distance between them}}{\text{Relative speed}}$$

chapter 16

PERCENT & PROFIT AND LOSS

PERCENT

The word 'percent' means 'per hundred' or 'out of hundred'. The symbol % is used to express the phrase 'percent'.

Thus, $7\% = 7 \text{ out of } 100 = \frac{7}{100}$.

1. To convert % into common fraction, divide by 100.

   e.g. $5\% = \frac{5}{100}$

   $7.5\% = \frac{7.5}{100}$

2. To convert common fraction into %, multiply by 100.

   e.g. $\frac{2}{5} = \frac{2}{5}$ $100\% = 40\%$

3. If there is an increase of x% in a quantity, then its value increase by (100 + x)% over its original value.

   Multiplying fraction to get the increased values is $\frac{100+x}{100}$.

4. If there is a decrease of x% in a quantity, then its value decreased by (100 – x) % over its original value.

   Multiplying fraction to get the decreased value is $\frac{100-x}{100}$.

COST PRICE

The price which a customer or a shopkeeper pays for an article at the time of purchasing is called its Cost Price (C.P) or Prime Cost.

SELLING PRICE

The price which a shopkeeper gets by selling an article is called its selling price (S.P).

$$\text{Profit} = \text{Selling Price} - \text{Cost Price (S.P.} - \text{C.P.)}$$

$$\text{Loss} = \text{Cost Price} - \text{Selling Price (C.P.} - \text{S.P.)}$$

Note : Profit and loss are always calculated on cost price.

$$\text{Profit\%} = \frac{(\text{S.P.} - \text{C.P.})}{\text{C.P.}} \quad 100$$

$$\text{Loss\%} = \frac{(\text{C.P.} - \text{S.P.})}{\text{C.P.}} \quad 100$$

$$\text{S.P.} = \frac{\text{C.P.} \times (100 - \text{Loss\%})}{100} \text{ (in case of Loss)}$$

$$\text{S.P.} = \frac{\text{C.P.} \times (100 + \text{Profit\%})}{100} \text{ (in case of Gain)}$$

$$\text{C.P.} = \frac{\text{S.P.} \times 100}{(100 + \text{profit\%})} \text{ (in case of Gain)}$$

$$\text{C.P.} = \frac{\text{S.P.} \times 100}{(100 - \text{Loss\%})} \text{ (in case of Loss)}$$

Note : Profit and loss percent (%) is the gain or loss on every100 of the cost price.

If (S.P.) > (C.P.), there is a gain.

If (S.P.) < (C.P.), there is a loss.

chapter 17

DISCOUNT

DISCOUNT

The amount deducted from the bill for cash payment is called discount.

$$\text{Discount} = \text{Sum due} - \text{Present worth.}$$

$$\text{Present worth} = \text{Sum payable} - \text{Discount}$$

$$\text{Sum due} = \frac{\text{S.I} \times \text{Discount}}{\text{S.I} - \text{Discount}}$$

CASH DISCOUNT

Cash discount is allowed to a retailer when he makes payment promptly or within stated period. The more the delay in making payment, the less the cash discount, i.e. the rates of cash discount vary from 1% to 5% according to the terms stated on the bill. Generally the terms are stated in the following ways.

Cash 5%, $\frac{3}{10}, \frac{2}{20}, \frac{n}{30}$

(*i*) Cash 5% means the cash discount of 5% will be allowed if payment is made on the spot promptly.

(*ii*) $\frac{3}{10}$ means that cash discount of 3% will be allowed if payment is made within 10 days.

(*iii*) $\frac{2}{20}$ means that cash discount of 2% on the amount of the bill will be allowed if it is paid upto the 20th day.

(*iv*) $\frac{n}{30}$ means that the net amount is due in 30 days after the date of the bill. The retailer is not entitled to any cash discount.

RETAIL DISCOUNT

In order to dispose off old, perishable or damaged goods, the dealers announce a special concession to their customers in the name of clearance sale. The amount offered as concession on such occasions is called retail *discount or retailers discount.* The original price is called the *marked price.* The retail discount is expressed as percent or a fraction of the marked price. The price which the customer pays for the goods is called the *selling price.*

TRADE DISCOUNT

The manufacturers who issue the list of various articles manufactured by them allow a discount on the list price. It is called the trade discount. Sometimes two or more discounts are applicable successively to a list price. They constitute a discount series. The first discount in the series is applied to the resulting price etc.

Example 1. Find the retails discount on a coat marked at Rs.80 and discounted at 15%.

Solution.

Marked price of the coat = Rs.80

Retail discount = 15%

Retail discount on Rs.100 = Rs.15

$\therefore$ Retails discount on Rs. 80 = Rs. $\left(\frac{15}{100}\right) \times 80$ = Rs.12

Example 2. A sofa set lists at Rs.650 and is quoted at 25% off on the list price. What is the cost price of the customer?

Solution.

Marked price of the sofa set = Rs. 650

Discount of the list price = 25%

$\therefore$ Actual discount allowed $= \left(\dfrac{25}{100}\right) \times 650 = \text{Rs.}162.50$

$\therefore$ Cost price of the customer $= \text{Rs.}650 - \text{Rs.}162.50$

$= \text{Rs.}487.50$

chapter 18

SAVINGS BANK ACCOUNT

Rules of Saving Bank Account in any nationalised bank.

1. Interest will be calculated for each calendar month on the lowest balance at credit between the 11th day and the end of the month.
2. Interest will be calculated at the rate of 5% per year after adjusting the amount to the nearest rupee.
3. Interest will be credited every six months that is in March and September for every year. Interest so calculated will be added to the principle and will form a part of the principle for the next six months.

chapter

19

PARTNERSHIP

Partnership is an association of two or more persons who put their money together in order to carry on a certain business.

Types. It is of two types.

1. **Simple partnership**
   If capital of the partners are invested for the same period, the partnership is called simple partnership.
2. **Compound partnership**
   If capital of the partners are invested for different lengths of time, then the partnership is called compound partnership.

Example. Three partners A, B and C invest Rs.1,600, Rs.1,800 and Rs.2,300 respectively in business. How should they divide a profit of Rs.1938 ?

Solution.

Profit should be divided in the ratios of the capitals, i.e. in the ratio 16:18:23.

Now, $16 + 18 + 23 = 57$

A's share $= \frac{16}{57}$ of Rs. 1,938 = Rs.544

B's share $= \frac{18}{57}$ of Rs. 1,938 = Rs.612

C's share $= \frac{23}{57}$ of Rs. 1,938 = Rs.782

chapter

20

SIMPLE AND COMPOUND INTEREST

INTEREST

It is the money paid for the use of money borrowed. It is generally a percentage of the sum borrowed. It is paid quarterly, half yearly or annually as agreed upon.

PRINCIPLE (P)

The actual money he borrowed is called principle.

AMOUNT (A)

The principle together with its interest is called amount.

RATE PERCENT PER ANNUM (R)

The sum paid on Rs. 100 of the loan for a year is called the rate percent per annum.

SIMPLE INTEREST

If throughout the loan period, interest is charged on the original sums borrowed (i.e. principal), it is called simple interest (S.I).

Formulae

1. Simple Interest (S.I.) $= \dfrac{P \times T \times R}{100}$

2. Principle (P) $= \dfrac{S.I. \times 100}{R \times T}$

3. Time (T) = $\dfrac{\text{S.I.} \times 100}{\text{P} \times \text{R}}$

4. Rate (R) = $\dfrac{\text{S.I.} \times 100}{\text{P} \times \text{T}}$

5. Amount (A) = Principle + Simple interest

6. To find out principle when amount is given

$$P = \frac{A \times 100}{100 + TR}$$

7. Amount (A) = $P\left(I + \dfrac{TR}{100}\right)$

where, A = amount

P = principle

T = number of years

R = rate % per annum

COMPOUND INTEREST

Money is said to be lent at compound interest when the interest due after a given time is added to the principal goes on increasing at the end of every year by an amount to the interest for that year. Difference between final amount and the original principle is called *compound interest.*

(*i*) *When interest is compounded annually :*

$$\text{Amount(A)} = P\left(I + \frac{R}{100}\right)^n$$

where, n = time in years.

(*ii*) Compound interest = Amount – Principle

(*iii*) Principle (P) = $\dfrac{A}{\left(1 + \dfrac{R}{100}\right)^n} = P\left[\left(1 + \dfrac{R}{100}\right)^n - 1\right]$

(*iv*) When rates are different for different years, say $R_1\%$, $R_2\%$, $R_3\%$ for 1st, 2nd and 3rd year respectively

then Amount $= P\left[1+\frac{R_1}{100}\right]\left[1+\frac{R_2}{100}\right]\left[1+\frac{R_3}{100}\right]$

REMEMBER
1. Compound interest for one year is equal to the simple interest for one year.
2. Difference between C.I. and S.I. on the same sum for 2 years is one year interest on the S.I. for 1 year.

chapter

21

MENSURATION

The word 'Mensuration' is derived from the Greek word 'Mensurato' meaning to measure and refers to that branch of geometry which deals with measurement of length, areas, volumes and so on.

AREAS AND DIMENSIONS OF PLANE FIGURES

1. Square

If the side of a square 'a', then

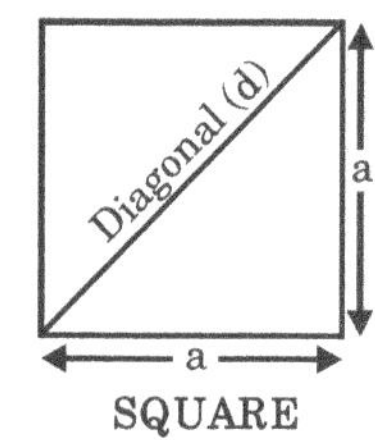

SQUARE

$$\text{Area (A)} = \text{side} \times \text{side} = (\text{side})^2 = a^2$$

$$\text{Side (a)} = \sqrt{\text{area}}$$

$$\text{Perimeter} = 4 \times \text{side} = 4a$$

$$\text{Diagonal (d)} = \sqrt{2(\text{side})^2} = \sqrt{2 \times \text{area}}$$

2. Rectangle

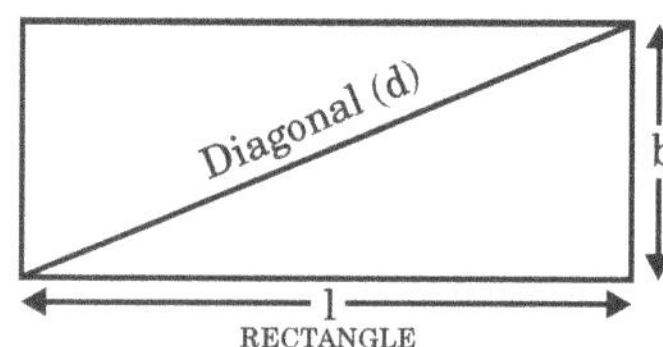

RECTANGLE

$$\text{Area (A)} = \text{Length} \times \text{Breadth} = l \times b$$

$$\text{Perimeter} = 2(\text{length} + \text{breadth})$$

$$= 2(l + b)$$

$$\text{Diagonal (d)} = \sqrt{l^2 + b^2}$$

3. **Parallelogram**

$$\text{Area (A)} = \text{Base} \times \text{Height}$$
$$= b \times h$$

$$\text{Base (b)} = \frac{\text{Area(A)}}{\text{Height(h)}}$$

$$\text{Height (h)} = \frac{\text{Area(A)}}{\text{Base(b)}}$$

4. **Rhombus**

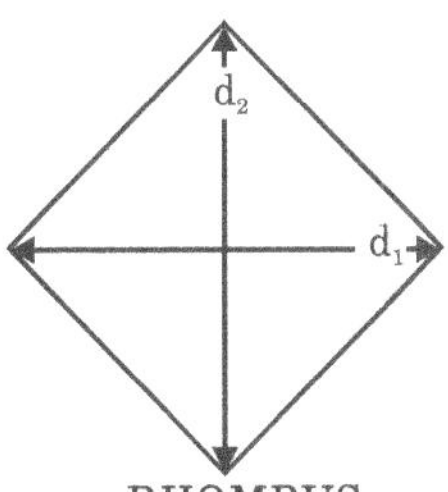

RHOMBUS

$$\text{Area (A)} = \frac{1}{2} \times \text{Product of its diagonals}$$
$$= \frac{1}{2} \times d_1 \times d_2$$

5. **Trapezium**

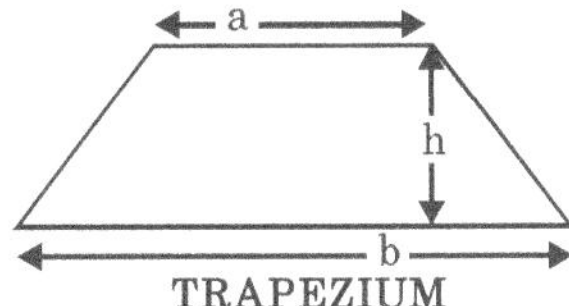

TRAPEZIUM

$$\text{Area (A)} = \frac{1}{2}\ (\text{Sum of parallel sides} \times \text{Height})$$
$$= \frac{1}{2}\ (a + b)\ h$$

6. **Trapezoid**

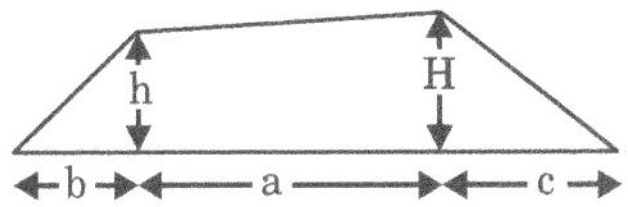

$$\text{Area (A)} = \frac{(H + h)a + bh + cH}{2}$$

A trapezoid can also be divided into two triangles. The area of each of these triangles is calculated and the result added to find the area of trapezoid.

7. **Right-angled Triangle**

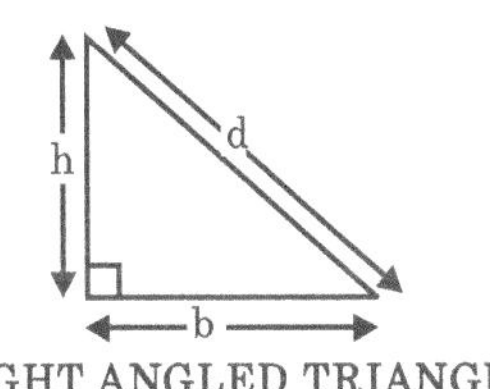

RIGHT ANGLED TRIANGLE

$$\text{Area (A)} = \frac{1}{2} \times \text{base} \times \text{height}$$
$$= \frac{1}{2} bh$$

Here $d^2 = b^2 + h^2$

$\therefore$ $d = \sqrt{b^2 + h^2}$

$b = \sqrt{d^2 - h^2}$

$h = \sqrt{d^2 - b^2}$

8. Acute-angled Triangle

Area (A) = $\sqrt{s(s-a)(s-b)(s-c)}$

where $s = \dfrac{a+b+c}{2}$

s is the semi-perimeter of the triangle

$$A = \frac{bh}{2} = \frac{b}{2}\sqrt{a^2 - \left(\frac{a^2 + b^2 - c^2}{2b}\right)^2}$$

9. Obtuse-angled Triangle

Area (A) = $\sqrt{s(s-a)(s-b)(s-c)}$

where, $s = \dfrac{a+b+c}{2}$

$$A = \frac{bh}{2}$$

$$= \frac{h}{2}\sqrt{a^2 - \left(\frac{c^2 - a^2 - b^2}{26}\right)^2}$$

10. Circle

Area of circle (A) = $\dfrac{22}{7} r^2 \left(\because \pi = \dfrac{22}{7}\right)$

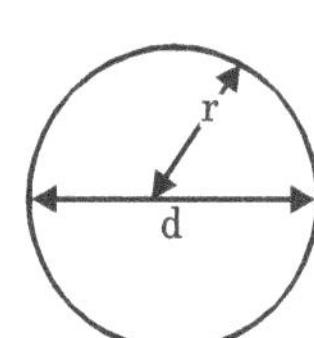

Circumference of circle = $2\pi r$

Diameter = $2 \times$ radius

11. Semi-circle

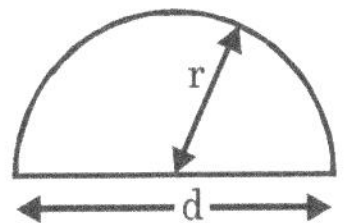

$$\text{Area (A)} = \frac{1}{2}\pi r^2$$

$$\text{Circumference} = \pi r + 2r = \frac{36}{7} r$$

12. Circular Sector

Let l = length of the arc,

θ = angle in degrees

$$\text{Area of sector (a)} = \frac{\theta}{360^\circ} \times \pi r^2$$

$$= \frac{1}{2}(\text{arc} \times r) = \frac{1}{2} \times l \times r$$

$$\text{Length of the arc } (l) = \frac{\theta}{360^\circ} \times 2\pi r$$

13. Circular Ring

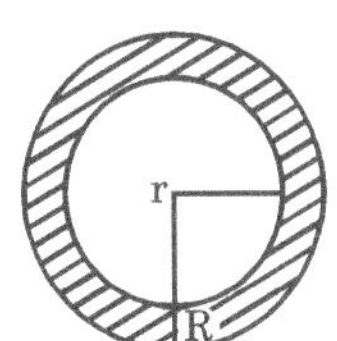

$$\text{Area (A)} = R^2 - r^2$$

$$= (R + r)(R - r)$$

14. Ellipse

$$\text{Area (A)} = \pi ab$$

$$\text{Perimeter (P)} = \pi\sqrt{2(a^2 + b^2)}$$

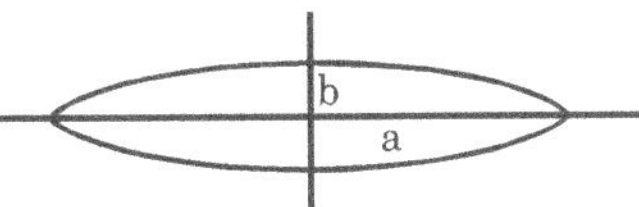

VOLUME OF SOLIDS

1. Cube

If 'a' is edge of the cube, then

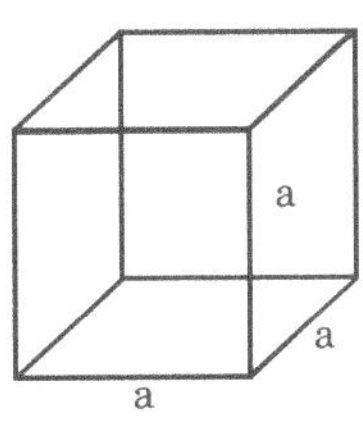

$$\text{Volume} = a^3$$

$$\text{Total surface area} = 6a^2$$

$$\text{Diagonal of the cube} = \sqrt{3} \times \text{edge}$$

$$= \sqrt{3} \times a$$

$$\text{Edge of a cube} = 3\sqrt{\text{volume}}$$

2. Cuboid

Let l = length,

b = breadth

h = height or depth of a cuboid, then

Volume = length × breadth × height

$= l \times b \times h$

$$\text{Length (l)} = \frac{\text{Volume}}{b \times h},$$

$$\text{Breadth (b)} = \frac{\text{Volume}}{l \times h}$$

$$\text{Height (h)} = \frac{\text{Volume}}{l \times b}$$

Total surface area = $2(lb + bh + hl)$

Diagonal of a cuboid = $\sqrt{l^2 + b^2 + h^2}$

3. Cylinder

Let r = radius of the base

h = height of the cylinder

d = diameter of the base, then

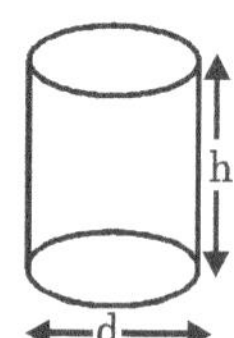

Area of the curved surface

$= 2\pi rh = \pi dh$

Total surface area = $2\pi r(h + r)$

$$= \pi d\left(\frac{d}{2} + h\right)$$

Volume of the cylinder = $\pi r^2 h = 0.7854\ d^2h$

4. Hollow Cylinder

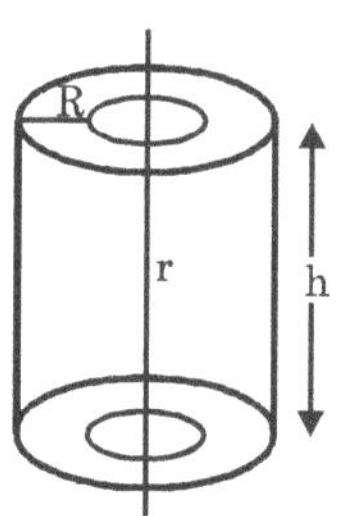

Volume of the hollow cylinder

$= (\pi R^2 - \pi r^2)\, h$

$= \pi(R^2 - r^2)h$

Area of the curved surface

$$= (2\pi Rh + 2\pi rh)$$
$$= 2\pi (R + r)h$$

Total surface area

$$= \text{area of curved surface} + 2\,(\text{area of base})$$
$$= 2\pi (R + r)h + 2\pi (R^2 - r^2)$$
$$= 2\pi (R + r)\, h + 2\pi (R + r)(R - r)$$
$$= 2\pi (R + r)(h + R - r)$$

5. Cone

Let s = slant height

r = radius of the base

h = vertical height, then

Area of curved surface $= \pi rs = \pi r\sqrt{(h^2 + r^2)}$

Total surface area = curved surface + area of the base

$$= \pi rs + \pi r^2 = \pi r\,(s + r)$$

Volume of the cone $= \dfrac{1}{3}\pi r^2 h$

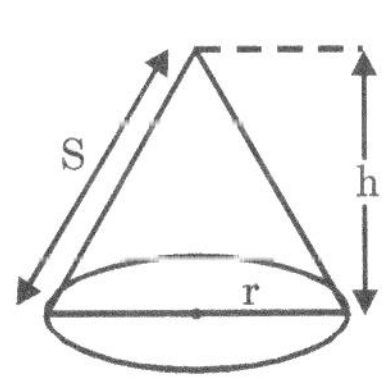

Also, $s^2 = h^2 + r^2$

$$s = \sqrt{h^2 + r^2}$$
$$h = \sqrt{s^2 - r^2}$$
$$r = \sqrt{s^2 - h^2}$$

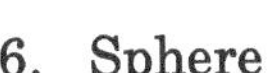
6. Sphere

Let r = radius of the sphere

d = diameter of the sphere, then

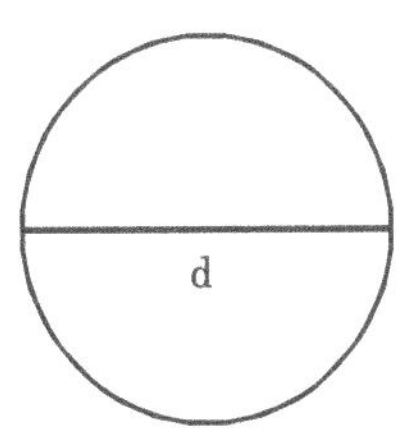

Surface area $= 4\pi r^2 = \pi d^2$

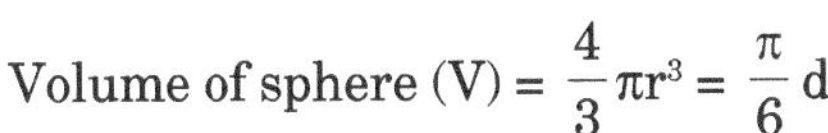
Volume of sphere (V) $= \dfrac{4}{3}\pi r^3 = \dfrac{\pi}{6} d^3$

Also, $r = 3\sqrt{\dfrac{3V}{4\pi}}$

7. Hallow Sphere

Volume of the hallow sphere

$$= \frac{4}{3}\pi R^3 - \frac{4}{3}\pi r^3$$

$$= \frac{4}{3}\pi R^3 - \frac{4}{3}\pi r^3 = \frac{4}{3}\pi(R^3 - r^3)$$

$$= \frac{\pi}{6}(D^3 - d^3)$$

8. Triangular Prism

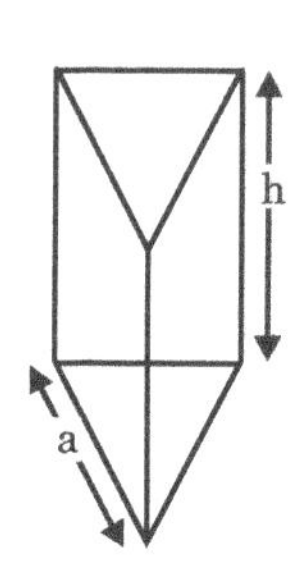

Area of triangle $= \frac{1}{2} \times \text{base} \times \text{height}$

$$= \sqrt{s(s-a)(s-b)(s-c)}$$

where, $s = \frac{a+b+c}{2}$

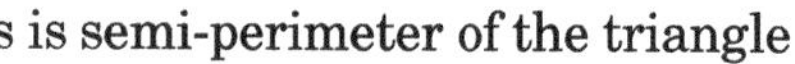
s is semi-perimeter of the triangle

Area of equilateral triangle $= \frac{\sqrt{3}}{4}(\text{side})^2 = \frac{\sqrt{3}}{4}a^2$

Volume $= A \times h = \frac{\sqrt{3}}{4}a^2 \times h$

Total surface area = Lateral surface + Sum of areas of two ends

$$= ah + ah + ah + \frac{\sqrt{3}}{4}a^2$$

$$= 3ah + \frac{\sqrt{3}}{4}a^2$$

9. Pentagonal Prism

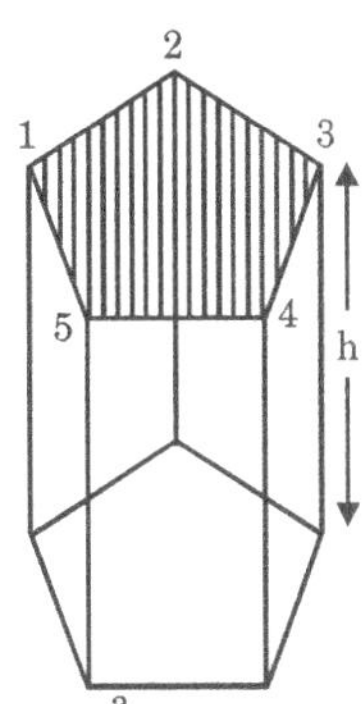

Surface area of pentagon = $\sqrt{3}\ a^2$

Volume = $\sqrt{3}\ a^2 \times h$

Total surface area

$$= 5\ ah + 2\sqrt{3}\ a^2$$

10. Hexagonal Prism

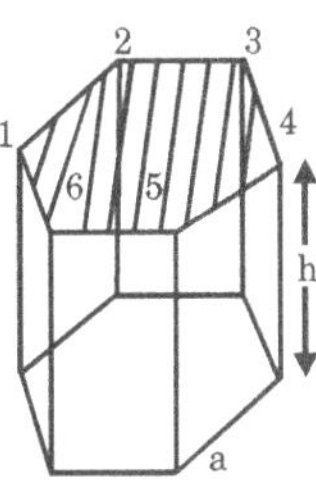

Surface area of the hexagonal (A) = $2.5981\ a^2$

Volume = $A \times h = 2.5981\ a^2 \times h$

Total surface area

$$= 6ah + 2 \times 2.5981\ a^2$$

11. Square Pyramid

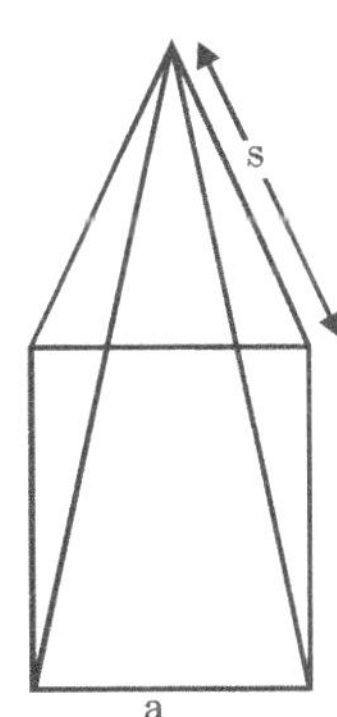

Area of lateral surface of the pyramid

$$= \frac{1}{2}(\text{perimeter}) \times \text{slant height}$$

$$= \frac{1}{2} \times 4a \times s$$

where, s = slant height

$$\text{Volume} = \frac{1}{3} \times h \times \text{area of the base}$$

$$= \frac{1}{3} \times h \times a^2$$

Total area of the pyramid

$$= \frac{1}{2} \times 4a \times s + a^2$$

12. Triangular Pyramid

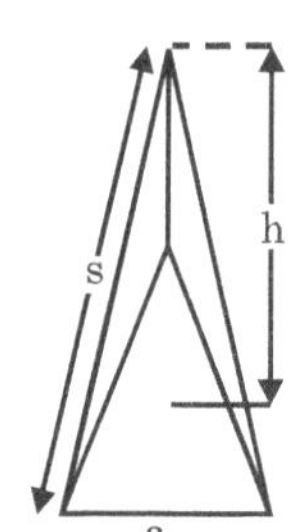

Area of lateral surface of the pyramid

$$= \frac{1}{2}\ (\text{perimeter}) \times (\text{slant height})$$

$$= \frac{1}{2} \times 3a \times s (s = \text{slant height})$$

$$\text{Volume} = \frac{1}{3} \times h \times \text{area of base}$$

$$= \frac{1}{3} h \times \frac{\sqrt{3}}{4} a^2$$

$$\text{Total area of the pyramid} = \frac{1}{2} 3as + \frac{\sqrt{3}}{4} a^2$$

13. Pentagonal Pyramid

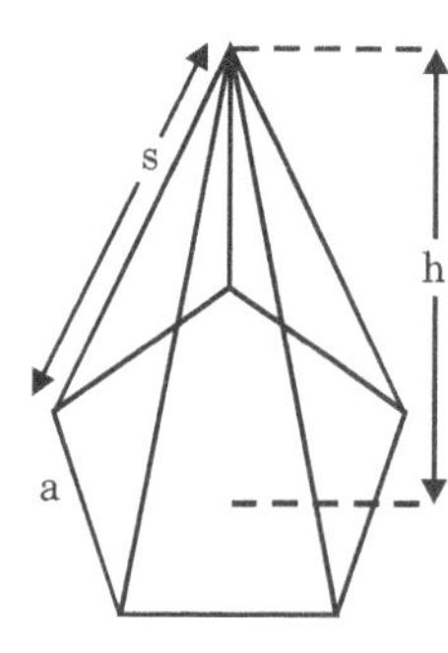

Total area of the pyramid

$$= \frac{1}{2} \times 5as + \sqrt{3}\ a^2$$

where, s is slant height

$$\text{Volume} = \frac{1}{3}\ h \times \text{area of base}$$

$$= \frac{1}{3} h \times \sqrt{3}\ a^2$$

14. Hexagonal Pyramid

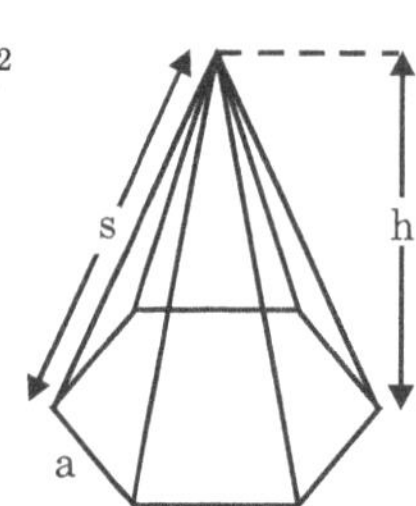

$$\text{Total surface area} = \frac{1}{2} \times 6as + 2.5981\ a^2$$

where s is slant height

$$\text{Volume} = \frac{1}{3} h \times \text{area of the base}$$

$$= \frac{1}{3} h \times 2.5981\ a^2$$

15. Area of the four walls of a room

(i) If l, b and h are the length, breadth and height, then

Total area of the four walls (A)

$$= \text{height of the room} \times \text{perimeter of the floor}$$

$$= h \times (2l + 2b)$$

$$= 2h (l + b)$$

(ii) If floor of a room is in the shape of a square whose side is l and h is height of the room, then total area of the four walls,

A = 4th square units.

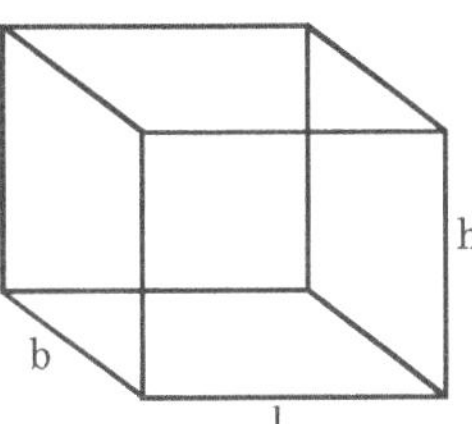

16. Rectangle Paths

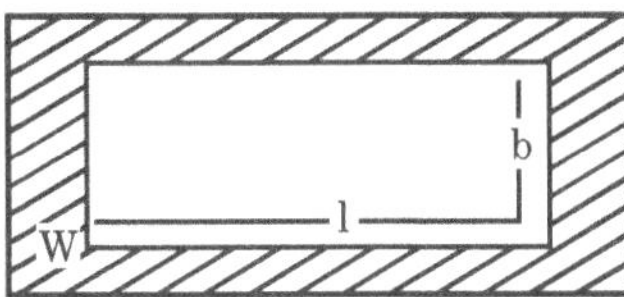

If a rectangular path of uniform width surrounds a rectangle, then length 'l' and breadth 'b' of the outer rectangle are obtained by adding twice width 'w' of the path to the length and breadth of the inner rectangle.

Area of outer rectangle

$$= (l + 2w)(b + 2w)$$

Area of path

$$= (l + 2w)(b + 2w) - lb$$

17. Tours (solid ring)

Tour is a solid of revolution of three dimensions obtained when a circle is rotated about an axis lying in its plane but not intersecting the circle.

e.g. a cycle tubes, rings, tennikoit ring, bangles, life belt.

If radius of the circle which rotates is 'r' and 'a' is the distance between centre of the surface of circle and the axis of revolution, then

Curved surface area of tours $= 2\pi r \times 2\pi a$

$= 4\pi^2 ra$ square units.

Volume of the tours $= \pi r^2 \times 2\pi a = 2\pi^2 r^2$ a cubic units.

Area of the ring around the top of the hemispherical vessel

$= \pi(R^2 - r^2)$ units.

Total surface area of a hemispherical vessel $= 3\pi\,(R^2 + r^2)\,(\text{units})^2$.

Where, R = outer radius

r = inner radius.

Solid Sphere

It is a solid formed by rotating semi circle having its diameter as an axis.

Hemisphere

A plane through the centre of a sphere divides it into two equal parts, each of which is called a *hemisphere.*

Spherical shell

Difference of two solid concentric spheres. Thickness of the shell is difference of the radii of two solid spheres determining it.

Chapter 22

SETS

German scientist George Cantor (1885-1915) developed it as the theory of sets.The theory of sets not only influenced and enriched every branch of Mathematics.

SET

A set is a well defined collection of objects.

Element of the set.

An object of a set is called an element of the set. The elements may be objects, animals, numbers or any other.

Sets are usually denoted by capital letters A, B, C...... X, Y, Z

Elements are usually denoted by small letters a,b,c....x, y, z.

Methods:

Sets are represented in two methods.

(*i*) **Roster form or List method**

In this method, we write all the elements, putting them in the brackets { } .

Suppose for a set S, whose elements are the digits from 0 to 9, we write

$$S = \{0, 1, 2, 3, 4, 5, 6, 7, 8, 9\}$$

While writing in the Roster form, we write an element only once even though it is repeated any number of times.

e.g. A = {x/x is a letter of the word "MISSISSIPI"}

A = {M,I,S,P}

(*ii*) Set-builder form or Characteristic form

In this method, we describe all the elements in the set by a common character.

The above set S can be written in set-builder form as

$$S = \{ x/x \in w.x\ 9\}$$

FINITE SET

A set is said to be finite according as the number of its elements is finite.

e.g. {a, e, i, o, u} ; {2, 3, 5}

INFINITE SET

A set is said to be infintie according as the number of its elements is infinite.

e.g. N = set of natural numbers

Z = set of integers

Q = set of rational number

R = set of real numbers

EQUAL SETS

If two or more sets contain the same elements, they are called equal sets. If A and B are equal sets, it is denoted by A = B.

e.g. if A = {1, 2, 3} and B = {2, 3, 1}

then A = B.

EQUIVALENT SETS

If any two sets have equal number of elements, they are called *equivalent sets.*

It is denoted by $A \leftrightarrow B$.

e.g. if A = {1, 2, 3} and B = {x, y, z}

then A and B are equivalent sets.

$\therefore$ $n(\phi) = 0$

NULL SETS

A set which contains no element is called *null set* or *empty set*. It is denoted by ϕ

i.e. $\phi = \{\ \}$.

e.g. The set of natural numbers less than zero.

The cardinal number of ϕ is '0'.

SUB SET

If every element in a set A is also an element of a set B, then A is called a *subset of B*.

If $x \in A \Rightarrow x \in B$, then $A \subseteq B$

Also, (*i*) $A \subseteq B$ and $B \subseteq A$, $\Rightarrow$ $A = B$

(*ii*) $A \subseteq A$.

PROPER SUBSET

If all the elements of A are contained in B and atleast one more in B than A, then A is called proper subset of B denoted by $A \subset B$ and B is a superset of A is denoted by $B \subset A$.

Theorems :

(*i*) ϕ is a subset of every set A.

(*ii*) $A \subseteq \phi$

$\Rightarrow$ $A = \phi$

(*iii*) $A \subseteq B$ and $B \subseteq C$

$\Rightarrow$ $A \subseteq C$

POWER SET

The set of all the subsets of a given set A is called *power set of A*. It is denoted by P(A).

e.g. if $A = \{1, 2\}$, then

$$P(A) = \{\phi, \{1\}, \{2\}, \{1, 2\}\}$$

- If A is a set with n elements, then P(A) consists of 2^n elements.
- The number of proper subsets to A is 2^{n-1} if n is the number of elements in A.

UNIVERSAL SET (μ)

If all the sets under consideration are the subsets of a fixed set S, then S (or) μ is called *universal set.*

COMPLEMENT

If μ is universal set, A is a subset, then complement of A is,

$$A = \{x/x \in \mu, x \notin A\}$$

UNION OF SETS (∪)

The union of sets A and B is the set of all elements which belong to A or B (or both) and is written as A ∪ B and is read as A union B.

The same is defined in the set builder form as

$$A \cup B = \{x/x \in A \text{ or } x \in B\}$$

INTERSECTION OF SETS (∩)

The intersection of sets A and B is the set of all elements which are common to A and B. It is denoted by A ∩ B and is read as A intersection B.

The same is defined is the set builder form as

$$A \cap B = \{x/x \in A \text{ or } x \in B\}$$

DIFFERENCE OF SETS

The difference of two sets A and B is the set of elements which belong to A but which do not belong to B. It is denoted by A – B.

∴ $A - B = \{x/x \in A \text{ and } x \notin B\}$,

Similarly, $B - A = \{x/x \in B \text{ and } x \notin A\}$

SYMMETRIC DIFFERENCE OF SETS

Symmetric difference of two sets A and B is $(A - B) \cup (B - A)$ and is written as $A \Delta B$.

Thus $$A \Delta B = (A - B) \cup (B - A)$$

In the set builder form

$$A \Delta B = \{x / x \in A \cup B \text{ and } x \notin A \cap B\}$$

Two sets are said to be disjoint sets, if they do not have any elements is common, then

$$A \cap B = \Phi$$

SINGLETON SET

A set which contains only one element is called *singleton set.*

1. Every set is a subset of itself.
2. Empty set is a subset of every set.
3. If $A \subseteq B$, then $A \cap B = A$.
4. If $A \subseteq B$, then $A \cup B = B$.
5. If $A \subset B$, then $A' \cup B = \mu$.
6. If $A \cup B = B$, then $A \subset B$.
7. If $A \cap B = A$, then $A \subset B$.
8. $A - B = A \cap B'$.
9. $B - A = B \cap A'$.
10. $A \cup B = \{x/x \in A \text{ or } x \in B\}$
11. $A \cap B = \{x/x \in A \text{ or } x \in B\}$
12. $A - B = \{x/x \in A \text{ or } x \notin B\}$
13. $B - A = \{x/x \in B \text{ or } x \notin A\}$
14. ϕ is identity for empty set.
15. μ is identity for universal.

16. A and A′ are disjoint sets.

17. $A \subseteq A$ (Reflexive)

18. If $A \subseteq B$ and $B \subseteq A$, then $A = B$ (anti-symmetric)

19. $n(A \cup B) = n(A) + n(B) - n(A \cap B)$

20. $n(A \cup B \cup C) = n(A) + n(B) + n(C) - n(A \cap B) - n(B \cap C) - n(C \cap A) + n(A \cap B \cap C)$.

De- Morgan's Laws :

$(A \cup B)' = A' \cap B'$

$(A \cap B)' = A' \cup B'$

BASIC LAWS OF ALGEBRA OF SETS

Property	Union ($\cup$)	Intersection ($\cap$)
Idempotent	$A \cup A = A$	$A \cap A = A$
Commutative	$A \cup B = B \cup A$	$A \cap B = B \cap A$
Associative	$(A \cup B) \cup C = A \cup (B \cup C)$	$(A \cap B) \cap C = A \cap (B \cap C)$
Identity	$A \cup \phi = A$	$A \cap \mu = A$
Identity	$A \cup \mu = \mu$	$A \cap \phi = \phi$
Distributive	$A \cup (B \cap C) = (A \cup B) \cap (A \cup C)$	$A \cap (B \cup C) = (A \cap B) \cup (A \cap C)$
Complement	$A \cup A' = \mu$	$A \cap A' = \phi$
Double	$(A')' = A$	$\mu' = \phi, \phi' = \mu$
Complement	Demorgan's Law	
Complement	$(A \cup B)' = A' \cap B'$	$(A \cap B)' = A' \cup B'$
Difference	$A - (B \cup C) = (A - B) \cap (A - C)$	$A - (B \cap C) = (A - B) \cup (A - C)$
Symmetric Difference	$A \Delta B = (A - B) \cup (B - A)$	$A \Delta B = (A \cup B) - (A \cap B)$

CARTESIAN PRODUCT SETS

Given two sets A and B, the set containing all the ordered pairs where the first element is taken from A and the second element is taken from B is called *Cartesian Product of A and B* and is denoted by $A \times B$ read as A cross B.

$$A \times B = \{(x,y)/\ x \in A \text{ and } y \in B\}$$

$$\therefore \qquad A \times B \neq B \times A.$$

- A relation is a subset at a cartesian product of two sets. It is a set of orered pairs.

  If $(a, b) = (x,y)$, then $\quad a = x,\ b = y.$

  $$\therefore \qquad (a, b) \neq (b, a)$$

- If $n(A) = p$, $n(B) = q$, then $n(A \times B) = n(A) \times n(B) = pq$.

  Here n(A) stands for number of elements in A otherwise called cardinal number of set A.

- If $A = \{\ \}$ or ϕ and $B = \{\ \}$ or ϕ, then $A \times B = \{\ \}$ or ϕ.

- If one of the sets of A and B is empty, then $A \times B = \{\ \}$

  Cartesian product of two sets is represented by

  (*i*) Arrow diagram

  (*ii*) Tree diagram

  (*iii*) Graphical Representation.

IMPORTANT VENN DIAGRAMS

(*i*)

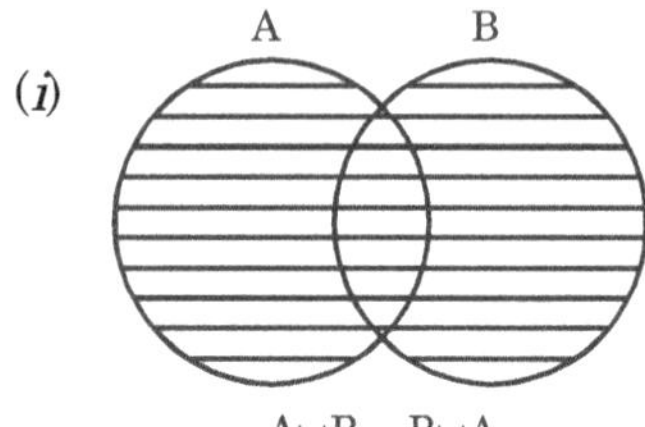

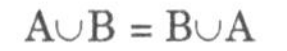

$A \cup B = B \cup A$

(*ii*)

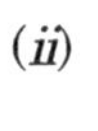

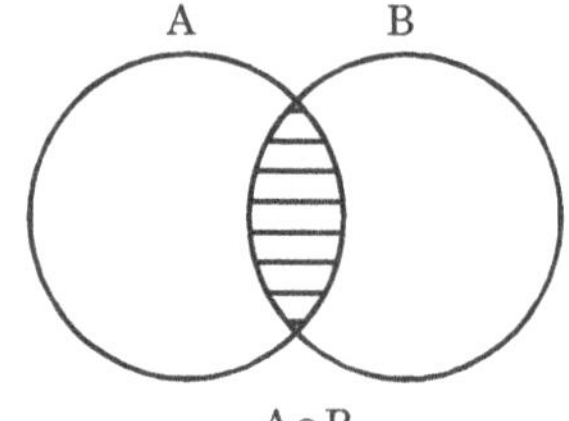

$A \cap B$

(*iii*)

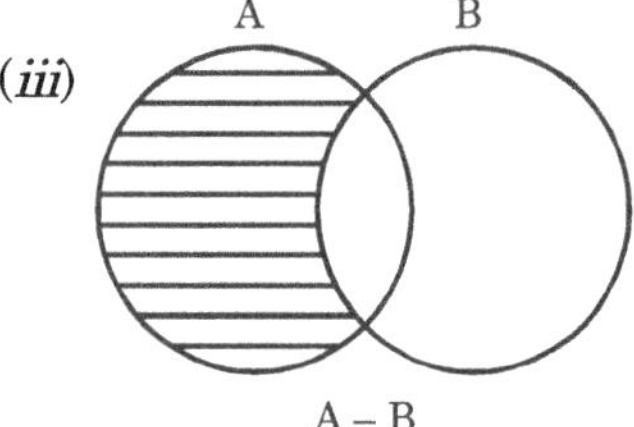

$A - B$

(*iv*)

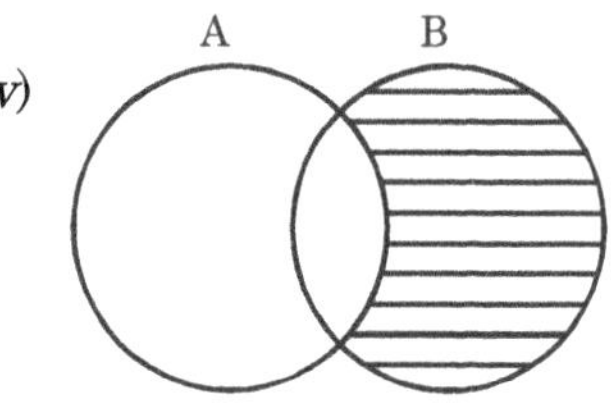

$B - A$

(*v*)

μ

A

$A' = \mu - A$

(*vi*)

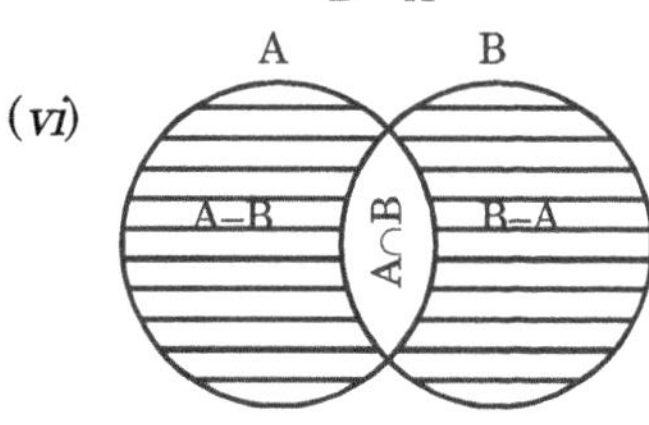

chapter

23

FUNCTIONS

FUNCTION (OR MAPPING)

It is a relation in which no two ordered pairs have the same first coordinate.

This is written as $f : A \rightarrow B$ (Read as f is a mapping from A to B)

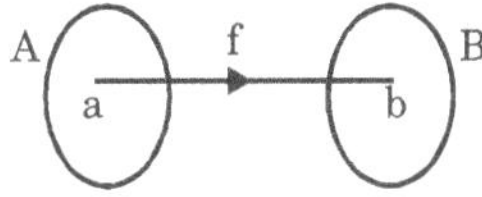

Note. Every function from A to B is a relation from A to B. But every relation from A to B need not be a function A to B.

Ordered Pairs

If a and b are any two objects, then pair (a, b) is called ordered pair. $(a, b) \neq (b, a)$

Relation is a set of ordered pairs.

Fundamental properties of ordered pairs.

(*i*) If $(a,b) \neq (b,a)$, then a is called *first co-ordinate* and 'b' is called *second co-ordinate*.

(*ii*) If $(x, y) = (2, 3)$, then $x = 2, y = 3$

Domain

A set consists of all first co-ordinates in the order pairs.

Range

A set consist of all second co-ordinates in the order pairs.

Cartesian Product of Sets

Given two sets A and B, the set containing all the ordered pairs where the first element is taken from A and the second element is taken from B is called cartesian product of A and B and is denoted by $A \times B$ read as A cross B.

$$A \times B = \{(x, y)/\ x \in A \text{ and } y \in B\}$$

1. If $A \subset C$ and $B \subset D$, then $A \times B \subset C \times D$
2. R is Relation $A \rightarrow B$, $R^{-1}: B \rightarrow A$
3. Domain of R = Range of R^{-1}
4. Domain of R^{-1} = Range of R.

CO-DOMAIN

Domain of $R \subseteq A$. Range of $R \subseteq B$.

If range of $R \neq B$, then B is called co-domain.

1. If A or B is the empty set, then A ´ B = f
2. If either A or B is infinite and the other non-empty, then $A \times B$ is infinite.

EVEN AND ODD FUNCTIONS

Even Function

A function 'f" is said to be even function of *x* if it remains unaltered in magnitude as well as in sign when x is replaced by $-x$.

$\therefore$ ϕ is even if $f(-x) = f(x)$.

e.g. $x^2 + 2x^4$, cosx are even functions of x.

Odd Functions

A function 'f' is said to be an odd function of x if it remains unaltered in magnitude but changes in sign when x is replaced by $-x$.

$\therefore$ f is odd if $f(-x) = -f(x)$

e.g. $x + 2x^3$, sin x are odd fucntions of x.

PROPERTIES OF RELATIONS

1. Reflexive

A relation is reflexive if every element of a given set is related with itself.
A relation R in $A \times A$ is reflexive, if $(x,x) \in R$ for every $x \in R$.

e.g. Every real number is equal to itself. So 'is equal to' real number is reflexive.

'is a subset of' real number is reflexive.

'is parallel to' real number is reflexive.

'is similar to' real number is reflexive.

'is congruent to' real number is also reflexive.

2. Symmetric relations

A relation R in set A is called symmetric if $(x, y) \in R$, then $(y, x) \in R$ if $R = R'$ then R is symmetric.

e.g. 'is equal to'

'is parallel to'

'is similar to'

'is congruent to'

3. Transitive Relation

A relation R is said to be transitive, if

$$(x, y) \in R \text{ and } (y, z) \in R \rightarrow (x, z) \in R.$$

e.g. 'is equal to' is a transitive relation for $a = b, b = c, \Rightarrow a = c$.

'is parallel to' is a transitive relation.

'is similar to' is a transitive relation.

4. Equivalence Relation

A relation which is

(*i*) reflexive

(*ii*) symmetric

(*iii*) transitive

is called an equivalence relation.

e.g. 'is congruent to' is an equivalence relation.

'is equal to' is an equivalence relation.

'is parallel to' is an equivalence relation.

EQUAL FUNCTIONS

Two functions f and g are said to be equal if

(*i*) they are defined on the same domain and co-domain.

(*ii*) $f(x) = g(x)$.

Anti Symmetric Property

A relation R in a set A is called anti symmetric if $(x, y) \in R$ and $(y, x) \in R$, then $x = y$.

$$A \times (B \cap C) = (A \times B) \cap (A \times C)$$

$$A \times (B \cup C) = (A \times B) \cup (A \times C)$$

IMAGE

If maps A to B and an element $a \in A$ is associated with an element $b \in B$, then b is called f image of a or b is called the image of a under the mapping f and is written as $f(a) = b$.

We may also say that f maps a into b. Also a is called pre-image or inverse image of b.

A relation is described in following five ways.

(*i*) Roster form or list form.

(*ii*) Set builder form.

(*iii*) Arrow diagram

(*iv*) Tree diagram

(*v*) Graphical Representation.

INVERSE RELATIONS

If R is relation from A into B and R^{-1} is the inverse relation of R, then

$$R = \{(x, y) / x, y \in R\}$$

and $R^{-1} = \{(y, x) / x, y \in R\}$

TYPES OF RELATIONS

1. **One to many relations.**
   If $R \subseteq A \times B$ and one element of A relates to more than one element of B, then R is called one to many relations.
2. **One to one relation.**
   If $R \subseteq A \times B$ and one element of A relates to only one element of B, then R is called one to one relation.
3. **Many to one relation.**
   If $R \subseteq A \times B$ and two or more elements of A relate to only one element of B, then R is called many to one relation.
4. **Many to many relations.**
   If $A \subseteq A \times B$ and two or more elements of A relate to two or more elements of B, then R is called many to many relation.

TYPES OF INTERVALS

1. **Closed interval** [a, b]

   $= \{x : x \in R; \ a \le x \le b\}$

   = Set of all real numbers lying between a and b including the end points a and b
2. **Open intervals** (a, b) **or**]a, b[

   $= \{x : x \in R ; a < x < b\}$

   = Set of all real numbers lying between a and b, excluding the end points a and b.
3. **Closed-open interval** [a, b) **and open-closed interval** (a, b]

   $[a, b) = \{x : x \in R; a \le x < b\}$

   $(a, b] = \{x : x \in R; a < x \le b\}$

TYPES OF FUNCTIONS

1. **One-One Function (Injection).**
A mapping f : A → B is called a one-one function if distinct elements of A have distinct images in B.

e.g.

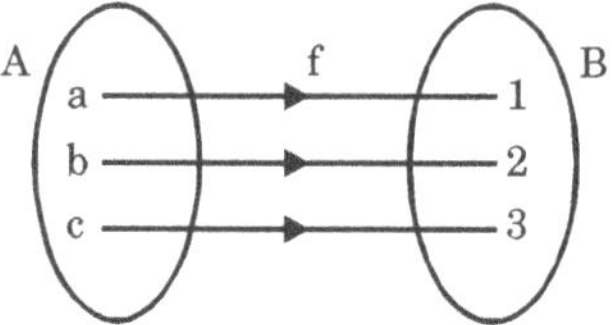

2. **Many-One Mapping.**
If the mapping f : A→B is such that two distinct elements a_1, a_2 of A have the same f-image in B, then the mapping is called many-one mapping or many-one function.

e.g.

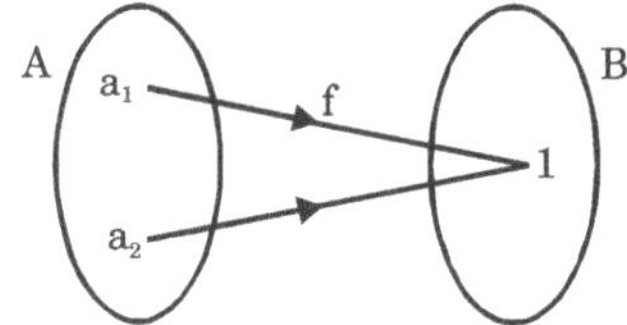

3. **Into Mapping.**
If the mapping f : A → B is such that there is atleast one element of B which is not the f-image of any element of A, then f is a mapping of A into B or f is an into function.

e.g.

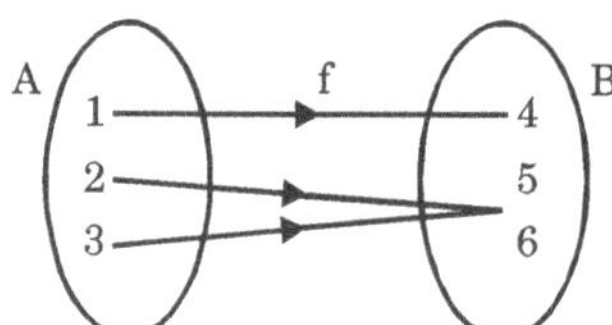

4. **On-to Function or Surjective Mapping.**
The mapping f : A→ B is called onto function if every element of B occurs as the image of atleast one of the elements of A.

e.g.

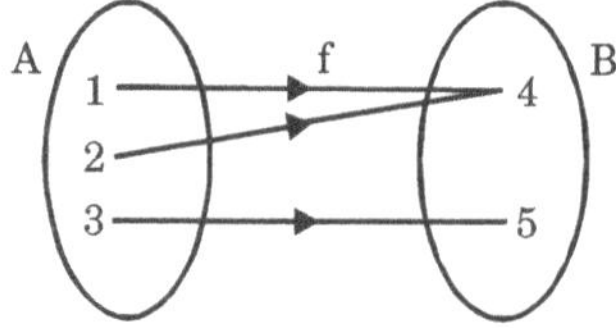

5. **Objective Function.**
If the function f is both one-one and on to, then it is called a one-one, on to or objective function.

6. **Identity Function.**
The mapping $f : A \to A$ defined by $f(x) = x$ is called identity function denoted by l_A or l.

i.e. every element of A is f image of itself.

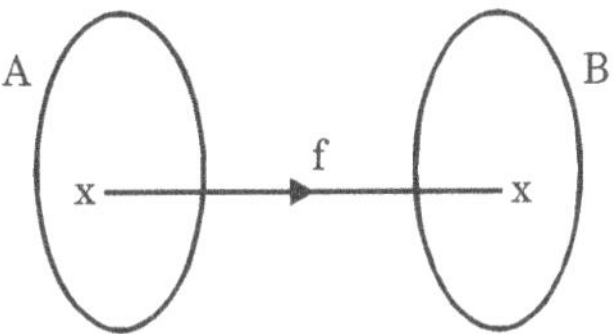

7. **Constant Function**
The function $f : A \to B$ is a constant function if the range of f consists of only one element.

e.g.

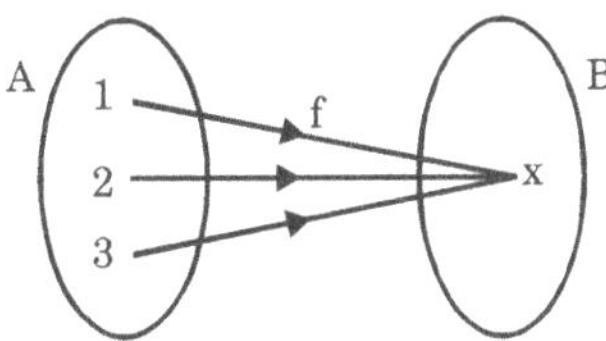

8. **Inverse Function**
If $f : A \to B$, then inverse of the function is a relation denoted by $f^{-1} : B \to A$.

e.g. $f : A \to B$, if $f(x) = y = ax + b$, then

$$f^{-1}(y) = x = \frac{y-b}{a}$$

$\therefore \quad f(x) = y$

$$\Rightarrow \quad x = f^{-1}(y) = \frac{y-b}{a}$$

> *Note.*
>
> (*i*) Inverse of a function need not be a function.
>
> (*ii*) Inverse of a function is also a function only if the given function is one-one and on to or objective function.

9. **Real Function.**

Let $f : A \rightarrow B$ and R is a set of real numbers.

(*i*) If domain A is a subset of R, f is said to be a function of a real variable.

(*ii*) If co-domain B is a subset of R, f is said to be a real valued function.

(*iii*) If both A and B are subsets of R, f is said to be a real function or real valued function of a real variable.

ZERO OF A FUNCTION

Let f be a function from a subset of real numbers into the set of real numbers. If $f(c) = 0$ where c is a number in the domain of f, then c is called a zero of f.

1. In the composite function, gof

(*i*) Range of f = Domain of g.

(*ii*) Domain of gof = Domain of f.

(*iii*) Range of gof = Domain of g.

2. If $f : A \rightarrow B$, $g : B \rightarrow C$ are one-one on to function, then

$$(gof)^{-1} = f^{-1} \text{ o } g^{-1}$$

3. **Periodic function**

A function f(x) is said to be a periodic function of x, with period of $T > 0$, such that $f(x + T) = f(x) \ \forall \ x \in R$

(*i*) sin x, cos x, sec x and cosec x are periodic functions with period 2π.

(*ii*) tan x, and cot x are periodic functions with period π.

(*iii*) If f(x) is periodic with period T, then $\frac{1}{f(x)}$ and $\sqrt{f(x)}$ are also periodic with same period T.

(*iv*) If f(x) is periodic with period T, then $k\,f(ax + b)$ is also periodic with period $\frac{T}{|a|}$.

4. If $f : A \to B$ and $g : B \to C$ and $h : C \to D$, then $g \circ f : A \to C$ defined by

   (*i*) $(g \circ f)(x) = g[f(x)]$

   (*ii*) $(f \circ g)(x) = f[g(x)]$

   (*iii*) $[h \circ (g \circ f)](x) = h\,[g \circ f)(x)] = h[g(f(x))]$

   (*iv*) $h \circ (g \circ f) = (h \circ g) \circ f$

   (*v*) $f \circ g = g \circ f$.

   If A and B are finite, then

   $$n(A \times B) = n(A) \times n(B)$$

5. Cartesian product of two sets A and B

   $$= A \times B = \{x, y); x \in A, \in B\}$$

6. Any subset of $A \times B$ in a relation from A to B.

7. f is a relation from, $A(\neq \phi)$ to $B(\neq \phi)$

   If to every element $a \in A$, there is a unique element $b \in B$ such that $(a, b) \in f$, then f is a function (or mapping) from A to B. It is denoted by

   $f : A \to B$. $b = f(a)$ = image of 'a'.

   $f^{-1}(b) = [a \in A ; f(a) = b]$ = the set of pre-images of 'b'.

8. If $f : A \to B$, then

   A = the domain of f

   B = the co-domain of f.

   $f(A)$ = range of f = $[b \in B; b = f(a)$ for some $a \in A]$.

   range of f $\leq$ co-domain of f.

9. The number of functions from A to B is $\{n(B)\}^{n(A)}$.

10. A function $f : A \to B$ is one-to one (or injective) if district elements of A have district images in B.

11. A function which is not one-to-one is many-to-one.

12. Let n(A) = r and n(B) = n,

 then condition to define an injection from A to B is

$$n(A) \leq n(B) \text{ or } r < n$$

 and number of such injection = n_{pr}.

13. A function f : A → B is onto (or sursective) if range of f = B. f : A → B is onto if every element of B has atleast one preimage in A.

14. If f : A → B is not onto, then it is said to be *into.*

15. The condition to define a surjection from A to B is

$$n(A) \geq n(B)$$

 i.e. $r \geq n.$

 In this case the number of such surjection from A to B

$$= \eta^r - \eta c_1 (\eta - 1)^r + \eta c_2 (\eta - 2)^r - \eta c_3 (\eta - 3)^r + ... + (-1)^{\eta-1} - \eta c_{\eta-1} 1^{r.}$$

16. A function which is one-one and on-to is called a *bisection.*

17. A bisection is possible from A to B (when they are finite and non-empty) only when

$$n(A) = n(B).$$

 The number of such bisection from A to B is n! where

$$n(A) = n(B) = n.$$

18. If n(A) = n(B) = n, then the number of injection (or subsection) from A to B is n!.

19. A function f : A → B is a constant function if the ranges of f contains only one element.

 The number of constant function from A to B = n(B).

20. Two functions f and g are equal if

 (*i*) domain of f = domain of g(A say), and

 (*ii*) f(x) = g(x) for all x ∈ A.

21. If $A \neq \phi$, then $f = \{x,x) ; x \varepsilon A\} = 1_A$ is the identity function on A.

e.g. if $A = \{2, 4, 6\}$ then

$$1_A = \{(2, 2), (4, 4) (6, 6)\}$$

22. If $f : A \rightarrow B$ is a bijection, then $f^{-1} : B \rightarrow A$ defined by

$f^{-1} = \{(b,a) : (a, b) \in f)$ is also a bisection.

f^{-1} is called the inverse of f.

23. If inverse of a function exists,then it is said to be invertible. The inverse of a function, if it exists, is unique. f is invertible (=) f is bisection.

24. 1_A is a bisection and $I_A^{-1} = 1_A$.

25. If $f : A \rightarrow B$ and $g : B \rightarrow C$ are functions, then

$$gof : A \rightarrow C \text{ defined by } (gof)$$

$(x) = g(f(x))$ for all $x \in A$ is a function and gof is called *composite function of f and g.*

(*i*) If $f : A \rightarrow B$ and $g : B \rightarrow C$ are one-one, then
$gof : A \rightarrow C$ is one-one.

(*ii*) If $f : A \rightarrow B$ and $g : B \rightarrow C$ are onto, then
$gof : A \rightarrow C$ is onto.

(*iii*) If $f : A \rightarrow B$ and $g : B \rightarrow C$ are bisections, then
$gof : A \rightarrow C$ is a bisection $(gof)^{-1} = f^{-1}og^{-1}$

(*iv*) If $gof : A \rightarrow c$ is one-one, then f is one-one.

(*v*) If $gof : A \rightarrow c$ is onto, then g is onto.

(*v*) If $f : A \rightarrow B$ is a functiont, then
$fol_A = 1_B\, of = f$.

(*vi*) If $f : A \rightarrow B$ is a bisection, then
$fof^{-1} = 1_B$, $f^{-1}of = 1_A$

(*vii*) If $f : A \rightarrow B$ and $g : B \rightarrow A$ are function such that
$gof = 1_A$ and $fog = 1_B$, then

$f : A \rightarrow B$ is abisection and $g = f^{-1}$

(*viii*) If f : A → A is a bisection, then

$$fof^{-1} = f^{-1} \text{ of} = 1_A$$

(*ix*) In general fog ≠ gof

(*x*) If f : A→ B g : B → C and h : C→D are functions, then

$$ho\ (gof) = (hog)\ of.$$

26. If the range of f ⊆ I_R, then f is real valued function.

27. If f = A → R and g : B → R (A, B ⊆ R), then

(*i*) $(f \pm g)(x) = f(x) \pm g(x)\ \forall\ x \in A \cap B.$

(*ii*) $(fg)(x) = f(x).\ g(x)\ \forall\ x \in Ao\cap B$

(*iii*) $\left(\frac{f}{g}\right)(x) = \frac{f(x)}{g(x)}$, v $x \in A \cap B.$

(*iv*) $(f \pm K)(x) = f(x) \pm K$, K is a real constant.

(*v*) $(Kf)(x) = K.f(x)$, K is a real constant.

(*vi*) $f^n(K) = \{f(x)\}^n, n>0$

(*vii*) $f(x) = \sqrt{f(x)}$, $f(x) \geq 0$, $x \in A.$

(*viii*) $|f|(x) = |f(x)|$, $x \in A.$

(*ix*) $(af + bg)(x) = a.f(x) + b.g(x)$, $x \in A \cap B$, a and b are real constant.

28. If f : A→ R, A $\overline{\subseteq R}$ and $f(-x) = f(x)$, ∀ x ∈ A, then f is an even function.

29. If f : A→R, A ⊆ R and $f(-x) = -f(x)$, ∀ x ∈ A, then f is an odd function.

30. If f : A→ R, A ⊂ R is defined by

$$f(x) = a_0x^n + a_1x^{n-1} + a_2x^{n-2} + \ldots + a_{n-1}\ x + a_n,\ a_0 \neq 0.$$

Here, $a_1, a_2 \ldots . a_n \subset R$

n is a non-negative

Integer is a polynomial function of degree n.

31. A function of the form $\frac{f(x)}{g(x)}$, where f(x) and g(x) are polynomial function and $g(x) \neq 0$ is called *rational function.*

32. A function obtained by a finite number of algebraic operation on polynomial function is called *algebraic function.*

33. If relation between independent varible x and dependent variable y is in the form f(x,y) = 0, then f is called *implicit function.*
e.g. $f(x,y) = x^2 + xy + y^2 - 4 = 0$

34. If $a \in R$, $a > 0$ then $f(x) = a^n$ is called *exponential function.*

35. If $\bar{a} \in R$ and a > O, x > 0 a≠1, then
$f(x) = \log_a x$ is called a *logarithmic function*;
its domain = (O,α) and range = (–α, α)

36. If x is any real number, then there exists integers n and n + 1 such that $n \leq x < n + 1$
Then greatest integral part of x = [x] = n.
e.g. [3] = 3, [–3.2] = –4, [1.6] = 1.

37. $f : R \rightarrow R$ defined by f(x) = [x] is called *step function*
Domain of f = R (–α, α), Range of f – Z.

38. If x is any real number, then
$$\{x\} = x - [x] = \text{the fractional part of x.}$$
Its domain = R = (–α, α); its range = [0,1].

39. If $a \in R$ and a > 0, then $f(x) = a^x$ is called *exponential functions*; its domain = $(-\infty, \infty)$ and range = $(0, \infty)$.

40. Modulus function
$$f(x) = |x| = \begin{cases} x, & \text{if } x > 0 \\ 0 & \text{if } x = 0 \\ -x & \text{if } x < 0 \end{cases}$$

41. Signum function
$$\text{sgn}(x) = \begin{cases} 1, & \text{if } x > 0 \\ 0 & \text{if } x = 0 \\ -1 & \text{if } x < 0 \end{cases}$$

Some Important Points

1. $(x-a)(x-b) > 0 \Rightarrow x < a$ or $x > b$, for $a < b$
2. $(x-a)(x-b) < 0 \Rightarrow a < x < b$, for $a < b$
3. For every $x \in R$, $|x| = \max\{x, -x\}$
4. For every $x \in R$, $|x| = \sqrt{x^2}$
5. $|x+y| \le |x| + |y|$
6. $|x-y| \ge |x| - |y|$
7. $|xy| = |x|\,|y|$
8. $|x| < a \Rightarrow -a < x < a$
9. $|x| > a \Rightarrow x < -a, x > a$
10. $\log_a x > \log_a y \Rightarrow \begin{Bmatrix} x > y & \text{if} & a > 1 \\ x < y, & \text{if} & 0 < a < 1 \end{Bmatrix}, \begin{matrix} a, x, y > 0 \\ a \ne 1 \end{matrix}$
11. $[x] \le x < [x] + 1$
12. $[x] + [-x] = \begin{Bmatrix} 0 & \text{if} & x \in Z \\ -1 & \text{if} & x \notin Z \end{Bmatrix}$
13. $\{x\} + \{-x\} = \begin{Bmatrix} 0, & \text{if} & x \in I \\ 1 & \text{if} & x \notin I \end{Bmatrix}$

Trigonometric functions

1. $\sin x$:

   Domain = R ; Range = [–1, 1]

2. $\cos x$:

   Domain = R ; Range = [–1, 1]

3. $\tan x$:

   Domain $= R \setminus \left\{ (2n+1)\frac{\pi}{2} \Big/ n \in I \right\}$; Range = R

4. $\cot x$:

   Domain $= R \setminus \{n\pi \mid n \in I\}$; Range = R

5. sec x :

Domain = $R\setminus\left\{(2n+1)\frac{\pi}{2}\Big/ n\in I\right\}$; Range = $(-\infty, -1]\cup[1, \infty)$

6. cosec x :

Domain = $R\setminus\{n\pi \mid n\in I\}$; Range = $(-\infty, -1]\cup[1, \infty)$

Inverse Trigonometric Functions

1. $\sin^{-1}x$:

Domain = $[-1, 1]$; Range = $\left[-\frac{\pi}{2}, \frac{\pi}{2}\right]$

2. $\cos^{-1}x$:

Domain = $[-1, 1]$; Range = $[0, \pi]$

3. $\tan^{-1}x$:

Domain = $(-\infty, \infty)$; Range = $\left(-\frac{\pi}{2}, \frac{\pi}{2}\right)$

4. $\cot^{-1}x$:

Domain = $(-\infty, \infty)$; Range = $(0, \pi)$

5. $\text{cosec}^{-1}x$:

Domain = $(-\infty, -1]\cup[1, \infty)$; Range= $\left[-\frac{\pi}{2}, 0\right)\cup\left(0, \frac{\pi}{2}\right]$

6. $\sec^{-1}x$:

Domain = $(-\infty, -1]\cup[1, \infty)$; Range = $\left[0, \frac{\pi}{2}\right)\cup\left(\frac{\pi}{2}, \pi\right]$

chapter 24

STATEMENTS

STATEMENT

A statement is a sentence which is either true or false but not both.

Statements are denoted by small letters such as p,q,r...........

OPEN SENTENCE

A sentence having one or more variable is called an open sentence.

NEGATION

If statement is modified with 'not', the new sentence so formed is called *Negation.*

If P is a statement then its negation is given by ~P.

If truth value of 'P' is True, then truth value of "~P" is False likewise controversy.

TRUTH TABLE

P	~P	~(~P)
T	F	T
F	T	F

CONNECTIVES

Many statements are the combination of simple statements with some connecting words. These words are called *connectives.*

COMPOUND STATEMENT.

A compound statement is a statement formed by joining two or more simple statements using one of the connectives 'and', 'of', '........ then .....' , if and only if".

CONJUNCTION [$\wedge$]

A statement formed by combining two or more simple statements by using the word 'and' is called *conjunction.*

TRUTH VALUE OF CONJUNCTION

If two statements P is true and Q is true; then their conjunction $P \wedge Q$ is True; otherwise False.

TRUTH TABLE

P	~P	$P \wedge Q$	$Q \wedge P$
T	T	T	T
T	F	F	F
F	T	F	F
F	F	F	F

DISJUNCTION [$\vee$]

A statement formed by combining two or more simple statements by using the word 'or' is called *Disjunction.*

TRUTH VALUE OF DISJUNCTION

If two statements P is False and Q is False, then their disjunction $P \vee Q$ is False; otherwise True.

TRUTH TABLE

P	Q	$P \vee Q$	$Q \vee P$
T	T	T	T
T	F	T	T
F	T	T	T
F	F	F	F

IMPLICATION [$\Rightarrow$]

A statement formed from two simple statements as an 'if..... then statement.In the implication '$P \Rightarrow Q$', (read 'P implies Q') in implication of a True statement cannot imply a False statement.

TRUTH VALUE OF IMPLICATION

If two statements P is True and Q is False then their implication P⇒Q is False; otherwise True.

TRUTH TABLE

P	Q	P ⇒ Q	Q ⇒ P
T	T	T	T
T	F	F	T
F	T	T	F
F	F	T	T

BI-IMPLICATION [⇔]

Conjunction of the two conditions P⇒Q, Q⇒P is called *bi-implication of P and Q*, it is written as P⇔Q and read as 'P if and only if Q'.

TRUTH VALUE OF BI-IMPLICATION

If two statements both P and Q are either True or False then their Bi-Implication P⇔Q is true; otherwise false.

TRUTH TABLE

P	Q	P ⇔ Q	Q ⇔ P
T	T	T	T
T	F	F	F
F	T	F	F
F	F	T	T

QUANTIFIERS

The phrases 'For all', 'For same', 'For no', 'For every' there exist atleast one convey the idea of an open statement called quantifiers.

UNIVERSAL QUANTIFIER. ["]

The quantifier 'for all' or 'for every' is called *universal quantifier.* It is denoted by the symbol "∀".

EXISTENTIAL QUANTIFIER [∃]

The quantifier 'some' 'or', there exists atleast one is called *existential quantifier.*It is denoted by the symbol "∃".

TAUTOLOGY

e.g. $P \vee \sim P$ is called Tautology

P	~P	P ∨ ~P
T	F	T
F	T	T

CONTRADICTION

A compound statement which is always False is called contradiction.

e.g. $P \wedge \sim P$ is called contradiction.

P	~P	P ∧ ~P
T	F	F
F	T	F

LAWS OF ALGEBRA STATEMENTS

1. **Idempotent laws**

   (*i*) $p \vee p \equiv p$

   (*ii*) $p \wedge p \equiv p$

2. **Associative Laws**

   (*i*) $(p \vee q) \vee r \equiv p \vee (q \vee r)$

   (*ii*) $(p \wedge q) \wedge r \equiv p \wedge (q \wedge r)$

3. **Commutative Laws**

   (*i*) $p \vee q \equiv q \vee p$

   (*ii*) $p \wedge q \equiv q \wedge p$.

4. **Distributive Laws**

   (*i*) $p \vee (q \wedge r) \equiv (p \vee q) \wedge (p \vee r)$

   (*ii*) $p \wedge (q \vee r) \equiv (p \wedge q) \vee (p \wedge r)$

5. De Morgan's Laws

(i) $\sim(p \vee q) \equiv (\sim p) \wedge (\sim q)$

(ii) $\sim(p \wedge q) \equiv \sim p) \vee (\sim q)$

6. Identity Laws

(i) $p \wedge F \equiv F$

(ii) $p \wedge T \equiv p$

7. Identity Laws

(i) $p \vee T \equiv T$

(ii) $p \vee F \equiv p$

8. Complement Laws

(i) $p \vee (\sim p) \equiv T$

(ii) $p \wedge (\sim p) \equiv F$

9. Complement Laws

(i) $\sim(\sim p) \equiv p$

(ii) $\sim T \equiv F$, $\sim F \equiv T$

An application (of truth tables) to switching networks.

chapter

25

ALGEBRAIC MULTIPLICATION & DIVISIBILITY PRINCIPLES

ALGEBRAIC MULTIPLICATION

(*i*) + ve number × + ve number = + ve number

(*ii*) – ve number × + ve number = – ve number

(*iii*) + ve number × – ve number = – ve number

(*iv*) – ve number × – ve number = + ve number

DIVISIBILITY PRINCIPLES

1. **Division Rule:**

$$\text{Divident} = \text{Quotient} \times \text{Divisor} + \text{Remainder}$$

or $$\frac{\text{Dividend}}{\text{Divisor}} = \text{Quotient} + \frac{\text{Re mainder}}{\text{Divisor}}$$

2. Division by zero is not defined.
3. Division by '1' for any whole number 'a'.

   e.g. a ÷ 1 = a
4. A natural number is divisible by 2 if and only if the digit in its units place is either 2, 4, 6, 8 or 10.
5. A natural number is divisible by 3 if and only if the sum of these digits is divisible by 3.
6. A natural number is divisible by 4 if and only if the number formed by the last two digits of the given number is divisible by 4.

7. A natural number is divisible by 5 if and only if its last digit is either 5 or zero.
8. If a number is divisible by 2 and 3, then it is divisible by their product 6.
9. A natural number is divisible by 8 if and only if the number formed by the last three digits of the given number is divisible by 8.
10. A natural number is divisible by 10 if its last digit is zero.
11. A natural number is divisible by 11 if and only if the difference between the sums of alternate digits is divisible by 11.

OPERATIONS WITH ZERO AND INFINITY

1. $\infty + x = \infty \quad \infty - x = \infty$
2. $x \times 0 = 0 \quad x \times \infty = \infty$
3. $\frac{0}{x} = 0 \qquad \frac{x}{0}$ = undefined ∞, i.e. $\frac{\text{Anything}}{\text{zero}}$ = undefined (i.e. ∞)
4. $\frac{x}{\infty} = 0 \qquad \frac{\infty}{x} = \infty$
5. $x^{\infty} = \infty$, if $x^2 > 1$
7. Illustration : $1^{\infty} = 1$
8. $x^{\infty} = 0$, if $x^2 < 1$
9. Illustration : $1^{-\infty} = 1$
10. $x^{-\infty} = 0$, if $x^2 > 1$
11. $x^{-\infty} = \infty$, if $x^2 < 1$
12. $\infty^{x} = \infty$
13. $0^{x} = 0$

chapter

26

IDENTITIES (GENERAL FORMULAE)

1. $(a+b)^2 = a^2 + 2ab + b^2$
2. $(a-b)^2 = a^2 - 2ab + b^2$
3. $(a+b)(a-b) = a^2 - b^2$
4. $(a+b)^2 + (a-b)^2 = 2(a^2 + b^2)$
5. $(a+b)^2 - (a-b)^2 = 4ab$
6. $(a+b+c)^2 = a^2 + b^2 + c^2 + 2ab + 2bc + 2ca$
7. $(a+b)^3 = a^3 + b^3 + 3ab(a+b) = a^3 + b^3 + 3a^2b + 3ab^2$
8. $(a-b)^3 = a^3 - b^3 - 3ab(a-b) = a^3 - b^3 - 3a^2b + 3ab^2$
9. $a^3 + b^3 = (a+b)(a^2 - ab + b^2) = (a+b)^3 - 3ab(a+b)$
10. $a^3 - b^3 = (a-b)(a^2 + ab + b^2) = (a-b)^3 + 3ab(a-b)$
11. $a^2 + b^2 = (a+b)^2 - 2ab$ or $(a-b)^2 + 2ab$
12. $a^3 + b^3 + c^3 - 3abc = (a+b+c)(a^2 + b^2 + c^2 - ab - bc - ca)$
13. If $a+b+c=0$, then
$$a^3 + b^3 + c^3 = 3abc$$
14. $(x+a)(x+b) = x^2 + x(a+b) + ab$
15. $(a+b)^4 = a^4 + 4a^3b + 6a^2b^2 + 4ab^3 + b^4$
16. $a^4 + a^2b^2 + b^4 = (a^2 + ab + b^2)(a^2 - ab + b^2)$
17. $a^4 - b^4 = (a+b)(a-b)(a^2 + b^2)$
18. $(a+b)^2 = (a-b)^2 + 4ab$

19. $(a - b)^2 = (a + b)^2 - 4ab$

20. $a^3 + b^3 + c^3 = (a + b + c)^3 - 3(a + b)(b + c)(c + a)$

21. $(a + b)(b + c)(c + a) = (a + b + c)(ab + bc + ca) - abc$

22. $a^2 + b^2 + c^2 - ab - bc - ca = \frac{1}{2}[(a-b)^2 + (b-c)^2 + (c-a)^2]$

23. If $a^2 + b^2 + c^2 - ab - bc - ca = 0$, then

$$a = b = c$$

24. $\left(a + \frac{1}{b}\right)^2 = a^2 + \frac{1}{b^2} + \frac{2a}{b}$

25. $\left(a - \frac{1}{b}\right)^2 = a^2 + \frac{1}{b^2} - \frac{2a}{b}$

chapter 27

POLYNOMIALS

An algebric expression of the form $ax^n + bx^{n-1} + cx^{n-2} + ...$

where $a \neq 0$, $n \in N$ is called a polynomial of degree n in x.

QUADRATIC EQUATION IN ONE VARIABLE

An equation of the type $ax^2 + bx + c = 0$ $(a \neq 0)$ where a, b, c are constant, is called a *quadratic equation* in the variable x or an equation of the second degree.

A quadratic equation has two roots generally represented by α and β.

$$\alpha = \frac{-b + \sqrt{b^2 - 4ac}}{2a} \quad \text{and} \quad \beta = \frac{-b - \sqrt{b^2 - 4ac}}{2a}$$

Discriminant

$b^2 - 4ac$ is called *discriminant* of the equation $ax^2 + bx + c = 0$ denoted by D or Δ.

1. If $b^2 - 4ac > 0$, then roots are unequal and real

   (*i*) If $\sqrt{b^2 - 4ac}$ is rational, then roots are real, unequal and rational.

   (*ii*) If $\sqrt{b^2 - 4ac}$ is irrational, then roots are real, unequal and irrational.

2. If $b^2 - 4ac = 0$, then roots are equal and real.
3. If $b^2 - 4ac < 0$, then roots are imaginary (complex).

Sum and Product of Roots

1. The quadratic equation having roots α and β is

$$x^2 - x(\alpha + \beta) + \alpha\beta = 0$$

i.e., $x^2 - x$ (sum of roots) + product of roots = 0.

2. Slope of $ax + by + c = 0$ is $-\frac{a}{b}$

$$\text{Slope (m)} = -\frac{\text{coefficient of x}}{\text{coefficient of y}} = -\frac{a}{b}$$

3. If α and β are roots of the quadratic equation $ax^2 + bx + c = 0$, then

$$\text{Sum of the roots } (\alpha + \beta) = \frac{\text{coefficient of x}}{\text{coefficient of } x^2} = \frac{-b}{a}$$

$$\text{Product of the roots } (\alpha\,\beta) = \frac{\text{constant term}}{\text{coefficient of } x^2} = \frac{c}{a}$$

REMAINDER THEOREM

If a rational integer funciton of x, say f(x) is divided by (x–a), then remainder is f(a).

FACTOR THEOREM

If f(x) is a rational integral function and f(a) = 0, then x – a is a factor of f(x).

1. (x + 1) is a factor of f(x), if sum of the coefficient of even powers of x is equal to sum of the co-efficient of odd powers of x.
2. (x – 1) is a factor of f(x), if sum of the coefficient of all powers of x in f(x) is zero.

VERY IMPORTANT POINTS
1. The set of polynomials has closure, commutative and associative properties under addition as well as multiplication. **Note:** Subtraction is not commutative in the set of polynomials.
2. '0' is the identity element under addition.
3. '1' is the identity element under multiplication.
4. Every polynomial has an additive and multiplicative inverse.

Equation of Higher Degree

$$f(x) = a_0x^n + a_1x^{n-1} + a_2\, x^{n-2} + \ldots\ldots\ldots a_{n-1}\, x + a_n = 0$$

where, $a_1, a_2 \ldots\ldots a_n \in R$, $a_0 \neq 0$ be a polynomial equation of degree n, having n roots $\alpha_1, \alpha_2 \ldots. \alpha_n$. Then

1. *Sum of roots:*

$$\alpha_1 + \alpha_2 + \ldots\ldots \alpha_n = (-1)^1 \frac{a_1}{a_0}$$

2. *Sum of product of two roots:*

$$\alpha_1 \alpha_2 + \alpha_1 \alpha_3 + \ldots\ldots = (-1)^2 \frac{a_2}{a_0}$$

3. *Sum of product of three roots:*

$$\alpha_1\, \alpha_2\, \alpha_3 + \alpha_2\alpha_3\alpha_4 + \ldots\ldots. = (-1)^3 \frac{a_3}{a_0}, \text{ so on.}$$

4. *Product of all roots*

$$\alpha_1 \alpha_2\, \alpha_3 \ldots\ldots \alpha_n = (-1)^n \frac{a_n}{a_0}$$

e.g. cubic equation: If α, β, γ are roots of the cubic equation $ax^3 + bx^2 + cx + d = 0$, then

$$\alpha + \beta + \gamma = -\frac{b}{a}$$

$$\alpha\beta + \beta\gamma + \gamma\alpha = \frac{c}{a}$$

chapter 28

PRINCIPLE OF MATHEMATICAL INDUCTION

If p(n) is a statement which is TRUE for n = 1 and is TRUE for n+1 whenever it is true for 1, 2.....n, then the statement p(n) is true for all natural numbers n.

Example. Prove $1 + 3 + 5 + \ldots\ldots\ldots\ldots + (2n - 1) = n^2$ using the principle of mathematical induction.

Proof.

We shall use the principle of induction on n.

The statement p(n) is

$$1 + 3 + 5 \ldots\ldots + (2n - 1) = n^2 \quad \ldots(1)$$

Clearly p(1) is true because $1 = 1^2$

Assume that the statement is true for n (this is called induction hypothesis)

i.e. $$1 + 3 + 5 + \ldots\ldots + (2n - 1) = n^2 \quad \ldots(2)$$

We have to prove the truth of p(n) for (n+1).

Adding $2(n + 1) - 1 = 2n + 1$, the term next to $2n - 1$ on both sides of (2), we get

$$1 + 3 + 5 + \ldots\ldots + (2n - 1) + (2n + 1) = n^2 + (2n + 1) = (n + 1)^2 \quad \ldots(3)$$

From (1) and (2), we can conclude that the result p(n) is true for all natural numbers.

SOME SPECIAL PRODUCTS

1. $(x + a)(x + b) = x^2 + x(a + b) + ab$
2. $(x + a)(x + b)(x + c) = x^3 + x^2(a + b + c) + x(ab + bc + ca) + abc$
3. $(ax + b)(cx + d) = acx^2 + x(ad + bc) + bd$.
4. If $x + \frac{1}{x} = K$, then

   (*i*) $x^2 + \frac{1}{x^2} = K^2 - 2$

   (*ii*) $x^3 + \frac{1}{x^3} = K^3 - 3K$

   e.g. If $x + \frac{1}{x} = 5 = 5$, then

   (*i*) $x^2 + \frac{1}{x^2} = 5^2 - 2 = 25 - 2 = 23$

   (*ii*) $x^3 + \frac{1}{x^3} = 5^3 - 3(5) = 125 - 15 = 110$

5. If $x - \frac{1}{x} = K$, then

   (*i*) $x^2 + \frac{1}{x^2} = K^2 + 2$

   (*ii*) $x^3 - \frac{1}{x^3} = K^3 + 3K$.

   e.g. If $x - \frac{1}{x} = 3$, then

   (*i*) $x^2 + \frac{1}{x^2} = 3^2 + 2 = 9 + 2 = 11$

   (*ii*) $x^3 - \frac{1}{x^3} = 3^3 + 3(3) = 27 + 9 = 36$.

CONCEPTS AND FORMULAE

1. A sub set A of R is said to be an inductive set, if $I \in A$ and $K \in A$ implies $K + I \in A$.
2. The intersection of all inductive sets in R is called the positive integer set (Z+) or natural number set (N).
3. Let $A \subseteq N$ be such that

   (*i*) $I \in A$

   (*ii*) $K \in A \Rightarrow K + I \in A$.

   then $A = N$
4. Every non empty subset of natural number set has the least element.
5. **Principle of mathematical induction :**
   Let f(n) be a statement for each $n \in N$. If f(1) is true and f(K) is True implies f(K+1) is True, the statement f(n) is true for all $n \in N$. This is called principle of *mathematical induction.*
6. Let a > O and b be two integers. Then there exists a unique pair of integers q and r, such that $b = aq + r$ and $0 \leq r \leq q$.

   If r = 0, then we say a divides b and we denotes it as a/b.
7. $1 + 2 + 3 + \ldots\ldots\ldots + n = \dfrac{n(n+1)}{2}$
8. $1^2 + 2^2 + 3^2 + \ldots\ldots\ldots + n^2 = \sum_{r=1}^{n} r^2 = \dfrac{n(n+1)(2n+1)}{6}$
9. $1^3 + 2^3 + 3^3 + \ldots\ldots + n^3 = \sum_{r=1}^{n} r^3 = \dfrac{n^2(n+1)^2}{4} = \left[\sum_{r=1}^{n} r^3\right]^2$
10. $1 + 3 + 5 + \ldots\ldots\ldots n$ terms $= n^2$
11. $2 + 4 + 6 + \ldots\ldots n$ terms $= n(n + 1)$.

chapter

29

SQUARE ROOTS

SQUARE ROOT

If a number is multiplied by itself, then the product is called square of that number.

e.g. 6 is the square root of 36, i.e. 6 . 6 = 36.

Note:

1. If $a^2 = b$, then a is the square root of b. The symbol for square root is $\sqrt{\ }$. It is called radical sign and is placed before the number whose square root is to be calculated.

   e.g. $\sqrt{9} = 3$, $\sqrt{16} = 4$, $\sqrt{25} = 5$ etc.,

2. The square root of x^2 is denoted by $\sqrt{x^2}$

   e.g. $\sqrt{x^2} = +x$ or $-x$

3. The positive equal factor of a number is called principle square root of that number.

   e.g. $\sqrt{49} = +7$ or -7

   because 7   7 = 49 and –7   –7 = 49

PERFECT SQUARE

If a number can be written as the product of two equal factors, then the number is called a perfect square.

e.g. 81 can be written as 81 = 9   9 (two equal factors)

so, 81 is a perfect square.

1, 4, 9, 16, 25, 36, ...are perfect square numbers.

2, 3, 5, 6, 7, 8, 10, 11, 12..........are not perfect square numbers.

Note:

1. Square roots for numbers which are perfect squares can be found by factorisation method.

   e.g. $81 = 3 \quad 27$

   $= 3 \quad 3 \quad 9$

   $= 3 \quad 3 \quad 3 \quad 3$

   $= (3 \quad 3) \quad (3 \quad 3)$

   $= 9 \quad 9 = 9^2$

   $\therefore \quad \sqrt{81} = 9$

2. The square of a number ends with any one of the digits 0, 1, 4, 5, 6, 9. The converse is not true.

3. Numbers ending with any one of the digits 2, 7, 8 ar enot perfect square numbers.

4. $x = \sqrt{x^2}$

   So $x^2 > 0$ implies that $\sqrt{\ }$ is applicable to non-negative real numbers.

   e.g. $\sqrt{-4}, \sqrt{-5}$ .... do not exist in the set of real numbers because –4, –5 are not non-negative.

   Square root of a negative number is called an imaginary numbers.

RELATIONS OF ALGEBRAIC EXPRESSIONS

1. $\sqrt{a} + \sqrt{b} \neq \sqrt{a+b}$
2. $\sqrt{a} - \sqrt{b} \neq \sqrt{a-b}$
3. $\sqrt{a} \times \sqrt{b} = \sqrt{ab}$.
4. $\sqrt{\frac{a}{b}} = \frac{\sqrt{a}}{\sqrt{b}}$
5. $\sqrt{x^2+y^2} \neq \sqrt{x^2} + \sqrt{y^2}$ or $x + y$
6. $\sqrt{x^2-y^2} \neq \sqrt{x^2} - \sqrt{y^2}$ or $x - y$

FINDING SQUARE ROOTS OF ALGEBRAIC EXPRESSIONS

Square roots of algebraic expressions can be found by following methods.

1. **Inspection Method (using special products).**

Example. Find the square root of $a^2 + 4ab + 4b^2$, using speical products.

Solution.

$$a^2 + 4ab + 4b^2 = a^2 + 2a(2b) + (2b)^2 = (a + 2b)^2$$

$$\therefore \qquad \sqrt{a^2 + 4ab + 4b^2} = a + 2b$$

2. **Division Method.**
Rule:

(*i*) Mark off the figure into periods of two, beginning from the decimal point and moving either way.

(*ii*) Find the greatest number whose square is obtained in the last period.

(*iii*) Write the square of this number below the last period and subtract.

(*iv*) Bring down the next period.

(*v*) Double the root figure already found for a trial divisor.

(*vi*) Divide the remainder, except the last digit by the trial divisor and get the next figure of the square root.

Example. Find the square root of the number 7225.

Solution.

.	85
8	7225 64
165	825 825
	0

Since all the digits are used and the last remainder is zero, the division as well as the extraction of the square root is completed.

$$\therefore \qquad \sqrt{7225} = 85$$

Example. Find the square root of the number 16129.

Solution.

	127
1	16129
	1
22	61
	44
247	1729
	1729
	0

$\therefore \qquad \sqrt{16129} = 127$

Example. Find the square root of the numbers 0.132496.

Solution.

	0.364
3	0.132496
	9
66	424
	396
724	2896
	2896
	0

$\therefore \qquad \sqrt{0.132496} = 0.364$

Note : If it is required to find the square root of a number upto decimal places, there must be 2n digits on the right of decimal point (if not, we create them by writing zero).

Example. Find the square root of 2 upto three places of decimal.

Solution.

To find square root upto 3 places of decimal point, we must have 2   3 = 6 digits on the right of the decimal point

Thus $3 = 3.000000$

	1.732
3	3.000000
	1
27	200
	189
343	1100
	1029
3462	7100
	6924
	176

∴ $\sqrt{3} = 1.732$ upto 3 decimal places.

Example. Find the square root of 321.865 upto four places of decimal point.

Solution.

To find square root upto 4 places of decimal, we must have 2 4 = 8 digits on the right of the decimal point.

Thus $321.865 = 321.86500000$

	17.9405
1	321.86500000
	1
27	221
	189
349	3286
	3141
3584	14550
	14336
358805	2140000
	1794025
	345975

∴ $\sqrt{321.865} = 17.9405$ upto 4 decimal places.

Example. Find square root of $x^4 - 2x^3 + 3x^2 - 2x + 1$ using the division method.

Solution.

$$
\begin{array}{r|l}
x^2 & x^4 - 2x^3 + 3x^2 - 2x + 1 \;(x^2 - x + 1 \\
 & x^4 \\
\hline
2x^2 - x & -2x^3 + 3x^2 \\
 & \underline{-2x^3 + x^2} \\
2x^2 - 2x + 1 & 2x^2 - 2x + 1 \\
 & \underline{2x^2 - 2x + 1} \\
 & 0
\end{array}
$$

3. **Method of Undetermined coefficients.**

Example 1. Find the square root of $x^4 + 6x^3 + 17x^2 + 24x + 16$.

Solution.

The given expression being of degree four its square root will be a quadratic expression. Therefore we may assume.

$$x^4 + 6x^3 + 17x^2 + 24x + 16 = (x^2 + Ix + m)^2$$

where l, m are to be determined.

$$(x^2 + lx + m)^2 = x^4 + 2lx^3 + (l^2 + 2m)x^2 + 2lmx + m^2$$

Thus,

$$x^4 + 6x^3 + 17x^2 + 24x + 16 = x^4 + 2lx^3 + (l^2 + 2m)x^2 + 2lmx + m^2$$

Comparing the coefficients of powers of x on either side, we get

$$2l = 6, \quad l^2 + 2m = 17, \quad 2lm = 24, \quad m^2 = 16$$

these give $\quad l = 3, m = 4$

Hence the square root is $\quad x^2 + lx + m = (x^2 + 3x + 4)$.

Example 2. If $ax^2 + bx + c$ is a perfect square, then prove that $b^2 = 4ac$.

Solution. Let $\quad ax^2 + bx + c = (lx + m)^2$

Then, $\quad ax^2 + bx + c = l^2x^2 + 2lmx + m^2$

Comparing coefficients of various powers of x on either side, we get

$$l^2 = a, \quad 2lm = b, \quad m^2 = c$$

$\Rightarrow$ $$2lm = b$$

Squaring on both sides, we get

$$4lm^2m^2 = b^2$$

Elimination of l, and m gives

$$4\ ac = b^2$$

$\therefore$ $$b^2 = 4ac$$

HOMOGENEOUS EXPRESSIONS

If all the terms of an algebraic expression are of the same degree, then such an expression is called a *homogeneous expression.*

1. ax + by is a first degree homogeneous expression in x and y.
2. $ax^2 + 2hxy + by^2$ is a second degree homogeneous expression in x and y.
3. $ax^3 + bxy + cx^2$ is not a homogeneous expression.

SYMMETRIC EXPRESSIONS

An algebraic expression f(x, y) in two variables x, y is called a symmetric expression if

$$f(x,y) = f(y,x)$$

e.g. (*i*) $f(x,y) = ax + ay = f(y,x)$

Hence ax + by is symmetric and also homogeneous.

(*ii*) $ax^2 + by^2$ is not symmetric but homogeneous.

(*iii*) $ax^2 + by^2 + c$ is neither homogeneous nor symmetric.

CYCLIC EXPRESSIONS

An algebraic expression f(x,y,z) in three variables x, y, z is said to be cyclic if

$$f(x, y, z) = f(y, z, x) = f(z, x, y)$$

e.g. (*i*) $\sum_{a,b} a^2b = a^2b + b^2a.$

(*ii*) $\sum_{a,b,c} a^2b = a^2b + b^2c + c^2a$

(*iii*) $\left(\sum_{a,b,c} a\right)^2 = (a + b + c)^2$

(*iv*) $\prod_{a,b,c} (a^2 + b^2) = (a^2 + b^2)\,(b^2 + c^2)\,(c^2 + a^2)$

IMPORTANT RESULTS

1. $\sum (x - y) = 0$

2. $\sum (x^2 - y^2) = 0$

3. $\sum (x^3 - y^2) = 0$

4. $\sum x(y - z) = 0$

5. $\sum x^2\,(y^2 - z^2) = 0$

6. $\sum x\,(y^2 - z^2) = (x - y)\,(y - z)\,(z - x)$

7. $\sum x^2\,(y - z) = -(x - y)\,(y - z)\,(z - x)$

8. $\sum (x - y)^3 = 3(x - y)\,(y - z)\,(z - x)$

chapter

30

LINEAR EQUATIONS AND INEQUATIONS

LINEAR EQUATION

Any equation of the first degree having two variables such as x and y is called a linear equation in two variables.

e.g. (*i*) $2x + 3y = 5$

(*ii*) $ax + by + c = 0$

NUMERICAL EXPRESSION

Expression of the form $7 + 5$, $6 - 4$, 5×7, $(10 + 8) - 9$, $10 \div 2$ etc., are called numerical expression.

MATHEMATICAL SENTENCE

If two numerical expressions are joined or connected by 'is equal to (=)' or 'is greater than (>)' or 'is less than (<)' etc, they are called mathematical sentence.

e.g. $7 + 4 = 11$, $8 + 4 > 10$, $5 \times 7 = 35$.

MATHEMATICAL STATEMENT

A mathematical sentence that can be verified as either True or False but not both is called a mathematical statement'.

EQUALITY

A true mathematical statement containing the sign 'is equal to (=)' is called an equality.

e.g. $5 + 4 = 9$.

SOLVING EQUATIONS HAVING TWO VARIABLES

For this we need two independent equations. We solve them by following methods:

1. The method of elimination
2. The method of substitution
3. The method of cross multiplication

Example. Solve the system of equations

$$5x - 24y = 16 \quad \text{...(1)}$$

$$4x - y = 31 \quad \text{...(2)}$$

Solution.

1. **Method of elimination.**

   Let us solve the system of equations by eliminating x.

   Coefficient of x in the two equations are 5 and 4. L.C.M. of 5 and 4 is 20. Let us make coefficient of x equal to the L.C.M. 20.

   Multiply both sides of (1) by 4, we get

   $$20x - 96y = 64 \quad \text{...(3)}$$

   Multiply both sides of (2) by 5, we get

   $$20x - 5y = 155 \quad \text{...(4)}$$

   Subtracting (4) from (3) [to eliminate x], we get

   $$-91y = -91$$

   $$\Rightarrow \quad y = 1$$

   Putting y = 1 in (1), we get

   $$5x - 24 \times 1 = 16$$

   $$\Rightarrow \quad 5x = 16 + 24$$

   $$\Rightarrow \quad x = \frac{40}{5} = 8.$$

   Hence the solution is x = 8, y = 1.

   i.e. the ordered pair (8, 1)

2. **Method of Substitution.**

From (2) we have

$$4x - y = 31$$

$$\therefore \quad y = 4x - 31 \qquad ...(3)$$

Substituting the value of y in (1), we get

$$5x - 24(4x - 31) = 16$$

$$\Rightarrow \quad 5x - 96x + 744 = 16$$

$$\Rightarrow \quad -91x = -728$$

$$\Rightarrow \quad x = \frac{-728}{-91} = 8$$

Putting x = 8 in (3), we get

$$y = 4(8) - 31 = 1$$

Hence the solution is x = 8, y = 1

i.e. the ordered pair (8,1).

3. **Method of Cross Multiplication.**

Rewrite the given equation so that Right Hand Sides (R.H.S.) of each is zero.

$$5x - 24y - 16 = 0$$

$$4x - y - 31 = 0$$

Now we write

$$\Rightarrow \quad \frac{x}{(-24)(-31)-(-1)(-16)} = \frac{y}{(-16)(4)-(-31)(5)}$$

$$= \frac{1}{(5)(-1)-(+4)(-24)}$$

$$\Rightarrow \quad \frac{x}{744 - 16} = \frac{y}{-64 + 155} = \frac{1}{-5 + 96}$$

$$\Rightarrow \quad \frac{x}{728} = \frac{y}{91} = \frac{1}{91}$$

$$\Rightarrow \quad x = \frac{728}{91} = 8, \quad y = \frac{91}{91} = 1$$

Hence the solution is x = 8, y = 1

i.e. the ordered pair is (8,1).

INEQUALITY

A true statement containing the signs '>' or '<' is called an *inequality*.

$x > 0$ means x is positive number, and

$x < 0$ means x is negative number.

INEQUATION

An open sentence containing one of the signs $\neq, <, \leq, >, \geq$ is called an inequation.

1. The line $ax + by + c = 0$ divides the cartesian plane into two half planes.

   One half-plane represents the inequation $ax + by + c > 0$

   Other half plane represents the inequation $ax + by + c < 0$.

2. Graph of a linear equation is a straight line

   Graph of a linear inequation is region.

chapter 31

SURDS

SURDS OR RADICALS

If 'a' is a positive rational number which cannot be expressed as the nth power of same rational number, then the irrational number

$\sqrt[n]{a}$ or $a^{1/n}$,

i.e. the positive nth root of 'a' is called a surd, i.e. an irrational real root of a rational number.

e.g. $\sqrt{2}$, $\sqrt{3}$, $\sqrt{5}$, are called quadratic surds or second order of surds.

$\sqrt[3]{2}$, $\sqrt[3]{3}$, $\sqrt[3]{5}$ are called cubic surds.

$\sqrt[4]{2}$, $\sqrt[4]{3}$, $\sqrt[4]{5}$ are called fourth order or biquadratic surds.

Radical Sign.

The symbol $\sqrt[n]{\ }$ is called the radical sign.

Order of the Surd.

In $\sqrt[n]{a}$, 'n' is called order of the surd or radical.

Radicand.

In $\sqrt[n]{a}$, 'a' is called radicand.

Surd in its Simplest form.

It has no factor which is the nth power of a rational number under the radical sign whose index is 'n'.

TYPES OF SURDS

1. **Pure and Mixed surds**

   A surd consisting of wholly of an irrational number is called *pure surd.*

   e.g. $\sqrt{2}, \sqrt[3]{5}$, etc.

   A surd consisting of the product of rational and an irrational number is called *mixed surd.*

   e.g. $a \times \sqrt{b}$, $3 \times \sqrt{5}$ etc.

2. **Compound surd**

   A surd which is the sum or difference of two or more surds is called *compound surd.*

   e.g. $\sqrt{3}+\sqrt{7}$, $\sqrt{2}+\sqrt[3]{5}-\sqrt[5]{7}$ etc.

3. **Binomial surd**

   A compound surd consisting of two surds is called a *binomial surd.*

   e.g. $\sqrt{2}+\sqrt[3]{5}, \sqrt{5}-\sqrt[3]{7}$ etc.

4. **Similar surd.**

   If two surds are different multiples of the same surd, then they are called *similar surds*, otherwise they are *dissimilar surds.*

   e.g. $\sqrt[3]{3}$, $\sqrt[4]{3}$, $\sqrt[-7]{3}$ etc. are similar surds.

   $\sqrt[6]{3}$, $\sqrt[5]{5}$ etc. are dissimilar surds.

   Note :

   Product or quotient of two similar monomial surds is a rational number.

   e.g. $\sqrt[2]{3} \times \sqrt[5]{3} = 10 \times 3 = 30$ is a rational number.

   $$\frac{\sqrt[2]{3}}{\sqrt[5]{3}} = \frac{2}{5}$$ is a rational number

5. **Quadratic surd**

   A surd of the second order is called *quadratic surd.*

6. **Conjugate surd**
   When bionomial expressions containing surds differing in the sign (+ or –) connecting them are said to be conjugate to each other.

   e.g. $x+\sqrt{y}$ and $x-\sqrt{y}$ are conjugate to each other.

COMPARISON OF SURDS

Surds of the same order can be compared by comparing their radicands.

- If $a+\sqrt{b}=c+\sqrt{d}$ where a, c are rational numbers and $\sqrt{b}$, $\sqrt{d}$ are surds, then

$$a=c,\ b=d.$$

- If 'a' is a rational number, then

$$a>0,\ \sqrt{a+\sqrt{a+\sqrt{a+\sqrt{a+\ldots\ldots\ldots\infty}}}}=\frac{1+\sqrt{1+4a}}{2}$$

$$a>0,\ \sqrt{a\sqrt{a\sqrt{a\sqrt{a\ldots\ldots\ldots\infty}}}}=a$$

$$a>0,\ \sqrt{a\sqrt{a\sqrt{a\sqrt{a\ldots\ldots\ldots n\,\text{times}}}}}=a^{1-\frac{1}{2^n}}$$

RATIONALISATION

If prodcut of two surds is rational, then one of them is called *rationalising factor* (R.F) of the other.

1. Rationalising factor of $a+\sqrt{b}$ is $a-\sqrt{b}$
2. Rationalising factor of $a-\sqrt{b}$ is $a+\sqrt{b}$
3. Rationalising factor of $\sqrt{a}+\sqrt{b}$ is $\sqrt{a}-\sqrt{b}$
4. Rationalising factor of $\sqrt{a}-\sqrt{b}$ is $\sqrt{a}+\sqrt{b}$
5. Rationalising factor of $a-\sqrt[3]{b}$ is $\left(a^2+a\sqrt[3]{b}+\sqrt[3]{b^2}\right)$
6. Rationalising factor of $a+\sqrt[3]{b}$ is $\left(a^2-a\sqrt[3]{b}+\sqrt[3]{b^2}\right)$

7. Rationalising factor of $\sqrt[3]{a} + \sqrt[3]{b}$ is $a^{2/3} - a^{1/3}b^{1/3} + b^{2/3}$

8. Rationalising factor of $\sqrt[3]{a} - \sqrt[3]{b}$ is $a^{2/3} + a^{1/3}b^{1/3} + b^{2/3}$

9. Rationalising factor of $a^{1/3} + b^{-1/3}$ is $a^{2/3} - a^{1/3}b^{-1/3} + b^{-2/3}$

10. Rationalising factor of $a^{1/3} - b^{-1/3}$ is $a^{2/3} + a^{1/3}b^{-1/3} + b^{-2/3}$

11. Rationalising factor of $\sqrt{x} + \sqrt{y} + \sqrt{z}$ is

$$\left(\sqrt{x} + \sqrt{y} - \sqrt{z}\right)\left(x + y - z - 2\sqrt{xy}\right)$$

12. Rationalising factor of $\sqrt[3]{x} + \sqrt[3]{y} + \sqrt[3]{z}$ is

$$\left[x^{2/3} + y^{2/3} + z^{2/3} - x^{1/3}y^{1/3} - y^{1/3}z^{1/3} - z^{1/3}x^{1/3}\right]$$

$$\left[(x + y + z)^2 + 3(x + y + z)(xyz)^{1/3} + 9(xyz)^{2/3}\right]$$

CONCEPTS AND FORMULAE

1. If $n\sqrt{a}$ is an irrational number where $n \in Z^+$, $a \in a^+$, then it is called a surd.

   When n = 2, it is called *quadratic surd.*

   When n = 3, it is called *cubic surd.*

   When n = 4, it is called *biquadratic surd.*

2. If 'a' is a rational number and $\sqrt{b}$ is a surd, then $a \pm \sqrt{b}$ is called *mixed surd.*

3. If the ratio of two surds is a rational number, then the two surds are called *like surds.*

   If their ratio is not a rational number, then they are called *dislike surds.*

4. If $\sqrt{a}$ and $\sqrt{b}$ are dislike surds, then there is no surd $\sqrt{c}$ such that $\sqrt{c} = \sqrt{a} + \sqrt{b}$

5. $a + \sqrt{b} = c + \sqrt{d}$ (= =) a = c, b = d.

6. $\sqrt{a \pm \sqrt{b}} = \sqrt{\frac{1}{2}\left(a+\sqrt{a^2-b}\right)} \pm \sqrt{\frac{1}{2}\left(a-\sqrt{a^2-b}\right)}$

7. If $\sqrt{a+\sqrt{b}} = \sqrt{x} + \sqrt{y}$, then $\sqrt{a-\sqrt{b}} = \sqrt{x} - \sqrt{y}$

8. If $\sqrt[3]{a+\sqrt{b}} = x + \sqrt{y}$, then $\sqrt[3]{a-\sqrt{b}} = x - \sqrt{y}$

9. If $\sqrt{a+\sqrt{b}+\sqrt{c}+\sqrt{d}} = \sqrt{x} + \sqrt{y} + \sqrt{z}$, then

$$x = \sqrt{\frac{bd}{4c}},\ y = \sqrt{\frac{bc}{4d}},\ z = \sqrt{\frac{cd}{4b}}$$

10. $a + \sqrt{b}$ and $a - \sqrt{b}$ are called conjugate surds.

11. $\sqrt{a+b+c+2\sqrt{ab}+2\sqrt{bc}+2\sqrt{ac}} = \sqrt{a}+\sqrt{b}+\sqrt{c}$

12. $\sqrt{a+b+c+2\sqrt{ab}-2\sqrt{bc}+2\sqrt{ac}}$

$$= \sqrt{a}+\sqrt{b}-\sqrt{c} \text{ if } \sqrt{a}+\sqrt{b} \geq \sqrt{c}$$

$$= \sqrt{c}-\sqrt{a}-\sqrt{b} \text{ if } \sqrt{a}+\sqrt{b} < \sqrt{c}$$

13. If $\sqrt[3]{a \pm \sqrt{b}} = x \pm \sqrt{y}$, then $x^3 + 3xy = a$, $x^2 - y = \sqrt[3]{a^2-b}$

14. A rationalising factor of $\sqrt[3]{a} \pm \sqrt[3]{b}$ is $\left[a^{2/3} \mp (ab)^{1/3} + b^{2/3}\right]$

15. A rationalising factor of $\sqrt[5]{a} \pm \sqrt[5]{b}$ is

$$\left[a^{4/5} \mp a^{3/5}b^{1/5} + a^{2/5}b^{2/5} \mp a^{1/5}b^{3/5} + b^{4/5}\right]$$

16. A rationalising factor of $\sqrt[6]{a} \mp \sqrt[6]{b}$ is

$$\left[a^{5/6} + a^{4/6}b^{1/6} + a^{3/6}b^{2/6} + a^{2/6}b^{3/6} + a^{1/6}b^{4/6} + b^{5/6}\right]$$

17. If $\left(a+\sqrt{b}\right)^{x^2-K} + \left(a-\sqrt{b}\right)^{x^2-K} = 2a$; $a^2 - b = 1$, then

$$x = \pm\sqrt{K \pm 1}$$

chapter

32

REAL NUMBERS

a^n is the product of n factors each of which is 'a' and 'n' is any natural number, n is called *index or exponent of the power* and a is called *base of the power.*

LAW OF INDICES

1. $a^{\circ} = 1$
2. $a^1 = a$
3. $a^m \times a^n = a^{m+n}$
4. $(a^m)^n = a^{mn}$
5. $(ab)^m = a^m b^m$
6. $a^{-m} = \dfrac{1}{a^m}$
7. $\left(\dfrac{a}{b}\right)^m = \dfrac{a^m}{b^m}$
8. $\dfrac{a^m}{b^n} = a^{m-n}$ if m > n

   $\dfrac{a^m}{a^n} = \dfrac{1}{a^{n-m}}$ if n > m
9. $\sqrt[n]{a} . \sqrt[n]{b} = \sqrt[n]{ab}$
10. $\sqrt[m]{a} . \sqrt[n]{a} = \sqrt[mn]{a^{m+n}}$
11. $\sqrt[m]{\sqrt[n]{a}} = \sqrt[mn]{a}$
12. $\dfrac{\sqrt[n]{a}}{\sqrt[m]{a}} = \sqrt[mn]{a^{m-n}}$

13. $p\sqrt[n]{a}\,.\,q\sqrt[n]{b} = pq\sqrt[n]{ab}$

14. If $x^n = y$, then $x = y^{1/n}$

$$\Rightarrow \qquad x = n\sqrt{y}$$

15. $\left(\sqrt{a}\right)^2 = a$

16. $\sqrt[n]{a^p} = a^{p/n}$

17. $\sqrt[n]{m\sqrt{\left(a^p\right)^m}} = {}^{mn}\sqrt{a^{pm}}$

18. $\sqrt[n]{a^n b} = a\sqrt[n]{b}$

OPERATIONS AND THEIR PROPERTIES

Let G be any set of numbers and o (operation) represent an operation over the elements of the set.

1. **Closure Property.**
   If a, b ∈ G and a o b ∈ G, then we say that G is closed under the operation 'o'.

2. **Associative Property.**
   If a, b, c ∈ G and ao(boc) = (aob) oc, then we say that p is assocaitive with respective to o.

3. **Identity Element.**
   If a is any element of G and there exist an element e ∈ G such that a o e = e o a = a, then a is called identity element in G with respective to 'o'.

4. **Inverse Property.**
   If a is any non zero element of G and there exists an element 'a' belonging to G such that $aoa' = a'oa = e$, then we say that 'a' is the inverse of 'a', with respective to 'o' in G.

5. **Commutative Property.**
   If a, b ∈ G and a o b = b o a, then G is commutative with respect to 'o'.

GROUP

A non empty set is called a group under a certain binary operation, if it satisfies the following properties:

1. Closure
2. Associative
3. Identity
4. Inverse

ABELIAN GROUP

If a group satisfies the commutative property, then it is called an abelian group.

e.g. (z, +) is a group. It is also a abelian group.

chapter

33

BINOMIAL THEOREM

DEFINITION

Any algebraic expression consisting of two terms is called *binomial expansion.*

e.g. $x + 2y$, $5x - y$ etc.

BINOMIAL THEOREM FOR POSITIVE INTEGRAL INDEX

Statement : If x and a are any real numbers and n is a positive integer, then

$$(x+a)^n = {}^nC_0 x^n + {}^nC_1 x^{n-1}a + {}^nC_2 x^{n-2}a^2 \ldots$$
$$ {}^nC_r\, x^{n-r}\, a^r + \ldots\ldots\ldots\ldots + {}^nC_n\, a^n$$

or $$(x+a)^n = \sum_{r=0}^{n} {}^nC_r\, x^{n-r} a^r$$

Note : (*i*) The expression of $(x + a)^n$ contains $(n + 1)$ terms.

(*ii*) Sum of the powers of x and 'a' in each term is equal to n.

General term.

The $(r+1)^{th}$ term is called *general term* and is denoted T_{r+1}

Thus $$T_{r+1} = {}^nC_r\, x^{n-r}\, a^r$$

Putting $r = 0, 1, 2, \ldots\ldots\ldots n$, all the terms of the expansion can be obtained.

Expansion of $(x - a)^n$.

Writing $-a$ for a in the expansion of $(x + a)^n$, we get by binomial theorem

$$(x-a)^n = {}^nC_0\, x^n - {}^nC_1\, x^{n-1}\, a + {}^nC_2\, x^{n-2} a^2 - \ldots\ldots$$
$$+ (-1)^r\, {}^nC_r\, x^{n-r}\, a^r + \ldots\ldots\ldots\ldots + (-1)^n\, {}^nC_n\, a^n$$

where, ${}^nC_0, {}^nC_1, {}^nC_2, \ldots\ldots {}^nC_r \ldots\ldots {}^nC_n$ are called binomial co-efficients.

General term.

$$T_{r+1\,c} = {}^nC_r x^{n-r} (-a)^r$$

Note :

1. $(x + a)^n + (x - a)^n = 2\,[{}^nC_0 x^n + {}^nC_2 x^{n-2}.\, a^2 + {}^nC_4 x^{n-4}.\, a^4 + \ldots]$
2. $(x + a)^n - (x - a)^n = 2\,[{}^nC_1 x^{n-1}.\, a + {}^nC_2 x^{n-3}.\, a^3 + {}^nC_5 x^{n-5}.\, a^5 + \ldots]$

PASCAL TRIANGLE

0							1							
1						1	Δ	1						
2					1	Δ	2	Δ	1					
3				1	Δ	3	Δ	3	Δ	1				
4			1	Δ	4	Δ	6	Δ	4	Δ	1			
5		1	Δ	5	Δ	10	Δ	10	Δ	5	Δ	1		
6	1		6		15		20		15		6		1	

Here, each row is bounded by 1, the above arrangement of the co-efficients is known as pascal triangle or the arithmetic triangle.

1. $n! = 1.\,2.\,3.\,4 \ldots\ldots\ldots (n-1).\, n$ or $n.\,(n-1).\,(n-2) \ldots.. 3.\,2.\,1.$
2. $0! = 1,\ 1! = 1$
3. $n! = n.\,(n-1)\,!$

   $= n.\,(n-1).\,(n-2)$

   $= n.\,(n-1)\,(n-2)\,(n-3)\,!$
4. ${}^nC_r = \dfrac{n!}{(n-r)\,!\,r!}$

5. $^nC_r = {^nC_{n-r}}$

6. $^nC_0 = {^nC_n} = 1$

7. $^nC_1 = n;\ {^nC_2} = \dfrac{n(n-1)}{2!} : {^nC_3} = \dfrac{n(n-1)(n-2)}{3!}$

8. $\dfrac{^nC_r}{^nC_{r-1}} = \dfrac{n-r+1}{r}$ if $1 \le r \le n$

9. $^nC_{r-1} + {^nC_r} = {^{n+1}C_r}$ if $1 \le r \le n$

10. $\dfrac{^nC_r}{^{n-1}C_{r-1}} = \dfrac{n}{r}$ if $1 \le r \le n$

11. $^nC_r = {^nC_s}$

$\Rightarrow\ r = s$ (or) $n = r + s$

RESULTS

1. The expansion $(x + a)^n$ has $n + 1$ terms.

2. The coefficient of x's in $\left(ax^p + \dfrac{b}{x^q}\right)^n$ is given by T_{r+1},

   where $r = \dfrac{np-s}{p+q}$

3. *Independent term of x.* The term which does not contain x is called the term independent of x or constant term.

   Independent term of x in $\left(ax^p + \dfrac{b}{x_q}\right)^n$ is T_{r+1},

   where $r = \dfrac{np}{p+q}$

   Constant term = ^nC_r, $a^{n-r}b^r$

Middle term in the expansion of $(x+a)^n$.

1. If n is even, middle term is $\left(\frac{n}{2}+1\right)^{th}$ term

i.e. $$t_{\frac{n}{2}+1} = {}^nC_{\frac{n}{2}}\ x^{\frac{n}{2}}.a^{\frac{n}{2}}$$

2. If n is odd, middle terms are $\left(\frac{n+1}{2}\right)^{th}$ and $\left(\frac{n+3}{2}\right)^{th}$.

i.e. $$t_{\frac{n+1}{2}} = t_{\frac{n-1}{2}}+1 = \frac{{}^nC_{n-1}}{2}x^{\frac{n+1}{2}}.a^{\frac{n-1}{2}}$$

$$t_{\frac{n+3}{2}} = t_{\frac{n+1}{2}}+1 = {}^nC_{\frac{n+1}{2}}\,x^{\frac{n-1}{2}}.a^{\frac{n+1}{2}}$$

BINOMIAL COEFFICIENTS

${}^nC_0, {}^nC_1, {}^nC_2, \ldots {}^nC_n$ are called *binomial coefficients* in the expansion of $(x + a)^n$. They are denoted by $C_0, C_1, C_2, \ldots C_4$ respectively.

Greatest Binomial Coefficient

Binomial coefficient of the middle term is *greatest binomial coefficient* in the expansion of $(x + a)^n$.

Greatest coefficient in the expansion of $(a + x)^n$ if

1. 'n' is even, is ${}^nC_{\frac{n}{2}}$.

   'n' is odd, is either ${}^nC_{\frac{n-1}{2}}$ or ${}^nC_{\frac{n+1}{2}}$ which are equal.

2. n is a positive integer, then

   $$(1+x)^n = {}^nC_0 + {}^nC_1x + {}^nC_2 + \ldots\ldots + {}^nC_rx^r + \ldots\ldots + {}^nC_nx^n$$

   Note :

   (*i*) General term, $t_{r+1} = {}^nC_rx^r$

   (*ii*) Coefficient of $x^r = {}^nC_r$

   (*iii*) Coefficient of rth term $= {}^nC_{r-1}$

3. If n is a positive integer, then

$$(1 - n)^n = {}^nC_0 - {}^nC_1 x + {}^nC_2 x^2 - \dots + (-1)^r\, {}^nC_r x^r + \dots + (-1)^n\, {}^nC_n x^n$$

General term, $t_{r+1} = (-1)^r\, {}^nC_r\, x^r$.

Note:

(*i*) $(1 + x)^n + (1-x)^n = 2\,[{}^nC_0 + {}^nC_2x^2 + {}^nC_4x^4 + \dots\dots\dots]$

(*ii*) $(1 + x)^n - (1 - x)^n = 2\,[{}^nC_1x + {}^nC_3x^3 + {}^nC_5x^5 + \dots\dots\dots]$

4. If n is a negative integer or fraction, then

(*a*) $(1 + x)^{-n} = 1 - nx + \dfrac{n(n+1)}{2!}x^2 - \dfrac{n(n+1)(n+2)}{3!}x^3 + \dots.$

(*b*) $(1 - x)^{-n} = 1 + nx + \dfrac{n(n+1)}{2!}x^2 + \dfrac{n(n+1)(n+2)}{3!}x^3 + \dots$

(*c*) $(1+x)^n = 1 + nx + \dfrac{n(n-1)}{2!}x^2 + \dfrac{n(n-1)(n-2)}{3!}x^3 + \dots$

(*d*) $(1+x)^{-1} = 1 - x + x^2 \dots (-1)^r x^r + \dots\infty$

(*e*) $(1 - x)^{-1} = 1 + x + x^2 \dots + x^r + \dots \infty$

(*f*) $(1 + x)^{-2} = 1 - 2x + 3x^2 - 4x^3 + \dots + (-1)^r (r + 1) x^r + \dots \infty$

(*g*) $(1 - x)^{-2} = 1 + 2x + 3x^2 + 4x^3 + \dots + (r + 1) x^r + \dots \infty$

(*h*) $(1 + x)^{-3} = \dfrac{1}{2!}[1.2 - 2.3x + 3.4x^2 - 4.5x^3 + \dots$
$+ (-1)^r (r+1)(r+2)x^r + \dots \infty]$

(*i*) $(1 - x)^{-3} = \dfrac{1}{2!}[1.2 + 2.3x + 3.4x^2 + 4.5x^3 + \dots$
$+ (r+1)(r+2)x^r + \dots \infty]$

(*j*) $(1+x)^{\frac{-p}{q}} = 1 - p\left(\dfrac{x}{q}\right) + \dfrac{p(p+q)}{2!}\left(\dfrac{x}{q}\right)^2$
$\dfrac{p(p+q)(p+2q)}{3!}\left(\dfrac{x}{q}\right)^3 + \dots\dots\infty$

(*k*) $(1-x)^{\frac{-p}{q}} = 1 + p\left(\frac{x}{q}\right) + \frac{p(p+q)}{2!}\left(\frac{x}{q}\right)^2$

$$+ \frac{p(p+q)\,(p+2q)}{3!}\left(\frac{x}{q}\right)^3 + ...\infty$$

(*l*) $(1+x)^{\frac{p}{q}} = 1 + p\left(\frac{x}{q}\right) + \frac{p(p-q)}{2!}\left(\frac{x}{q}\right)^2$

$$+ \frac{p(p-q)(p-2q)}{3!}\left(\frac{x}{q}\right)^3 + ... +$$

$$\frac{p(p-q)(p-2q)....\left[p-(r-1)q\right]}{\angle r}\left(\frac{x}{q}\right)^r + ...\infty$$

(*m*) $(1-x)^{\frac{p}{q}} = 1 - p\left(\frac{x}{q}\right) + \frac{p(p-q)}{2!}\left(\frac{x}{q}\right)^2 - \frac{p(p-q)(p-2q)}{3!}\left(\frac{x}{q}\right)^3$

$$+...+ \frac{p(p-q)(p-2q).....\left[p-(r-1)q\right]}{\angle r}(-1)^r\left(\frac{x}{q}\right)^r + ...\infty$$

(*n*) Let f(x) be any polynomial in x, then

(*i*) sum of the coefficients = f(1)

(*ii*) sum of the coefficients of even powers of x = $\frac{f(1)+f(-1)}{2}$

(*iii*) sum of the coefficient of odd powers of x = $\frac{f(1)+f(-1)}{2}$

PROPERTIES OF BINOMIAL CO-EFFICIENTS

1. $^nC_k + {}^nC_{k+1} = (n+1)_{C_{k+1}}$

2. $^nC_0 + {}^nC_1 + {}^nC_2 + ... {}^nC_n = 2^n$

3. $^nC_0 - {}^nC_1 + {}^nC_2 ....(-1)^n\, {}^nC_n = 0$

4. $^nC_n + {}^{(n+1)}C_n + {}^{(n+2)}C_n + ...+ {}^{(n+m)}C_n = {}^{n+m+1}C_{n+1}$

5. $^{n}C_0 + {}^{n}C_2 + {}^{n}C_4 + \ldots\ldots = 2^{n-1}$

6. $^{n}C_1 + {}^{n}C_3 + {}^{n}C_5 + \ldots\ldots = 2^{n-1}$

7. $1^{n}C_1 - 2^{n}C_2 + \ldots\ldots(-1)^{n+1}n\ {}^{n}C_n = 0$

8. Let $C_0, C_1, C_2 \ldots C_n$ are the binomial coefficients in the expansion of $(1+x)^n$, then

(*a*) $C_0 + \frac{C_1}{2}x + \frac{C_2}{3}x^2 + \ldots\ldots + \frac{C_n}{n+1}x^n = \frac{(1+x)^{n+1} - 1}{(n+1)x}$

(*b*) $C_0 + \frac{C_1}{2} + \frac{C_2}{3} + \ldots\ldots + \frac{C_n}{n+1}x^n = \frac{2^{n+1} - 1}{n+1}$

(*c*) $C_0 - \frac{C_1}{2} + \frac{C_2}{3} - \frac{C_3}{4} + \ldots\ldots + (-1)^n \frac{C_n}{n+1} = \frac{1}{n+1}$

(*d*) $C_0 + \frac{C_2}{3} + \frac{C_4}{5} + \ldots\ldots = \frac{2^n}{n+1}$

(*e*) $\frac{C_1}{2} + \frac{C_3}{4} + \frac{C_5}{6} + \ldots\ldots = \frac{2^n - 1}{n+1}$

(*f*) $a.C_0 + (a+d).C_1 + (a+2d).C_2 + \ldots + (a+nd).C_n = (2a+nd)2^{n-1}$

(*g*) $a.C_0 - (a+d).C_1 + (a+2d).C_2 \ldots\ldots + (-1)^n(a+nd).C_n = 0.$

(*h*) $C_0^2 + C_1^2 + C_2^2 + \ldots\ldots + C_n^2 = {}^{2n}C_n$

(*i*) $C_0^2 - C_1^2 + C_2^2 - C_3^2 + \ldots + (-1)^n C_n^2 = (-1)^{n/2}\ {}^{n}C_{n/2}$ if n is even.

$= 0$ if n is odd.

(*j*) $a.C_0^2 + (a+d).C_1^2 + (a+2d).C_2^2 + \ldots\ldots + (a+nd).C_n^2$

$$= \left(\frac{2a+nd}{2}\right)^2\ {}^{n}C_n.$$

chapter

34

DECIMALS

DECIMAL NUMBERS

The numbers written in decimal form are called decimal numbers or simple decimals.

e.g. 0.3, 0.47, 3.125 etc.

Decimal parts.

These are whole number part and decimal part of the decimal number offer the decimal.

Decimal places.

The number of digits contained in the decimal part of a decimal gives the number of its decimal places.

e.g. 7.35 has 2 decimal places.

Like decimals.

Decimals having the same number of decimal places are called like decimals.

e.g. 2.68, 11.54 etc.

Unlike decimals.

Decimals not having the same number of decimal places are called unlike decimals.

e.g. 3.08, 10.987, 0.8 etc.

TO CONVERT DECIMAL INTO A FRACTION

Step 1 : Remove the decimal point and write the resulting number as the numerator.

Step 2 : Write 1 followed by as many zeros as is the number of decimal places, as denominator.

Step 3 : Reduce the above fraction in simplest form.

e.g. $0.6 = \frac{6}{10} = \frac{3}{5}$

TO FIND HCF AND LCM OF GIVEN DECIMALS

Step 1 : Convert the given decimal into like decimals.

Step 2 : Find HCF or LCM of numbers without the decimal points.

Step 3 : In the result, mark the decimal point to have as many decimal places as are there in each decimal, taken in step 1.

TERMINATING DECIMALS

While expressing a fraction into a decimal, if the division comes to an end after a finite number of steps, then such decimal is a terminating decimal.

e.g. $\frac{1}{2} = 0.5$, $\frac{3}{4} = 0.75$ etc.

REPEATING OR RECURRING DECIMALS

When a digit or a set of digits are repeated in the decimal part of a decimal, then it is called recurring decimal.

e.g. $\frac{1}{3} = 0.333........ = 0.\overline{3}$

$\frac{5}{6} = 0.8333...... = 0.8\overline{3}$

PURE RECURRING DECIMALS

A recurring decimal is said to be pure recurring, if a set of digits just after the decimal point is repeated.

e.g. $\frac{1}{3} = 0.\overline{3}$

MIXED RECURRING DECIMALS

A recurring decimal is said to be mixed recurring, if some of the digits after decimal point are not repeated and then a set of digits is repeated.

e.g. $\frac{5}{6} = 0.8333 = 0.8\overline{3}$

chapter

35

CALCULUS

LIMITS

The concept of a limit is the most basic concept of calculus. Calculus had its origin integration and differentiation.

DEFINITION

A function f(x) is said to tend to l as $x \to a$ if corresponding to any pre-assigned positive number $\in$, however small, we can find a positive number δ (depending on $\in$) such that

$$|f(x) - \lambda < \in \text{for } 0 < |x - a| < \delta| .$$

We can write the above as $\underset{x \to a}{\text{Lt}} f(x) = l$

SOME IMPORTANT RELATIONS

1. If $\underset{x \to a}{\text{Lt}} f(x) = l$ and $\underset{x \to a}{\text{Lt}} g(x) = m$, then

   (*i*) $\underset{x \to a}{\text{Lt}}\left[f(x) \pm g(x)\right] = \underset{x \to a}{\text{Lt}} f(x) \pm \underset{x \to a}{\text{Lt}} g(x) = l \pm m$

   (*ii*) $\underset{x \to a}{\text{Lt}}\left[f(x).g(x)\right] = \underset{x \to a}{\text{Lt}} f(x).\underset{x \to a}{\text{Lt}} g(x) = l.m$

   (*iii*) $\underset{x \to a}{\text{Lt}}\left[\dfrac{f(x)}{g(x)}\right] = \dfrac{\underset{x \to a}{\text{Lt}} f(x)}{\underset{x \to a}{\text{Lt}} g(x)} = \dfrac{1}{m}$ $(m \neq 0)$

   (*iv*) $\underset{x \to a}{\text{Lt}} k f(x) = k \underset{x \to a}{\text{Lt}} f(x) = kl$

2. $\underset{x \to 0}{\text{Lt}} \dfrac{\sin x}{x} = 1 = \underset{x \to 0}{\text{Lt}} \dfrac{\sin^{-1} x}{x}$

   and $\underset{x \to 0}{\text{Lt}} \dfrac{\sin ax}{x} = a$ (x is measured in radian)

3. $\underset{x\to 0}{\text{Lt}} \frac{x^n - a^n}{x - a} = n\, a^{n-1}$

4. $\underset{x\to 0}{\text{Lt}} \frac{\tan x}{x} = 1 = \underset{x\to 0}{\text{Lt}} \frac{\tan^{-1} x}{x}$

and $\underset{x\to 0}{\text{Lt}} \frac{\tan ax}{x} = a$ (x is measured in radian)

5. $\underset{x\to 0}{\text{Lt}} (1 + x)^{1/x} = \underset{x\to \infty}{\text{Lt}} \left(1 + \frac{1}{x}\right)^x = e$

6. $\underset{x\to 0}{\text{Lt}} (1 - x)^{1/x} = \underset{x\to \infty}{\text{Lt}} \left(1 - \frac{1}{x}\right)^x = e^{-1} = \frac{1}{e}$

7. $\underset{x\to 0}{\text{Lt}} \frac{e^x - 1}{x} = 1$

and $\underset{x\to 0}{\text{Lt}} \frac{e^{ax} - 1}{x} = a$

8. $\underset{x\to 0}{\text{Lt}} \frac{a^x - 1}{x} = \log a$

and $\underset{x\to 0}{\text{Lt}} \frac{a^{kx} - 1}{x} = k \log a$

9. $\underset{x\to 0}{\text{Lt}} \left(\frac{a^x + b^x}{2}\right)^{1/x} = \sqrt{ab}$

10. $\underset{x\to 0}{\text{Lt}} \frac{\sin^{-1} x}{x} = 1$

11. $\underset{x\to 0}{\text{Lt}} \frac{(1+x)^n - 1}{x} = n$

12. $\underset{x\to 0}{\text{Lt}} \frac{\sqrt[n]{1 + x} - 1}{x} = \frac{1}{n}$

13. $\underset{x \to 0}{\text{Lt}} \dfrac{\sqrt[n]{a+x} - \sqrt[n]{a-x}}{x} = \dfrac{2}{n} a^{\frac{1}{n}-1}$

14. *Based on Modulus:*

$$
\begin{aligned}
|x - a| &= x - a, \text{ if } x > a \\
&= -(x - a), \text{ if } x < a \\
&= 0, \text{ if } x = a
\end{aligned}
$$

If $a = 0$,

$$
\begin{aligned}
|x| &= x, \text{ if } x > 0 \\
&= -x, \text{ if } x < 0 \\
&= 0, \text{ if } x = 0
\end{aligned}
$$

SOME USEFUL EXPANSIONS

1. $\sin x = x - \dfrac{x^3}{3!} + \dfrac{x^5}{5!} - \dfrac{x^7}{7!} + \ldots\ldots.$

2. $\cos x = 1 - \dfrac{x^2}{2!} + \dfrac{x^4}{4!} - \dfrac{x^6}{6!} + \ldots\ldots$

3. $\tan x = x + \dfrac{x^3}{3} + \dfrac{2}{15}x^5 + \dfrac{17}{315}x^7 + \ldots\ldots\ldots..; \ |x| < \dfrac{\pi}{2}$

4. $\sec x = 1 + \dfrac{x^2}{2} + \dfrac{5}{24}x^4 + \dfrac{61}{720}x^6 + \ldots\ldots\ldots.; \ 0 < |x| < \dfrac{\pi}{2}$

5. $\text{cosec } x = \dfrac{1}{x} + \dfrac{x}{6} + \dfrac{7}{360}x^3 + \dfrac{31}{15120}x^5 + \ldots\ldots; \ 0 < |x| < \pi$

6. $\cot x = \dfrac{1}{x} - \dfrac{x}{3} - \dfrac{x^3}{45} - \dfrac{2}{945}x^5 \ \ldots\ldots; \ 0 < |x| < \pi$

7. $\sin^{-1} x = x + \dfrac{1}{2}\dfrac{x^3}{3} + \dfrac{1.3}{2.4}\cdot\dfrac{x^5}{5} + \dfrac{1.3.5}{2.4.6}\cdot\dfrac{x^7}{7} + \ldots..; \ |x| < 1$

8. $\cos^{-1} x = \dfrac{\pi}{2} - \sin^{-1}x = \dfrac{\pi}{2} - \left\{x + \dfrac{1}{2}\dfrac{x^3}{3} + \dfrac{1.3}{2.4}\cdot\dfrac{x^5}{5} + \ldots..\right\}; \ |x| < 1$

9. $\tan^{-1}x = \begin{cases} x - \dfrac{x^3}{3} + \dfrac{x^5}{5} - \dfrac{x^7}{7} + \ldots\ldots.; |x| < 1 \\ \pm\dfrac{\pi}{2} - \dfrac{1}{x} + \dfrac{1}{3x^3} - \dfrac{1}{5x^5} + \dfrac{1}{7x^7} \ldots.; \begin{cases} + \text{if } x \geq 1 \\ - \text{ if } x \leq -1 \end{cases} \end{cases}$

10. $e^x = 1 + \frac{x}{1!} + \frac{x^2}{2!} + \frac{x^3}{3!} + ...$

11. $e^{-x} = 1 - \frac{x}{1!} + \frac{x^2}{2!} - \frac{x^3}{3!} + ...$

12. $\log_e (1 + x) = x - \frac{x^2}{2} + \frac{x^3}{3} - ...., -1 < x \leq 1$

13. $\log_e (1 - x) = -x - \frac{x^2}{2} - \frac{x^3}{3} - ...., -1 \leq x < 1$

14. $a^x = 1 + x \log a + \frac{(x \log a)^2}{2!} + ...$

CONCEPTS AND FORMULAE

1. (*i*) **Real functions.**
   If $f : A \to B$, A and B are sub-sets of R, then f is called *real function.*

   (*ii*) **Logarithmic Function.**
   Function $f : R^+ \to R$; $R+ = \{x \in R / x > 0\}$, $f(x) = \log_e x$ (or $\log x$) is called *natural logarithmic function.*

   (*iii*) **Exponential Function.**
   $R \to R^+$, $f(x) = e^x$, is called *exponential function.*

   (*iv*) **Greatest Integer Function.**
   $R \to R$, $f(x) = [x]$ is called the greatest integer function.

2. (*i*) If $f(x) \leq g(x)$ for every x in a deleted nhd of 'a',
   then $\underset{x \to a}{\text{Lt}} f(x) \leq \underset{x \to a}{\text{Lt}} g(x)$.

   (*ii*) If $f(x) \leq g(x) \leq h(x)$ for every x in a delected nhd of 'a'
   and $\underset{x \to a}{\text{Lt}} f(x) = l = \underset{x \to a}{\text{Lt}} h(x)$, then
   $\underset{x \to a}{\text{Lt}} g(x) = l$

   (*iii*) $\underset{x \to a}{\text{Lt}} (fog)(x) = f\left[\underset{x \to a}{\text{Lt}} g(x)\right]$

   (*iv*) If $\underset{x \to a}{\text{Lt}} f(x) = \alpha$ or $-\alpha$, then $\underset{x \to a}{\text{Lt}} \frac{1}{f(a)} = 0.$

STANDARD LIMITS

If f(x) and g(x) are two polynomials such that deg f(x) = m and deg g(x) = n, then

$$\underset{x \to \alpha}{Lt} \frac{f(x)}{g(x)} = 0 \text{ for } m < n$$

$$\underset{x \to \alpha}{Lt} \frac{f(x)}{g(x)} = \alpha \text{ for } m > n$$

$$\underset{x \to \alpha}{Lt} \frac{f(x)}{g(x)} = \frac{\text{coefficient of } x^n \text{in } f(x)}{\text{coefficient of } x^n \text{ is } g(x)} \text{ for } m = n.$$

L'HOSPITAL'S RULE

If f(x) and g(x) are two functions of 'x' such that

$$\underset{x \to a}{Lt} f(x) = 0 = \underset{x \to a}{Lt} g(x)$$

and f'(x), g'(x) and g''(x) are continuous at the point x = a,

then $$\underset{x \to a}{Lt} \frac{f(x)}{g(x)} = \underset{x \to a}{Lt} \frac{f'(x)}{g'(x)}$$

If in addition f'(a) = 0 and g'(a) = 0, applying the rule again, we get

$$\underset{x \to a}{Lt} \frac{f(x)}{g(x)} = \underset{x \to a}{Lt} \frac{f'(x)}{g'(x)} = \underset{x \to a}{Lt} \frac{f''(x)}{g''(x)}$$

Sometimes it may be necessary to repeat this process a number of times till our goal is achieved.

This rule is also applicable if

$$\underset{x \to a}{Lt} f(x) = \alpha \quad \text{and} \quad \underset{x \to a}{Lt} g(x) = \alpha$$

In this case also, $$\underset{x \to a}{Lt} \frac{f(x)}{g(x)} = \underset{x \to a}{Lt} \frac{f'(x)}{g'(x)} = \ldots\ldots$$

$$\frac{d}{dx} \int_{\phi(x)}^{\psi(x)} f(n)dx = \int (\varphi(x))\, \varphi'(x) - f(\phi(x)\, \phi'(x)$$

Evaluation of Left hand and Right hand limits

(i) Left hand limit, L.H.L. = $\underset{x \to \bar{a}}{Lt}\ f(n) = \underset{n \to 0}{Lt}\ f(a-h),\ h > 0$

(ii) Right hand limit, R.H.L = $\underset{x \to a+}{Lt}\ f(n) = \underset{h \to 0}{Lt}\ f(a+h),\ h > 0$

(iii) If $\underset{a \to a-}{Lt}\ f(n) = \underset{a \to a+}{Lt}\ f(n) = I \Leftrightarrow \underset{x \to a}{Lt}\ f(n) = I.$

(iv) If a function f is defined on some right neighbourhood of 'a' and is not defined on any left neighbourhood of 'a', then

$$\underset{x \to a-}{Lt}\ f(x) = \underset{x \to a+}{Lt}\ f(x)$$

Note: $$\underset{x \to a-}{Lt}\ \sqrt{x-a} = \underset{x \to a+}{Lt}\ \sqrt{x-a} = 0$$

(v) If a function f is defined on some left neighbourhood of 'a' and is not defined on any right neighbourhood of 'a', then

$$\underset{x \to a}{Lt}\ f(x) = \underset{x \to \bar{a}}{Lt}\ f(x)$$

Note: $$\underset{x \to a}{Lt}\ \sqrt{a-x} = \underset{x \to \bar{a}}{Lt}\ \sqrt{a-x} = 0$$

CONTINUITY AND DISCONTUNITY

Let $D \subseteq R$ and f be a real valued function defined on D.
Let $a \in D$. f is said to be continuous at a, if, for each $\in > 0$, there exists a $\delta > 0$ such that

$$x \in D \text{ and } |x-a| < \delta \Rightarrow > \{f(x)\ f(a)\} < \in$$

If f is not continous at 'a', then we say that f is discontinuous at 'a' or 'a' is a point discontinuity of f.

Note : For the continuity or discontinuity of f at 'a', the point 'a' must be necessarily in the domain of f.

(*i*) When 'a' is an interior point of D, i.e. $(a - \alpha, a + \alpha) \subseteq D$ for some $(\in > 0)$, then f is continuous at $\Leftrightarrow \underset{x \to a}{Lt}\ f(x) = f(a)$.

(*ii*) When the domain of f is an interval [a,b], then

f is continous at a $\Leftrightarrow \underset{x \to a+}{\text{Lt}} f(x) = f(a)$

and f is continous at b $\Leftrightarrow \underset{x \to b^-}{\text{Lt}} f(x) = f(b)$.

(*iii*) If there is $\alpha > 0$ such that $(a - \alpha,, a + \alpha) \wedge D = \{a\}$, then any function $f : D \to R$ is continuous at 'a'.

DIFFERENTIATION

Differentiation had its origin to the problem of tangents to curve.

Let y = f(x) be a given function of x, and let δy be a change in y corresponding to a change dx in x, then limiting value of the ratio

$\frac{\delta y}{\delta x}$ when $\delta x \to 0$ is called *differential coefficient of 'y'* with respective

'x' and is denoted by $\frac{dy}{dx}$ or y_1 or Dy.

Some Important Differentiations

1. $\frac{d}{dx}(C) = 0$, where C = constant

2. $\frac{d}{dx}(x^n) = n\, x^{n-1}$

3. $\frac{d}{dx}(\sqrt{x}) = \frac{1}{2\sqrt{x}}$

4. $\frac{d}{dx}(ax + b)^n = n\,(ax + b)^{n-1}\, a$

5. $\frac{d}{dx}(\log_e x) = \frac{1}{x}$

6. $\frac{d}{dx}(\log_a x) = \frac{\log_a e}{x}$ $a \neq 0,1$

7. $\frac{d}{dx}(e^x) = e^x$

8. $\dfrac{d}{dx}\left(a^{x}\right) = a^{x} \log a, \quad \text{where } a = \text{constant}$

9. $\dfrac{d}{dx}(U \pm V) = \dfrac{dU}{dx} \pm \dfrac{dV}{dx}$

10. $\dfrac{d}{dx}(UV) = U\dfrac{dV}{dx} + \dfrac{dU}{dx}V$

11. $\dfrac{d}{dx}(UVW) = UV\dfrac{dW}{dx} + U\dfrac{dV}{dx}W + \dfrac{dU}{dx}VW$

12. $\dfrac{d}{dx}\left(\dfrac{U}{V}\right) = \dfrac{V\dfrac{dU}{dx} - U\dfrac{dV}{dx}}{V^2}$

13. $\dfrac{d}{dx}(\sin x) = \cos x$

14. $\dfrac{d}{dx}(\cos x) = -\sin x$

15. $\dfrac{d}{dx}(\tan x) = \sec^2 x$

16. $\dfrac{d}{dx}(\cot x) = -\operatorname{cosec}^2 x$

17. $\dfrac{d}{dx}(\sec x) = \sec x \tan x$

18. $\dfrac{d}{dx}(\operatorname{cosec} x) = -\operatorname{cosec} x \cot x$

19. $\dfrac{d}{dx}\left(\sin^{-1} x\right) = \dfrac{1}{\sqrt{1 - x^2}}$

20. $\dfrac{d}{dx}\left(\cos^{-1} x\right) = -\dfrac{1}{\sqrt{1 - x^2}}$

21. $\frac{d}{dx}\left(\tan^{-1}x\right) = \frac{1}{1+x^2}$

22. $\frac{d}{dx}\left(\cot^{-1}x\right) = \frac{-1}{1+x^2}$

23. $\frac{d}{dx}\left(\sec^{-1}x\right) = \frac{1}{|x|\sqrt{x^2-1}}$ for $|x| > 1$

24. $\frac{d}{dx}\left(\text{cosec}^{-1}x\right) = \frac{-1}{|x|\sqrt{x^2-1}}$ for $|x| > 1$

25. $\frac{d}{dx}e^{mx} = e^{mx}.m$

26. $\frac{d}{dx}kx = k$

27. $\frac{d}{dx}\ kx^n = knx^{n-1}$

28. $\frac{d}{dx}\ \frac{1}{x} = -\frac{1}{x}$

29. $\frac{d}{dx}\ \frac{1}{x^2} = -\frac{2}{x^3}$

30. $\frac{d}{dx}\ \frac{1}{x^n} = -\frac{n}{x^{n+1}}$

31. $\frac{d}{dx}\sqrt{ax+b} = \frac{1}{2\sqrt{ax+b}}.a$

32. $\frac{d}{dx}\ \frac{1}{\sqrt{x}} = -\frac{1}{2x\sqrt{x}}$

CONCEPTS AND FORMULAE

1. Let 'a' be a point in the Domain of f(x).

   If $\underset{x\to a}{\text{Lt}} \frac{f(x)-f(a)}{x-a}$ or $\underset{h\to 0}{\text{Lt}} \frac{f(a+h)-f(a)}{h}$ exists and finite, then the function f(x) is called differentiable at x = a and the limit value is denoted by f′(a).

   $$\text{i.e. } f'(a) = \underset{x\to a}{\text{Lt}} \frac{f(x)-f(a)}{x-a} = \underset{h\to 0}{\text{Lt}} \frac{f(a+h)-f(a)}{h}$$

   here f′(a) is called derivation or differential coefficient of f(x) at x = 0.

2. A function f is called differentiable if it is differentiable at each point in the domain of f.

3. Let 'a' be a point in the domain of f(x).

   If $\underset{x\to a^-}{\text{Lt}} \frac{f(x)-f(a)}{x-a} = \underset{h\to 0^+}{\text{Lt}} \frac{f(a-h)-f(a)}{-h}$ exist and finite, then the function f(x) is called left differentiable at x = a, the limit value is denoted by f′(a) or $f'(a^-)$ and is called left derivative of f(x) at x = a.

4. Let 'a' be a point in the domain of f(x).

   If $\underset{x\to a^+}{\text{Lt}} \frac{f(x)-f(a)}{x-a} = \underset{h\to 0^+}{\text{Lt}} \frac{f(a+h)-f(a)}{h}$ exist and finite, then the function f(x) is said to be right differentiable at x = a, the limit value is denoted by R f′(a) or f′(a+) and is called right derivative of f(x) at x = a.

5. (*i*) Every differentiable function is continuous but the converse is not true.

   (*ii*) If L f′(a) and R f′(a) exist and finite, then f is continous at 'a'.

6. f(x) is differntiable at x = a (=) L f′ (a) and Rf′(a) exist and equal.

7. If $y = f(x)$ is a function which is differentiable at each point in the Domain of 'f', then function $f'(x) = \underset{h \to 0^+}{\text{Lt}} \frac{f(x+h) - f(x)}{h}$ will be denoted by $\frac{df}{dx}$ or $\frac{dy}{dx}$ or $\frac{df(x)}{dx}$ or $D\{f(x)\}$ or Dy or y' and it is called derivative of $y = f(x)$ with respect to 'x'.

8. If $u(x)$, $v(x)$ are two functions having the same Domain D and $u(x)$, $v(x)$ are differentiable at each point in D, then

   (*i*) $\frac{d}{dx}(ku(x)) = k\frac{d}{dx}(u(x))$, where k is a constant.

   (*ii*) $\frac{d}{dx}(u(x) \pm v(x)) = \frac{d}{dx}(u(x)) \pm \frac{d}{dx}(v(x))$.

   (*iii*) $\frac{d}{dx}\{u(x)v(x)\} = u(x)\frac{d}{dx}v(x) + v(x)\frac{d}{dx}u(x)$

   (*iv*) $\frac{d}{dx}\left\{\frac{u(x)}{v(x)}\right\} = \frac{v(x)\frac{d}{dx}u(x) - u(x)\frac{d}{dx}v(x)}{[v(x)]^2}$ provided $v(x) \neq 0$.

9. If f is a differentiable function at x and g is a differentiable function at $f(x)$, then g o f is differentiable at x and

$$(gof)'(x) = g'(f(x))f'(x).$$

10. If $y = f(t)$ and $x = g(t)$ are two differentiable functions and if $g'(t) \neq 0$, then $\frac{dy}{dx} = \frac{f'(t)}{g'(t)} = \frac{\frac{dy}{dt}}{\frac{dx}{dt}}$

11. If f is differentiable at 'x' and $f'(x) \neq 0$, then f^{-1} is differentiable at $f(x)$ and $(f^{-1})'(f(x)) = \frac{1}{f'(x)}$ provided f is a bijection.

DERIVATIVES

Derivative of

1. $\sinh x = \cosh x$
2. $\cosh x = \sinh x$
3. $\tanh x = \text{sech}^2 x$
4. $\coth x = -\text{cosech}^2 x$
5. $\coth x = -\text{sech } x.\ \tanh x$
6. $\text{cosech } x = -\text{cosech } x.\ \coth x$
7. $\sinh^{-1} x = \sqrt{1+x^2}$
8. $\cosh^{-1} x = \dfrac{1}{\sqrt{x^2-1}}$
9. $\tanh^{-1} x = \dfrac{1}{1-x^2}$
10. $\coth^{-1} x = \dfrac{-1}{1-x^2}$
11. $\text{sech}^{-1} x = \dfrac{1}{|x|\sqrt{1-x^2}}$
12. $\text{cosech}^{-1} x = \dfrac{-1}{|x|\sqrt{x^2+1}}$

If for all $x_1, y \in R$, $f(x + y) = f(x)\, f(y)$ and if $f'(o)$ exists, then

$$f'(x) = f(x). \quad f'(o) \text{ for all real x.}$$

INDEFINITE INTEGRAL

Integration had its origin to the problem of finding the areas.

If $\dfrac{d}{dx}(f(x) + c) = g(x)$, then $\int g(x) = f(x) + c$

where c is called *constant of integration* and, f(x) + c is called *indefinite integral* of g(x).

Some Important Integrals

1. $\int dx = x + c$
2. $\int a\, dx = a \int dx = ax + c.$
3. $\int (U + V + W + \ldots\ldots.)\, dx = \int U\, dx + \int V\, dx + \int W\, dx + \ldots\ldots\ldots$
4. $\int x^n\, dx = \dfrac{x^{n+1}}{n+1} + c; \quad (n \neq -1)$
5. $\int x^{-1}\, dx = \int \dfrac{1}{x} dx = \log x + c$
6. $\int e^x\, dx = e^x + c.$
7. $\int a^x\, dx = \dfrac{a^x}{\log a} + c.$
8. $\int \sin x\, dx = -\cos x + c$
9. $\int \cos x\, dx = \sin x + c$
10. $\int \tan x\, dx = \log |\sec x| + c = -\log |\cos x| + c$
11. $\int \cot x\, dx = \log |\sin x| + c = -\log |\text{cosec } x| + c$
12. $\int \sec x\, dx = \log (\sec x + \tan x) + c = \log \left(\tan \dfrac{x}{2} + \dfrac{\pi}{4}\right) + c$
13. $\int \text{cosec } x\, dx = \log (\text{cosec } x - \cot x) + c = \log \left(\tan \dfrac{x}{2}\right)$
14. $\int \sec^2 x\, dx = \tan x + c.$
15. $\int \text{cosec}^2 x\, dx = -\cot x + c$
16. $\int \sec x \tan x\, dx = \sec x + c$
17. $\int \text{cosec } x \cot x\, dx = -\text{cosec } x + c$
18. $\int e^{ax}.dx = \dfrac{e^{ax}}{a}$

CONCEPTS AND FORMULAE

1. $\int \frac{1}{a^2+x^2}\,dx = \frac{1}{a}\tan^{-1}\left(\frac{x}{a}\right) + c$

2. $\frac{1}{a^2-x^2}\,dx = \frac{1}{2a}\log\left|\frac{a+x}{a-x}\right| + c$ or $\frac{1}{a}\tan h^{-1}\left(\frac{x}{a}\right) + c$

3. $\int \frac{1}{x^2-a^2}\,dx = \frac{1}{2a}\log\left(\frac{x-a}{x+a}\right) + c$

4. $\int \frac{1}{\sqrt{a^2-x^2}}\,dx = \sin^{-1}\left(\frac{x}{a}\right) + c$ (or) $-\cos^{-1}\left(\frac{x}{a}\right) + c$

5. $\int \frac{1}{\sqrt{x^2-a^2}}\,dx = \cosh^{-1}\left(\frac{x}{a}\right) + c$ (or) $\log\left|x+\sqrt{x^2-a^2}\right| + c$

6. $\int \frac{1}{\sqrt{a^2+x^2}}\,dx = \sinh^{-1}\left(\frac{x}{a}\right) + c$ (or) $\log\left|x+\sqrt{a^2+x^2}\right| + c$

7. $\int \sinh x\,dx = \cosh x + c$

8. $\int \cosh x\,dx = \sinh x + c$

9. $\int \text{sech}^2 x\,dx = \tanh x + c$

10. $\int \text{sech}\,x \tanh x\,dx = -\text{sech}\,x + c$

11. $\int \text{cosech}\,x \coth x\,dx = -\,\text{cosech}\,x + c$

12. $\int \tanh x\,dx = \log|\cosh x| + c$

13. $\int \coth x\,dx = \log|\sinh x| + c$

14. $\int (ax+b)\,dx = \frac{1}{a}\int f(t)\,dx$, where $t = ax + b$

15. $\int \sqrt{a^2-x^2}\,dx = \frac{x}{2}\sqrt{a^2-x^2} + \frac{a^2}{2}\sin^{-1}\left(\frac{x}{a}\right) + c$

16. $\int \sqrt{x^2 - a^2}\, dx = \frac{x}{2}\sqrt{x^2 - a^2} - \frac{a^2}{2}\cosh^{-1}\left(\frac{x}{a}\right) + c$, or

$$= \frac{x}{2}\sqrt{x^2 - a^2} - \frac{a^2}{2}\log\left|x + \sqrt{x^2 - a^2}\right| + c$$

17. $\int \sqrt{a^2 + x^2}\, dx = \frac{x}{2}\sqrt{a^2 + x^2} + \frac{a^2}{2}\sinh^{-1}\left(\frac{x}{a}\right) + c$, or

$$= \frac{x}{2}\sqrt{a^2 + x^2} + \frac{a^2}{2}\log\left|x + \sqrt{a^2 + x^2}\right| + c$$

18. $\int e^{ax} \sin bx\, dx = \frac{e^{ax}}{a^2 + b^2}(a \sin bx - b\cos bx) + c$

19. $\int e^{ax} \cos bx\, dx = \frac{e^{ax}}{a^2 + b^2}(a \cos bx + b \sin bx) + c$

20. $\int \frac{f'(x)}{f(x)} dx = \log |f(x)| + c$

21. $\int \frac{f'(x)}{f(x)} dx = 2\sqrt{f(x)} + c$

22. $\int [f(x)]^n . f'(x) dx = \frac{[f(x)]^{n+1}}{n+1} + c; (n \neq 1)$

23. $\int f(x).\, g(x)\, dx = f(x) \int g(x)\, dx - \int f'(x) \left[\int g(x)\, dx\right] dx$

24. $\int e^x [f(x) + f'(x)] dx = e^x f(x) + c$

25. $\int \tan^n x\, dx = \frac{\tan^{n-1}}{n-1} - \int \tan^{n-2} x\, dx, \ (n \geq 2, n \in N).$

26. $\int \sin^n x\, dx = -\frac{\sin^{n-1} x \cos x}{n} + \frac{n-1}{n}\int \sin^{n-2} x\, dx, (n \in N).$

27. $\int \cos^n x dx = \frac{\cos^{n-1} x \sin x}{n} + \frac{n-1}{n} \int \cos^{n-2} x, dx \; (n \in N)$

28. $\int \frac{1}{|x|\sqrt{x^2-1}} = \sec^{-1} x + c$ or

$= -\text{cosec}^{-1} x + c$

DEFINITE INTEGRAL

1. If F(x) is a continuously differentiable function on [a,b] and $F'(x) = f(x)$ for all $x \in [a, b]$, then

$$\int_a^b f(x)dx = \lim_{\substack{n\to\infty \\ h\to 0 \\ nh = b-a}} h \sum_{r=1}^{n} f(a+rh) = F(b) - F(a)$$

2. $\int_a^a f(x)\, dx = 0$

3. $\int_b^a f(x)\, dx = -\int_a^b f(x)\, d(x)$

4. If $f(x) \le g(x)$; $x \in [a,b]$, then

$$\int_a^b f(x)\, dx \le \int_a^b g(x)dx$$

5. $\int_a^b [c_1 f(x) + c_2 g(x)]dx = c_1 \int_a^b f(x)dx + c_2 \int_a^b g(x)dx$

6. $\left|\int_a^b f(x)dx\right| \le \int_a^b |f(x)|dx$

7. If a < c < b, then

$$\int_a^b f(x)(dx) = \int_a^c f(x)\,dx + \int_c^b f(x)dx$$

8. If f(x) is an even function on [–a, a], then

$$\int_{-a}^{a} f(x)dx = 2\int_0^a f(x)dx$$

9. If f(x) is an odd function on [–a, a], then

$$\int_{-a}^{a} f(x)dx = 0$$

10. $\int_{-a}^{a} f(x)dx = \int_a^b f(a+b-x)\,dx$.

11. $\int_a^b f(x)fx = \int_a^b f(t)dt$

12. $\int_0^a f(x)dx = \int_0^a f(a- \ x)\ dx$

13. $\int_0^{na} f(x)dx = n\int_0^a f(x)dx \ \text{ if } f\,(a{+}x) = f(x)$

i.e. f(x) is a periodic function of period ‘a’.

14. $\int_0^k f(x)dx = \underset{n\to a}{Lf}\ \frac{1}{n}\sum_{r=0}^{nk-1} f\left(\frac{r}{n}\right);\ k \in N.$

15. $\int_0^{\pi/2} \sin^n x dx = \int_0^{\pi/2} \cos^n x dx$

$$= \left(\frac{n-1}{n}\right)\left(\frac{n-3}{n-2}\right)\left(\frac{n-5}{n-4}\right)\cdots\cdots\frac{1}{2}\frac{\pi}{2} \text{ if 'n' is even}$$

$$= \left(\frac{n-1}{n}\right)\left(\frac{n-3}{n-2}\right)\left(\frac{n-5}{n-4}\right)\cdots\cdots\frac{2}{3}.1 \text{ if 'n' is odd.}$$

16. $I_h = \int_0^{\pi/4} \tan^n x\, dx = \frac{1}{n-1} - I_{n-2}$

17. $\int_0^{\pi/2} \sin^m x.\cos^n x dx$

$$= \frac{[(m-1)(m-3)-2 \text{or} 1][(n-1)(n-3)-2 \text{or} 1]}{(m+n)(m+n-2)(m+n-n)-2 \text{or} 1}$$

Multiply the above by $\frac{\pi}{2}$ when both m and n are even only.

APPLICATIONS OF DERIVATIVES

1. Equation of Tangent to a curve at point (x_1, y_1)

$$y - y_1 = \left(\frac{dy}{dx}\right)_{(x_1, y_1)} (x - x_1)$$

2. Slope of Normal to a curve at point (x_1, y_1)

$$= \frac{-1}{\text{slope of tangent}} = \frac{-1}{\left(\frac{dy}{dx}\right)_{(x_1, y_1)}} = -\left(\frac{dx}{dy}\right)_{(x_1, y_1)}$$

3. Equation of Normal to a curve at point (x_1, y_1)

$$(y - y_1) = \frac{-1}{\left(\frac{dy}{dx}\right)_{(x_1, y_1)}} (x - y_1)$$

4. Angle of intersection of two curves

$$\tan\theta = \pm\frac{m_1 - m_2}{1 + m_1 m_2} = \pm\frac{f'(x) - \phi\, g'(x)}{1 + f'(x)g'(x)}$$

5. Length of the tangent = $\left|\frac{y\sqrt{1+\left(\frac{dy}{dx}\right)^2}}{\frac{dy}{dx}}\right|$

6. Length of the normal = $\left|y\sqrt{1+\left(\frac{dy}{dx}\right)^2}\right|$

Increasing and Decreasing Functions

Increasing function:

$$x_1 < x_2 \Rightarrow f(x_1) \le f(x_2)$$

Strictly increasing function:

$$x_1 < x_2 \Rightarrow f(x_1) < f(x_2)$$

Decreasing function:

$$x_1 < x_2 \Rightarrow f(x_1) \ge f(x_2)$$

Strictly decreasing function:

$$x_1 < x_2 \Rightarrow f(x_1) > f(x_2)$$

Monotonic function

A function f is called monotonic on an interval I if it is either increasing or decreasing on I.

ROLLE'S AND LAGRANGE'S MEAN THEOREM

Rolle's Theorem

If a function f, defined on the closed interval [a, b], is

(*i*) continuous on [a, b]

(*ii*) derivable on (a, b) and

(*iii*) f(a) = f(b),

then there exists at least one real number 'c' between a and b (a < c < b) such that f′(c) = 0

Lagrange's Mean Value Theorem

If a function f defined on the closed interval [a, b], is

(*i*) continuous on [a, b] and

(*ii*) derivable on (a, b),

then there exists at least one real number 'c' between a and b ($a < c < b$) such that

$$f'(c) = \frac{f(b) - f(a)}{b - a}$$

Maxima and Minima of Functions

For the function > = f(x)

Let, $f'(x) = 0$ have roots a, b, c ... etc. then

At point $x = a$

if $f''(a) < 0$, then $x = a$ is a point of local maxima.

if $f''(a) > 0$, then $x = a$ is a point of local minima.

if $f''(a) = 0$, we cannot say anything.

Point of Inflexion

If at $x = a$, shape of the curves changes from concave to convex or from convex to concave, then $x = a$ is called point of inflexion. $f''(x)$ changes sign as x passes through the point a.

Differentiablility of a function at a point 'c'

f is differentiable at an interior point $c \in I$ provided

$$\underset{x \to c}{\text{Lt}} \frac{f(x) - f(c)}{x - c} = \underset{x \to c^-}{\text{Lt}} \frac{f(x) - f(c^-)}{x - c} = f'(c) = \underset{x \to c^+}{\text{Lt}} \frac{f(x) - f(c^+)}{x - c}$$

ORDER AND DEGREE OF A DIFFERENTIAL EQUATIONS

Order

Order of the differential equation is order of the highest differential coefficient involved.

Degree

Degree of the equation is the power to which the highest differential coefficient is raised.

e.g.

(*i*) $\frac{dy}{dx} + y = x^2$

Order = 1, Degree = 1

(*ii*) $\frac{d^3y}{dx^3} + \frac{d^2y}{dx^2} + \frac{dy}{dx} + y = x$

Order = 3, Degree = 1

(*iii*) $\left(\frac{d^2y}{dx^2}\right) + \left(\frac{dy}{dx}\right)^3 + 3y = x^2$ Order = 2, Degree = 1

(*iv*) $\left(\frac{d^3y}{dx^3}\right)^2 + \left(\frac{dy}{dx}\right) = x$

Order = 3 Degree = 2

(*v*) $\left[1 + \left(\frac{dy}{dx}\right)^2\right]^{3/2} = \frac{d^3y}{dx^3}$

Order = 3, Degree = 2

chapter

36

MATRICES

A matrix is a rectangular array of m × n elements arranged in m rows and n columns. The order of matrix is the number of rows by columns. An English mathematician Arthur Caylay introudced this system in mathematics. James Joseph Sylvester, another English mathematician give the name "Matrix".

MATRIX

A set of numbers, real or complex arranged in the form of square or rectangular array having rows and columns is called matrix. It is denoted by [ ] or ( ).

e.g. $\begin{bmatrix} a & b \\ c & d \end{bmatrix}, \begin{bmatrix} 1 & 2 & 3 \\ 4 & 5 & 6 \end{bmatrix}$ etc.

Notations:

(*i*) Matrices are generally denoted by capital letters of the alphabet viz., A, B, C, D..........etc.

(*ii*) The elements are generally denoted by corresponding small letters viz., a, b, c, d.........p, q, r, s........

ORDER OF MATRIX

The number of rows x number of columns of a matrix is called *order of the matrix.*

i.e., m rows and n columns, the matrix is m × n type or order.

ELEMENTS

The numbers arranged in rows and columns in a matrix are called *elements of the matrix.*

TYPE OF MATRIX

1. **Rectangular Matrix.**
   If the number of rows and columns of a matrix are not equal, the matrix is called *rectangular matrix.*

   e.g. $\begin{bmatrix} a_1 & b_1 & c_1 \\ a_2 & b_2 & c_2 \end{bmatrix}$

2. **Information Matrices.**
   The matrices which serve as store houses of information are called *information matrices.*

3. **Route Matrices.**
   We can show by means of matrix how many direct routes there are joining different places. Such matrices are called *route matrices.*

4. **Row Matrix.**
   A matrix containing only one row is called *row matrix.*

   e.g. $[1, 2, 3]_{1\times 3}$

5. **Column Matrix.**
   A matrix having only one column is called *column matrix.*

   e.g. $\begin{bmatrix} 1 \\ 2 \\ 3 \end{bmatrix}_{3\times 1}$

6. **Null Matrix or Zero Matrix.**
   If every element of a matrix is 0, then it is called *null matrix.*

   e.g. $\begin{bmatrix} 0 & 0 & 0 \\ 0 & 0 & 0 \end{bmatrix}_{2\times 3}$

7. **Square Matrix.**
   A matrix in which the number of rows is equal to number of columns is called *square matrix.*

   e.g. $\begin{bmatrix} 1 & 2 \\ 3 & 4 \end{bmatrix}_{2\times 2}$

8. Scalar Matrix.

A scalar matrix in which all the elements in the principla diagonal are equal and rest of the elements are zero is called *scalar matrix.*

e.g. $\begin{bmatrix} 5 & 0 & 0 \\ 0 & 5 & 0 \\ 0 & 0 & 5 \end{bmatrix}_{3\times 3}$

9. Diagonal Matrix.

A square matrix in which except the leading diagonal elements all other elements are zeroes is called *diagonal matrix.*

e.g. (*i*) $\begin{bmatrix} 1 & 0 & 0 \\ 0 & 2 & 0 \\ 0 & 0 & 3 \end{bmatrix}$

(*ii*) $\begin{bmatrix} a & 0 & 0 \\ 0 & b & 0 \\ 0 & 0 & c \end{bmatrix}$; a, b, c, ∈ R are all diagonal matrices.

10. Upper Triangular Matrix.

A square matrix in which all the elements below the principal diagonal are zeroes is called *upper triangular matrix.*

e.g. $\begin{bmatrix} 1 & 2 & 3 \\ 0 & 4 & 5 \\ 0 & 0 & 6 \end{bmatrix}$

11. Lower Triangular Matrix.

A square matrix in which all the elements above the principal diagonal are zeroes is called *lower triangular matrix.*

e.g. $\begin{bmatrix} 1 & 0 & 0 \\ 2 & 3 & 0 \\ 4 & 5 & 6 \end{bmatrix}$

TRANSPOSE OF A MATRIX

The matrix obtained by the interchange of the rows and columns of the given matrix A is called transpose of A and is denoted by A^T or A^I.

e.g. if $A = \begin{bmatrix} 1 & 2 \\ 3 & 4 \end{bmatrix}$; then $A^T = \begin{bmatrix} 1 & 3 \\ 2 & 4 \end{bmatrix}$

Formulae.

1. $(A^T)^T = A$

2. $(A + B)^T = A^T + B^T$

3. $(A\,B)^T = B^T A^T$

4. $(kA)^T = kA^T$ k is scaler

5. $(A^2)^T = (A^T)^2$

6. $AB^T = (BA^T)^T$

PRINCIPAL DIAGONAL OF SQUARE MATRIX

The diagonal from first element of the first row to the last element of the last row is called *principal diagonal of the square matrix.*

e.g. $\begin{bmatrix} 1 & 2 & 3 \\ 4 & 5 & 6 \\ 7 & 8 & 9 \end{bmatrix}$

Principal diagonal of the adjoining matrix contains elements 1, 5, 9.

Symmetric Matrix.

If a matrix is equal to its transpose, it is called *symmetric matrix.*

e.g. If $A = \begin{bmatrix} 1 & -2 \\ -2 & 3 \end{bmatrix}$ then $A^T = \begin{bmatrix} 1 & -2 \\ -2 & 3 \end{bmatrix}$

But $A = A^T$

hence A is called symmetric matrix.

SKEW-SYMMETRIC MATRIX

If transpose of a given matrix is equal to its additive inverse, i.e. if $A^T = -A$, then that matrix is called skew symmetrix matrix.

e.g. $\begin{bmatrix} 0 & 1 & 2 \\ -1 & 0 & 3 \\ -2 & -3 & 0 \end{bmatrix}$

Note: The diagonal elements of a skew-symmetric matrix are zeroes.

MINOR OF A MATRIX

If n-p rows and m-p columns from matrix $A_{n \times m}$ are removed, then remaining square submatrix of p rows and p columns is left. The determinant of a square submatrix of order $p \times p$ is called minor of A or order p.

RANK OF A MATRIX

A positive integer r is called rank of a non-zero matrix A, if

1. there exists at least one minor in A of order r which is not zero.
2. every minor in A of order greater than r is zero. It is denoted by

$$p(A) = r.$$

Properties of Rank

1. Rank of a matrix remains unaltered by elementary transformations.
2. Rank of matrix A = Rank of matrix A'
3. AA' has the same rank as A
4. If $p(A) = p(B) = r$, then $p(AB) = p(BA) = r$
5. If A is an $n \times m$ matrix, then $p(A) \leq \text{Min}(n, m)$

Echelon Form of a Matrix

A non-zero matrix A is said to be in Echelon form if A satisfies the following conditions:

(*i*) All the non-zero rows of A, if any precede the zero rows.

(*ii*) The number of zeroes preceding the first non- zero element in a row is less than the number of such zeros in the succeeding row.

(*iii*) The first non-zero element in a row is unity.

$$A = \begin{bmatrix} 1 & 5 & 3 & 2 & 6 \\ 0 & 1 & 2 & 3 & 4 \\ 0 & 0 & 1 & 5 & 2 \\ 0 & 0 & 0 & 0 & 0 \end{bmatrix}, p(A) = 3$$

EQUALITY OF TWO MATRICES

Two matrices are equal if and only if they have same order and corresponding elements are identical.

e.g. $A = \begin{pmatrix} 1 & 2 \\ 3 & 4 \end{pmatrix}; B = \begin{pmatrix} 1 & 2 \\ 3 & 4 \end{pmatrix}$

Hence matrices A and B are of the same order and their corresponding elements are also equal A = B).

Identity Matrix (or) Unit Matrix

A square matrix in which the leading diagonal elements are each 1 and all other elements are 0. It is denoted by l.

e.g. $l_2 = \begin{bmatrix} 1 & 0 \\ 0 & 1 \end{bmatrix}; \; l_3 = \begin{bmatrix} 1 & 0 & 0 \\ 0 & 1 & 0 \\ 0 & 0 & 1 \end{bmatrix}$

Addition of Matrices

If A and B are two matrices same type, then their sum is written as A + B and is defined to be the matrix of the same type obtained by adding the corresponding elements of A and B and putting in the corresponding place.

e.g. If $A = \begin{bmatrix} 1 & 2 \\ 3 & 4 \end{bmatrix}$ and $B = \begin{bmatrix} 5 & 6 \\ 7 & 8 \end{bmatrix}$

then $A + B = \begin{bmatrix} 1+5 & 2+6 \\ 3+7 & 4+8 \end{bmatrix} = \begin{bmatrix} 6 & 8 \\ 10 & 12 \end{bmatrix}$

ADDITION PROPERTIES

1. **Closer property.**
   If A and B are two matrices, then A + B is also a matrix.

2. **Associative property.**
   If A, B and C belong to same size, then
   $$(A + B) + C = A + (B + C)$$

3. **Additive Identity.**
   Let A be any matrix and 'O' be a zero matrix of the same size as 'A', then
   $$A + 0 = 0 + A = A.$$
   Zero is the additive identity matrix for addition.

4. **Additive Inverse.**
   If A is any matrix of order m x n, then

$$A + (-A) = (-A) + A = 0$$

   The matrix –A is called additive inverse of A.

5. **Distributive Property.**
   A matrix multiplication is distributive over addition.

   If A, B and C are three matrices, then

$$A(B + C) = AB + AC.$$

6. **Commutative Property.**
   If A and B are same size matrices, then

$$A + B = B + A.$$

   (*i*) $k(A + B) = kA + kB$

   (*ii*) $(k + m) A = kA + mA$

   (*iii*) $m(nA) = n(mA) = mnA.$

MATRICES MULTIPLICATION

Two matrices are called conformable for multiplication, if number of columns of the first matrix are equal to number of rows of the second matrix. Then their product is denoted by AB. AB is obtained by multiplying rows of first matrix with columns of second matrix.

e.g. If $A = \begin{bmatrix} a & b \\ c & d \end{bmatrix}$; and $B = \begin{bmatrix} p & q \\ r & s \end{bmatrix}$

then $A \times B = \begin{bmatrix} ap + br & aq + bs \\ cp + dr & cq + ds \end{bmatrix}$

Multiplication Properties.

1. If $AC = BC$ and $C \neq 0$, then A need not be equal to B.
2. If a square matrix A is multiplied by identity matrix l, we get the same matrix A,

   i.e. $Al = lA = A.$

3. If AB = BA = A, then B is called unit matrix denoted by I.
4. If A is a square matrix of order

$$A \times A = A^2$$
$$A \times A \times A = A^3$$
$$A \times A \times A \times \text{.............m times} = A^m$$

are all square matrices of order n.

Also, we define $A = I_n$.

5. For any positive integer n,

$$I^n = I.$$

6. If A is a square matrix such that $A^2 = I$, then A is called *involuntary matrix.*
7. If A is m x n size matrix, B is n x p size matrix, then size of the product matrix AB is m x p.
8. Even if AB and BA exist they need not necessarily be equal, i.e. $AB \neq BA$
9. Matrix multiplication is associative

i.e. $(AB)C = A(BC)$

10. Multiplication distributes over addition

i.e. $A \times (B + C) = (A \times B) + (A \times C)$.

DETERMINANT OF SQUARE MATRIX

Determinant of square matrix $\begin{bmatrix} a & b \\ c & d \end{bmatrix}$; a, b, c, d $\in$R is the real number ad – bc. It is denoted by $\begin{vmatrix} a & b \\ c & d \end{vmatrix}$ or det $\begin{vmatrix} a & b \\ c & d \end{vmatrix}$

If $A = \begin{bmatrix} a_{11} & a_{12} \\ a_{21} & a_{22} \end{bmatrix}_{2 \times 2}$, then

$$|A| = \det A = \begin{vmatrix} a_{11} & a_{12} \\ a_{21} & a_{22} \end{vmatrix}$$

$= a_{11}a_{22} - a_{12}a_{21}$ is called second order determinent.

e.g. If $A = \begin{bmatrix} 5 & 3 \\ 1 & 2 \end{bmatrix}$, then $|A| = \begin{vmatrix} 5 & 3 \\ 1 & 2 \end{vmatrix} = 5 \times 2 - 3 \times 1 = 10 - 3 = 7$

and if $A = \begin{bmatrix} -1 & 2 \\ 3 & 4 \end{bmatrix}$, then $|A| = \begin{vmatrix} -1 & 2 \\ 3 & 4 \end{vmatrix} = (-1) \times 4 - 2 \times 3$

$= -4 - 6 = -10$

If A is any square matrix, then $|A| = |A^T|$

SINGULAR AND NON-SINGULAR MATRIX

Singular Matrix.

Square matrix A whose determinant is zero, i.e. $|A| = 0$ is called *singular matrix.*

Non-singular Matrix.

Square matrix A whose determinent is non-zero, i.e. $|A| \neq 0$ is called *non-singular matrix.*

MULTIPLICATIVE INVERSE OF A MATRIX

1. If A is a non singular matrix, then a non-singular matrix B of the same order satisfying AB = I, where I is identity matrix, is called multiplicative inverse of A. The multiplicative inverse of A is denoted by A^{-1}.

   We write as $B = A^{-1}$

   or $A = B^{-1}$

   i.e. $BB^{-1} = AA^{-1} = A^{-1}B = I$

   (*i*) Only square matrix can have inverse

   (*ii*) If B is the inverse of A, then A is inverse of B.

   (*iii*) Inverse of a square matrix if it exist is unique.

2. If $A \times B = K.I.$ where $K \in R$, then $A^{-1} = \frac{1}{K}.B.$

3. If $A = \begin{bmatrix} a & b \\ c & d \end{bmatrix}$ then, $A^{-1} = \frac{1}{ad - bc}\begin{bmatrix} d & -b \\ -c & a \end{bmatrix}$; where $ad - bc \neq 0$.

Formulae.

(*i*) $(A^{-1})^{-1} = A$

(*ii*) $(AB)^{-1} = B^{-1} A^{-1}$

(*iii*) $(A^T)^{-1} = (A^{-1})^T$

Working rule for solving the linear equations.

Let $$a_1x + b_1y = c_1$$
$$a_2x + b_2y = c_2$$

Step I : Write down the given system of equation in a single matrix equation $AX = B$

where, $A = \begin{bmatrix} a_1 & b_1 \\ a_2 & b_2 \end{bmatrix}, \quad X = \begin{bmatrix} x \\ y \end{bmatrix}, B = \begin{bmatrix} c_1 \\ c_2 \end{bmatrix}$

Step II : Evaluation $|A|$, i.e. find $|A| = a_1 b_2 - a_2b_1$

Step III : If the matrix A is non-singular, i.e. $|A| \neq 0$, then A^{-1} exists and find A^{-1}.

Step IV : Pre-multiply both sides of the equation $AX = B$ by A^{-1}, so that we have

$$A^{-1} AX = A^{-1}B$$

$\Rightarrow$ $$1X = A^{-1} B \quad [\because A^{-1} A = I].$$

$\Rightarrow$ $$X = A^{-1} B.$$

Step V : Equate the two matrices and get the values of x and y.

Note: When $|A| = 0$, then in this case A^{-1} does not exist.

MINORS AND COFACTORS OF DETERMINANTS

1. **Minor**

   Minor of any element a_{ij} in $|A|$ is a determinant of the sub-matrix obtained from A, by deleting the row and the columns containing a_{ij}. It is denoted by M_{ij}.

$$|A| = \begin{vmatrix} a_{11} & a_{12} & a_{13} \\ a_{21} & a_{22} & a_{23} \\ a_{31} & a_{32} & a_{33} \end{vmatrix}$$

The minor of a_{11} is $M_{11} = \begin{vmatrix} a_{22} & a_{23} \\ a_{32} & a_{33} \end{vmatrix}$

The minor of a_{12} is $M_{12} = \begin{vmatrix} a_{21} & a_{23} \\ a_{31} & a_{33} \end{vmatrix}$

2. **Co-factor**

Co-factor of any element a_{ij}, denoted by C_{ij} is defined as $(-1)^{i+j} M_{ij}$

where i + j is sum of the rows number i and column number j in which the element a_{ij} lies.

$$C_{ij} = (-1)^{i+j} \times \text{minor of element } a_{ij}$$

$$= \begin{vmatrix} M_{ij} \text{ if } i+j \text{ is even} \\ -M_{ij} \text{ if } i+j \text{ is odd} \end{vmatrix}$$

Co-factor of a_{11} is $C_{11} = (-)^{1+1} M_{11} = M_{11}$

Co-factor of a_{12} is $C_{12} = (-1)^{1+2} M_{12} = -M_{12}$

CRAMMER'S RULE

(1) Consider two linear equations in two unknowns.

$$a_1x + b_1y = c_1 \qquad ...(1)$$

$$a_2x + b_2y = c_2 \qquad ...(2)$$

Let D is determinant of the coefficient of x, y in equations (1) and (2).

$$D = \begin{vmatrix} a_1 & b_1 \\ a_2 & b_2 \end{vmatrix}$$

Replacing elements of first column by c_1, c_2, we get

$$\therefore \qquad D_1 = \begin{vmatrix} c_1 & b_1 \\ c_2 & b_2 \end{vmatrix}$$

Replacing elements of second column by c_1, c_2, we get

$$D_2 = \begin{vmatrix} a_1 & c_1 \\ a_2 & c_2 \end{vmatrix}$$

Find determinants of the matrices D_1 and D_2 and write solution for the given set of equations.

$$\therefore \qquad x = \frac{D_1}{D}; \; y = \frac{D_2}{D} \qquad (\because D \neq 0)$$

(2) Consider three linear equations in three unknowns.

$$a_1x + b_1y + c_1z = d_1$$

$$a_2x + b_2y + c_2z = d_2$$

$$a_3x + b_3y + c_3z = d_3$$

The solution of the system of equations is given by

$$x = \frac{D_1}{D}, \; y = \frac{D_2}{D}, \; z = \frac{D_3}{D},$$

where

$$D = \begin{vmatrix} a_1 & b_1 & c_1 \\ a_2 & b_2 & c_2 \\ a_3 & b_3 & c_3 \end{vmatrix}; \quad D_1 = \begin{vmatrix} d_1 & b_1 & c_1 \\ d_2 & b_2 & c_2 \\ d_3 & b_3 & c_3 \end{vmatrix}$$

$$D_2 = \begin{vmatrix} a_1 & d_1 & c_1 \\ a_2 & d_2 & c_2 \\ a_3 & d_3 & c_3 \end{vmatrix}; \quad D_3 = \begin{vmatrix} a_1 & b_1 & d_1 \\ a_2 & b_2 & d_2 \\ a_3 & b_3 & d_3 \end{vmatrix}$$

Provided $D \neq 0$

Conditions for Consistency

(*i*) If $D \neq 0$, then the system is consistent, and has a unique solution

$$x = \frac{D_1}{D}, \; y = \frac{D_2}{D}, \; z = \frac{D_3}{D}$$

(*ii*) If $D = 0$ and atleast one of the determinants D_1, D_2, D_3 is non-zero, then given system is inconsistent, i.e. it has no solution.

(*iii*) If $D = 0$ and $D_1 = D_2 = D_3 = 0$, then system is consistent and dependent and has infinitely many solutions.

Homogeneous and Non-homogeneous System

1. If $D_1 = D_2 = D_3 = 0$, then the system is called homogeneous, othewise it is called non-homogeneous.

2. If the system of equations is homogeneous, then
   (i) If $D \neq 0$, the system has only trivial solution $(x = y = z = 0)$

   (ii) If $D = 0$, the system has a non-trivial solution, it has infinitely many solutions.

IDEMPOTENT MATRIX.

A matrix such that $A^2 = A$ is called idempotent matrix.

e.g. If AB = A and BA = B, then both A and B are idempotent.

$$A A^{-1} = I = A^{-1} A, \quad (A^1)^{-1} = A$$

i.e. inverse of a unit Matrix is itself.

ADJOINT OF A.

Let A be a square matrix. Then transpose of the matrix got from A by replacing the elements of A by the corresponding co-factors is called the adjoint of A. It is denoted by Adj A.

1. If A is an $n \times n$ non-singluar matrix, then

$$A^{-1} = \frac{\text{Adj} A}{|A|}, \text{ and } \quad \text{Adj } A = |A| A^{-1}$$

2. $(\text{Adj } A)^{-1} = \dfrac{A}{|A|} = \text{Adj } (A^{-1})$
3. $\text{Adj } A^T = (\text{Adj } A)^T$
4. $\text{Det } (A^{-1}) = (\text{Det } A)^{-1}$
5. $|\text{Adj } A| = |A|^{n-1}$
6. $\text{Adj } (\text{Adj } A) = |A|^{n-2} A$
7. For any scalar K, $\quad \text{Adj } (KA) = K^{n-1} \text{Adj } A$
8. $|\text{Adj Adj } A| = |A| (n-1)^2$
9. $|\text{Adj Adj Adj } A| = |A| (n-1)^3$
10. If A and B are wo non-singular matrices of the same type, then
$$\text{Adj } (AB) = (\text{Adj } B) (\text{Adj } A)$$
11. $|\text{Adj } (AB)| = |\text{Adj } B| \; |\text{Adj } A|$

CONCEPT AND FORMULAE.

1. If rows and columns in a square matrix are interchanged then value of its determinants remains unaltered.
2. Let A be an $n \times n$ matrix, then

$$\det(A) = \det(\Delta T)$$

$$\det(KA) = K^n \, |A|$$

3. Determinant of a square matrix changes it sign when any two rows or columns are interchanged.
4. If two rows or columns of a square matrix are identical or in the same ratio, then value of the determinant is zero.
5. If all the elements of a row (or column) of a square matrix are multiplied by a number 'K', then determinant of the resulting matrix is equal to 'K' times the determinant of the original matrix.
6. If det $A = \alpha + \beta i$, then

$$\det A = \alpha - i\beta$$

7. A square matrix A is called symmetric matrix, if

$$A^T = A.$$

8. If A is a symmetric matrix, then

$$A^T = \det A.$$

9. A square matrix A is called skew-symmetry, if

$$A^T = -A$$

10. If $A_{n \times n}$ is a skew symmetric, then

$$|A| = 0; \text{ 'n' is odd.}$$

11. A square matrix A is called Hermitian (Charles Hermite 1822-1901) if transpose conjugate of A is itself, i.e.

$$(A)^T = A.$$

12. A square matrix is called Skew-Hermitian, if

$$(A)^T = -A$$

13. If A is a square matrix, and $A = \frac{A^T + A}{2} + \frac{A - A^T}{2}$,

then $\frac{A^T + A}{2}$ is symmetric part, and $\frac{A - A^T}{2}$ is skew-symmatrix part.

14. If elements of a square matrix are polynomials in x and

(*i*) if two rows or columns become identical, when x = a, then (x – a) is a factor of its determinant.

(*ii*) if three rows are identical, then $(x - a)^2$ is a factor of determinant.

15. Sum of the principal (main) diagonal elements $a_{11}, a_{22}, \ldots\ldots. a_{nn}$ of a square matrix A is called trace of A.

$$\text{Trace } A = \text{Tr } D = a_{11} + a_{22} + \ldots\ldots. + a_{nn}$$

(*i*) If A and B are of order n, then

$$\text{Tr } (A + B) = \text{Trace } A + \text{Trace } B.$$

(*ii*) If C is of order m × n and G is of order n × m, then

$$\text{Tr } CG = \text{Tr } GC.$$

(*iii*) Let A, B, C be three matrices of order n, then

$$\text{Tr } ABC = \text{Tr } BCA = \text{Tr } CAB$$

$$= -\text{Tr } ACB = -\text{Tr } BAC = -\text{Tr } CBA.$$

16. Let A and B be two matrices of order n, then AB – BA is called commutator of A and B.

If A and B commute, then commutator of A and B is zero.

chapter

37

STATISTICS

The word 'Statistics' derived from Latin word 'Status' which means 'a political state'. In ancient days numerical statistics pertaining to population and their details to the military required for the protection of the state were collected in the form of numbers. The details are called statistics.

LIMIT AND BOUNDARIES

Limit of the Class.

The starting and end values of each class are called "LOWER LIMIT" and UPPER LIMIT".

e.g. if '0-10' represents a class, then '0' is its lower limit and 10 is its upper limit.

Class Boundaries.

Average of the upper limit of a class and lower limit of the succeeding class is called *upper boundary* of that class.

Upper boundary of a class becomes lower boundary of the next class. These boundaries are also called 'TRUE CLASS LIMIT'.

Class Interval.

The difference between upper and lower boundary of a class is called 'class interval' or 'size of the class'.

Range.

The difference between highest element and lowest element of a data is called its range.

Frequency.

When data is presented in a frequency table, then number of items (values) that fall in any particular class is called 'frequency' of that class.

Frequency Table or Frequency Distribution.

If data is classified in a convenient way and presented in a table, then it is called 'frequency table' or 'frequency distribution'.

CUMULATIVE FREQUENCY

Cumulative frequency corresponding to any value of the variate (or a class) is sum of all the frequencies upto and including that variate-value (or class).

Cumulative Frequency Distribution.

1. **Less than Cumulative Frequency** : The number of elements from the beginning to the upper boundary of a particular class of a frequency distribution is called 'less than cumulative frequency'.

2. **Greater than Cumulative Frequency** : The number of elements from the end to the lower boundary of a particular class of a frequency distribution is called 'greater than cumulative frequency'.

The average of a number of quantities of the same kind is their sum divided by their number.

$$\text{Average} = \frac{\text{Sum of the quantities}}{\text{Number of the quantities}}$$

$$\text{Sum of the quantities} = \text{Average} \times \text{Number of the quantities.}$$

$$\text{Number of the quantities} = \frac{\text{Sum of the quantities}}{\text{Average}}$$

ARITHMETIC MEAN (A.M.)

The value obtained on dividing the sum of items by the number of items is called arithmetic mean.

1. **Arithmetic mean of ungrouped data.**

If x_1, x_2, x_3, x_4 .... x_n are 'n' items, then

$$\text{Arithmetic mean, } \bar{x} = \frac{x_1 + x_2 + x_3 + x_4 + \ldots\ldots\ldots x_n}{n} = \frac{\sum_{i=1}^{n} x_i}{n}$$

2. **Arithmetic mean of grouped data.**

If x_1, x_2, x_3 ...... x_4 are mid values and f_1, f_2, f_3 ....f_n are frequencies of the receptive class intervals of a frequency distribution, then

$$\text{Arithmetic mean, } \bar{x} = \frac{f_1x_1 + f_2x_2 + f_3x_3 + \ldots\ldots\ldots f_nx_n}{f_1 + f_2 + f_3 + \ldots\ldots\ldots + f_n} = \frac{\sum_{i=1}^{n} f_ix_i}{\sum_{i=1}^{n} f_i}$$

3. **Arithmetic of combined data.**

If P and Q are number of items and x, y are arithmetic means of datas, then

$$\text{A.M. of combined data} = \frac{Px + Qy}{P + Q}$$

(*i*) If two terms are in A.P., then the terms may be taken as

$a - d, a + d$.

(*ii*) If three terms are in A.P., then the terms may taken as

$a-d, a, a + d$.

(*iii*) If four terms are in A.P., then the terms may be taken as

$a - 3d, a - d, a + d, a + 3d$.

(*iv*) If five terms are in A.P., then the terms may be taken as

$a - 2d, a - d, a, a + d, a + 2d$.

MEDIAN

If the observations are arranged in increasing or decreasing order, the median is defined as the middle observation.

e.g. To find the median of the numbers 2, 5, 4, 9, 1.

First write them in the increasing order, i.e. 1, 2, 4, 5, 9.

Clearly the middle one or median = 4.

1. **Median of Ungrouped data :**
   If 'n' items in the data are arranged in ascending or descending order and

   if 'n' is odd, then $\frac{n+1}{2}$ then item is called median.

   if 'n' is even, then the average of $\frac{n}{2}$ th and $\left(\frac{n}{2}+1\right)$ th item is called median.

2. **Median of Grouped data :**

$$\text{Median} = l + \frac{\left(\frac{n}{2} - m\right) * c}{f}$$

Here, l = lower boundary of the median class

n = total number of observations or total frequency

m = cummulative frequencies of the class preceeding the median class.

c = class interval

f = frequency of the median class

MODE

The item having maximum frequency is called mode.

1. **Mode of Ungrouped data :**
   The item which repeats more is the mode.

2. **Mode of Grouped data :**
The class containing maximum frequency is called *modal class.*

$$\text{Mode} = l + \frac{f - f_1}{2f - (f_1 + f_2)} \times c$$

Here l = lower boundary of the modal class

f = frequency in the class immeditely lower than the modal class

c = class interval

Also, $$\text{Mode} = l + \frac{\Delta_1}{\Delta_1 + \Delta_2} . c$$

where, $\Delta_1 = f - f_1$

$\Delta_2 = f - f_2$

Relation between mean, median and mode :

$$\text{Mean} - \text{Mode} = 3(\text{Mean} - \text{Median})$$

$$\Rightarrow \quad \text{Mode} = 3\ \text{Median} - 2\ \text{Mean}$$

Deviation Method for Mean of a Grouped data.

$$\bar{x} = \Lambda \mid \frac{1}{n} \sum_{i=1}^{K} f_i \mu_i$$

where, A = assumed value among the mid values

C = length of the class interval

K = number of classes of the frequency distribution

$\mu_i = \dfrac{x_i - A}{C}$; i = 1, 2 .... K

x_i = mid value of the ith class

n = total frequency = $\sum_{i=1}^{K} f_1$

QUARTILES

Quartiles are the values which divide the total frequency into four equal parts.

Quartile Deviation.

$$\text{First quartile, } Q_1 = l_1 + \left[\frac{\frac{N}{4} - m_1}{f_1}\right] \times c$$

$$\text{Third quartile, } Q_3 = l_2 + \left[\frac{\frac{3N}{4} - m_2}{f_2}\right] \times c$$

where, N = total frequency of the frequency distribution.

l_1 and l_2 = lower boundaries of respective quartile classes.

m_1 and m_2 = cumulative frequencies upto the class above the quartile classes.

f_1 and f_2 = frequencies of respective quartile classes.

$$\text{Quartile Deviation (Q. D.)} = \frac{Q_3 - Q_1}{2}$$

$$\text{Lower quartile, } Q_1 = \frac{n+1}{4} \text{th observation, if n is odd,}$$

$$= \frac{n}{4} \text{th observation, if n is even.}$$

$$\text{Upper quartile, } Q_3 = \frac{3(n+1)}{4} \text{th observation, if n is odd}$$

$$= \frac{3n}{4} \text{th observation, if n is even.}$$

$$\text{Inter quartile rang} = Q_3 - Q_1$$

$$\text{Semi inter quartile range} = \frac{Q_3 - Q_1}{2}$$

MEAN DEVIATION

It is defined as mean of the absolute values of the deviations from the mean (or median or mode).

$$\text{Mean deviation} = \frac{\sum |X - M|}{n}$$

where, X = the score

M = average from which deviations are taken

n = number of scores

In a frequency distribution,

$$\text{Mean deviation} = \frac{\sum |f(X-M)|}{\sum f} = \frac{\sum |fd|}{\sum f}$$

where, X = mid value of the class.

f = frequency of the class

M = average

$$d = X - M$$

STANDARD DEVIATION (σ).

Square root of the arithmetic mean of the squares of deviations of the items in the data with arithmetic mean is called standard deviation.

1. **Standard deviation for Ungrouped data :**
   If x_1, x_2, x_3, ... x_n are n items in the data and x be their arithmetic mean, then

$$\sigma = \sqrt{\frac{\sum (x_i - \bar{x})^2}{n}} = \sqrt{\frac{\sum x_i^{\,2}}{n} - (\bar{x})^2}$$

2. **Standard deviation for Grouped data :**
   If $x_1, x_2, x_3, \ldots\ldots\ldots x_n$ are mid values; $f_1, f_2, f_3, \ldots\ldots\ldots f_n$ are frequencies of n classes of a frequency distribution and x arithmetic mean, then

$$\sigma = \sqrt{\frac{\sum f_i x_i}{n} - (\overline{x})^2}$$

3. **Standard Deviation of Combined data :**
   If x, y are arithmetic means of two data containing p, q items respectively, and σ_1, σ_2 are standard deviations, and σ is the standard deviation of combined data, then

$$\sigma = \frac{p\sigma_1^2 + q\sigma_2^2}{p+q} + \frac{pq}{(p+q)^2}(x-y)^2$$

VARIANCE (σ^2)

Variance of a distribution is defined as the square of the standard deviation.

$$\text{Spearman's Rank Correlation } (r) = 1 - \frac{6\sum d^2}{n(n^2-1)}$$

Note : r lies between + 1 and – 1

(*i*) r = 1 for perfect positive correlation.

(*ii*) r = – 1 for perfect negative correlation.

(*iii*) r = 0 for complete absence of correlation.

MEASURES OF THE DISPERSION OR VARIATION IN COMMON USE

1. Range
2. Quartile deviation
3. Mean deviation
4. Standard deviation

$$\text{Coefficient of range} = \frac{\text{Maximum value} - \text{Minimum value}}{\text{Maximum value} + \text{Minimum value}}$$

$$\text{Coefficient of Quartile deviation (Q.D.)} = \frac{Q_3 - Q_1}{Q_3 + Q_1}$$

$$\text{Coefficient of mean deviation} = \frac{\text{Mean deviation}}{\text{Average}}$$

$$\text{Coefficient of variance} = \frac{\text{S.D.}}{\text{A.M.}}$$

$$\text{Q.D.} = \frac{2}{3}\ \text{S.D.}$$

$$\text{M.D.} = \frac{4}{5}\ \text{S.D.}$$

chapter

38

PERMUTATIONS AND COMBINATIONS

FUNDAMENTAL PRINCIPLE OF COUNTING

Addition Principle

If an operation can be performed in m ways and if another operation can be performed in n ways and only one operation can be done at a time, then either of the two operations can be performed in (m+n) ways.

Multiplication Principle

If an operation can be performed in m ways and if another operation in n ways independent of the first, then the number of ways of performing both operations simultaneously is $(m \times n)$.

PERMUTATIONS

Each of the arrangement that can be made by taking some or all of a number of things (objects) is called a *permutation*.

Thus, $n! = 1.\ 2.\ 3 \ldots\ldots\ldots\ldots\ldots\ldots\ n$

or $n! = n\,(n-1)\,(n-2) \ldots \ldots .\ 3.\ 2.\ 1$

or $n! = n\,(n-1)!$

or $n\,(n-1)\,(n-2)\,! \ldots \ldots ..$

e.g. $4! = 4.3.2.1 = 24$

$3! = 3.2.1 = 6$

$$2! = 2.1 = 2$$

$$1! = 1$$

$$0! = 0$$

If order of the thing is changed, we get a different permutation.

Product of the first 'n' natural numbers is called 'factorial n' and is denoted by n', or $\angle n$.

Number of permutations of n different objects taken r at a time is usually denoted by the symbol ${}^nP_r$ or p(n,r).

Formulae

1. ${}^nP_r = n\,(n-1)\,(n-2)\,..........\,(n-r+1) = \dfrac{n!}{(n-r)!}$

2. ${}^nP_r = n.\ {}^{n-1}P_{r-1}$

   $= n.\,(n-1)\,.\ {}^{n-2}P_{r-2} = ...$

   $= {}^nP_1 . {}^{n-1}P_{r-1} = ...$

   $= {}^nP_2 . {}^{n-2}P_{r-2}$

   $= {}^nP_s . {}^{n-s}P_{r-s}\ (\because\ s \le r)$

3. ${}^{n+1}P_r = {}^nP_r + r.\,{}^nP_{r-1}$

4. ${}^nP_n = n!,\ \forall\, n \in N.$

5. ${}^nP_o = 1$ and ${}^nP_n = n!$

6. Number of permutations of n different objects taken r at a time in which each object is repeated r times in any arrangements is n^r.

7. ${}^nP_r = n.\ {}^{n-1}P_{r-1}$

8. $\frac{^nP_r}{^nP_{r-1}} = n - r + 1$

9. The number of permutations of n things taken all at a time when p of them are alike and the rest are different is $\frac{n!}{p!}$.

10. Number of permutations of n things taken all at a time when p of them are alike of one kind, 'q' of them are alike of second kind, 'r' of them are alike of third kind and the rest are all different is $\frac{n!}{p!q!r!}$.

Linear permutation.

An arrangement of things in a line is called a linear *permutation.*

- Number of permutations of n different things taken r at a time, when a particular thing is to be always included in each arrangement is $r.\,^{n-1}P_{r-1}$.
- Number of permutations of n different things, taken r at a time, when s particular things are to be always included in each arrangement is

$$s!\,(r - s + 1)\,!\,^{n-s}P_{r-s}$$

- Number of permutations of n different things, taken r at a time, when a particular thing is never taken in each arrangement, is $^{n-1}P_r$

Circular permutation

An arrangement of things around a circle is called a *circular permutation.*

- Number of circular permutations of n dissimilar things taken all at a time is $(n - 1)!$
- Number of circular permutations of "n" dissimilar things taken all at a time when the direction is not considered is $\frac{(n-1)!}{2}$.
- Number of circular permutations of n dissimilar things taken "r" at a time is $\frac{^np_r}{r}$.

COMBINATION

The different selections or groups that can be formed out of a given number of things some or all of them at a time are called *combinations.*

Number of combinations of n different object taken r at a time is usually denoted by the symbol ${}^nC_r$ or C(n, r).

Formulae

1. $${}^nC_r = \frac{n(n-1)(n-2)......(n-r+1)}{r.(r-1).....3.2.1} = \frac{{}^nP_r}{r!} = \frac{n!}{(n-r)!\,r!}$$

2. ${}^nC_r = {}^nC_{n-r}$

3. ${}^nC_0 = {}^nC_n = 1$

4. ${}^nC_1 = {}^nC_{n-1} = n.$

5. $${}^nC_r = \frac{{}^nP_r}{r!}$$

6. ${}^nC_{r-1} + {}^nC_r = {}^{n+1}C_r$

7. $$\frac{{}^nC_r}{{}^nC_{r-1}} = \frac{n-r+1}{r}$$

8. ${}^nC_r = {}^nC_s$

   $\Rightarrow r = s$ or $r + s = n$.

9. Number of ways in which 2n things can be divided equally into two groups is $\frac{(2n)!}{2!(n!)^2}$.

10. Number of combinations in which (m + n + p) things can be divided into three groups, which contains m, n and p things respectively is $\frac{(m+n+p)!}{m!n!p!}$.

11. Number of combinations in which 3n things can be divided equally into three groups is $\frac{(3n)!}{3!(n!)^3}$.

12. Total number of combinations of n different things taken one or more at a time is 2^{n-1}.

    Number of permutations of n things taken all at a time, where p of things are alike and of one kind,

    q of things are alike and of another kind,

    r of things are alike and of another kind,

    and so on, is

$$x = \frac{n!}{p!q!r!} \quad \ldots.$$

chapter

39

PROGRESSIONS

The study of progressions in Mathematics started with the study of natural numbers. Aryabhata gave a formula for finding the sum of 'n' terms of an arithmetic progression starting with any term.

ARITHMETIC PROGRESSION (A.P.)

When a term is subtracted from the term following (for every term) it, we get a constant, that series is called arithmetic progression.

General form of an A.P. whose first term a and common difference d is

$$a + (a + d) + (a + 2d), \dots\dots\dots\dots$$

Formulae

1. In A.P. common difference, $d = t_2 - t_1$.

   Let $t_1, t_2, t_3, \dots\dots t_n$ are first, second, third, ……… n^{th} terms of a series, then

   $$n^{th} \text{ term, } t_n = a + (n - 1)\, d$$

2. Sum of n terms, $S_n = a + (a + d) + (a + 2d) + \dots\dots + a + (n - 1)d$

   $$= \frac{n}{2}\{2a + (n - 1)\, d\}$$

   Here a is called first term, and

   d is called common difference.

3. If a, b and c are in A.P., then arithmetic mean, $b = \frac{a+c}{2}$

   If a, $x_1, x_2, x_3, \dots\dots\dots x_n$, b are in A.P, then $x_1, x_2, x_3, \dots\dots\dots x_n$ are called 'n' arithmetic means between a and b, and

   $$d = \frac{b-a}{n+1}$$

GEOMETRIC PROGRESSION (G.P.)

If every term bears a constant ratio to the term preceeding it, we call that series a geometric progression (G.P.). This constant ratio is called common ratio.

General form of a G.P. whose first term is 'a' and common ratio 'r' is

$$a + ar + ar^2 + ar^3 + \dots \dots \dots .$$

Formulae

1. Sum of n terms, $S_n = a + ar + ar^2 + \dots\dots + ar^{n-1}$

$$= \frac{a[r^n - 1]}{r-1} \text{ if } r > 1.$$

$$= \frac{a(1-r^n)}{1-r} \text{ if } r < 1$$

Here, a = first term.

b = common ratio.

n = number of terms.

2. n^{th} term, $t_n = a\, r^{n-1}$

3. Common ratio, $r = \frac{t_n}{t_{n-1}}$ or $\left(\frac{t_n}{a}\right)^{1/n-1}$

4. If a. b. c are in G.P, then

$$b^2 = ac \qquad \text{or} \qquad b = \sqrt{ac}\,.$$

5. Sum to infinity

If $|r| < 1$, as $n \to \infty$, then $\quad S_\infty = \frac{a}{1-r}$.

6. If in a series $\frac{t_n}{t_{n-1}}$ is independent of n, then it is a geometric series.

7. If every term of a G.P. is multiplied or divided by a fixed number, then the resulting series is also G.P.

8. If every term of a G.P. is raised to the same power, then resulting one is also G.P.
9. The reciprocals of all the terms of a G.P. also form a G.P.
10. If three numbers are in G.P., then they are taken as $\frac{a}{r}$, a, ar.
11. If four numbers are in G.P., then they are taken as $\frac{a}{r^3}$, $\frac{a}{r}$, ar, ar^3.

HARMONIC PROGRESSION (H.P.)

If reciprocals of the terms of a series from an A.P., then the series is called a Harmonic progression (H.P.).

Formulae

1. nth term, $t_n = \frac{1}{a+(n-1)d}$
2. If a, b and c are in H.P., then

$$\text{Harmonic mean, } b = \frac{2ac}{a+c}$$

3. The series obtained by reciprocals of the terms of an A.P. in the same order as in H.P.
4. If A, G, H are the A.M., G.M., H.M. of two numbers respectively, then

   (*i*) $G^2 = A.H$

   (*ii*) $A > G > H$.
5. Largest among A.M., G.M. and H.M. of two numbers is A.M.
6. If $\frac{1}{t_n} - \frac{1}{t_{n-1}}$ is independent of n, then progression is a H.P.
7. If a, a + d, a + 2d ... ... are in A.P. and a, ar. ar^2 .... are in G.P., then a, (a + d)r, (a + 2d)r^2 ...... are in Arithmetico Geometric Series.

   n^{th} term in Arithmetico Geometric series,

$$t_n = [a + (n-1)\, d]r^{n-1}$$

Sigma Notations

(*i*) Sum of the first 'n' natural numbers,

i.e. $1 + 2 + 3 + \ldots\ldots\ldots\ldots\ldots\ldots + n = \Sigma n = \frac{n(n+1)}{2}$.

(*ii*) Sum of the squares of the first 'n' natural numbers,

i.e. $1^2 + 2^2 + 3^2 + \ldots\ldots\ldots\ldots + n^2 = \Sigma n^2 = \frac{n(n+1)(2n+1)}{6}$.

(*iii*) Sum of the cubes of the first "n" natural numbers,

i.e. $1^3 + 2^3 + 3^3 + \ldots\ldots\ldots\ldots + n^3 = \Sigma n^3 = \frac{n^2(n+1)^2}{4} = [\Sigma n]^2$.

chapter 40

LINEAR PROGRAMMING

LINEAR EQUATION IN TWO VARIABLES

An equation of the type $ax + by + c = 0$ in two variables is called *linear equation.*

where 'a' and 'b' are not simultaneously zero.

Slope of the line $ax + by + c = 0$ is

$$= -\frac{\text{coefficient of } x}{\text{coefficient of } y} = -\frac{a}{b}$$

Formulae

1. If $A(x_1, y_1)$ and $B(x_2, y_2)$ are two points on a line, then

$$\text{slope at that line} = \frac{y_2 - y_1}{x_2 - x_1} = \frac{\text{difference in y-cordinates}}{\text{difference in x-cordinates}}$$

2. If a line makes an angle 'θ' with x-axis in the positive direction, then slope of that line is $\tan\theta$.

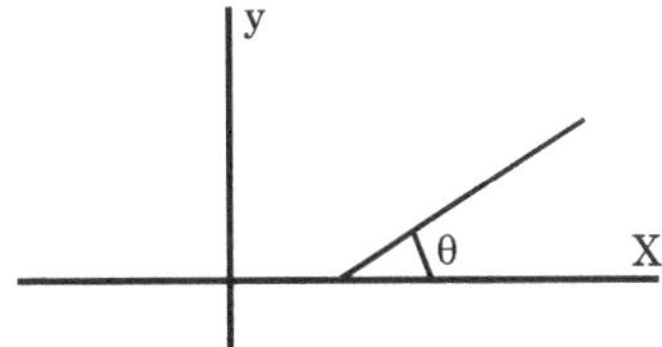

$ax + by + c = 0$, where $a, b, c \in R$ always represents a straight line.

(*i*) $A(x_1, y_1)$ belongs to line if $ax_1 + by_1 + c = 0$.

(*ii*) One half of the plane divided by the line if $ax_1 + by_1 + c > 0$.

(*iii*) One half of the plane divided by the line if $ax_1 + by_1 + c < 0$.

(*iv*) Two points (x_1, y_1), (x_2, y_2) belongs to the same half plane and opposite plane if $ax_1 + by_1 + c = 0$, $ax_2 + by_2 + c = 0$ all of the same sign and if they are of opposite signs respectively.

FUNDAMENTAL THEOREM

If values of the expression $f = ax + by$ are considered over set of points constituting a non-empty closed convex polygon, then maximum (or minimum) of f occurs on atleast one of the vertices of the polygon.

OBJECTIVE FUNCTION

A linear programming problem consists of minimising (or maximizing) a function $f = ax + by$, where $a, b \in R$ subject to certain constraints expressed as linear in equation in x and y. Such function f is called *objective function* (or profit function).

Convex Set.

It has the property that the line segment joining any pair of points in the set lies entirely in the set.

Closed Convex Polygon.

The set of all points within and on some polygon with a finite number of vertices is called *closed convex polygon.*

Open Convex Polygon.

The set of all points within and on some polygon, which is open on one side with a finite number of vertices.

Feasible Region.

The polygon region which is intersection of a finite number of closed half planes is called *feasible region.*

Note:

1. Feasible region is always convex polygon.
2. If none of the feasible solutions minimized or maximized the objective function, then problem has no solution.
3. If iso-profit line coincides with the boundary of the polygonal regions, then problem has infinite solutions.

4. Solution set of linear inequations is a set of points called the polyhedral set.
5. If $a_1x + b_1y + c_1 = 0$ and $a_2x + b_2y + c_2 = 0$ represents a pair of parallel lines, then

$$\frac{a_1}{a_2} = \frac{b_1}{b_2} \neq \frac{c_1}{c_2}$$

6. If $a_1x + b_1y + c_1 = 0$ and $a_2x + b_2y + c_2 = 0$ are coincident, then

$$\frac{a_1}{a_2} = \frac{b_1}{b_2} = \frac{c_1}{c_2}$$

c h a p t e r

41

PROBABILITY

Probability of an event A, denoted by P(A), is defined as

$$P(A) = \frac{\text{Number of cases favourable to A}}{\text{Number of possible outcomes}}$$

Formulae:

1. If an event A can happen in m ways and fails in n ways then probability of happening of the event A is

$$p = P(A) = \frac{m}{m+n}$$

And probability of non-occurrence of the event A is

$$q = P(\overline{A}) = \frac{n}{m+n}$$

Note:

(*i*) $p + q = 1$

(*ii*) $0 \le p, q \le 1$

(*iii*) $p = 1$, event is certain to occur

(*iv*) $p = 0$, event is impossible

2. Complement of an event E, is denoted by $\overline{E}$ or E' or E^c, is the set of all sample points of the space other than the sample points in E.

3. Mutually exclusive events are the events if occurrence of one precludes or rules out of the happening of other.

$$A \cap B = \phi.$$

4. Equally likely events are the events if there is no reason to expect anyone in preference to the other.

5. Exhaustive events is the total number of all possible outcomes of any trial.
6. Mutually exclusive and exhaustive events

$$E_1 \cup E_2 \cup .... \cup E_n = S$$

and $\quad E_i \cap E_j = \phi$ for all $i \neq j$

7. $A \cap B$ means both A and B occur.
8. $A \cup B$ at least one of A and B occurs.
9. $A - B$ or $A \cap \overline{B}$ means A occur but b not occur.
10. $\overline{A} \cap \overline{B}$ means neither A nor B occur.
11. $P(A \cup B) = P(A) + P(B) - P(A \cap B)$
12. If A and B are mutually exclusive events, then

$$P(A \cap B) = 0$$

and $\quad P(A \cup B) = P(A) + P(B).$

13. Two events A and B are said to be independent event if occurrence (or non occurrence) of one does not affect probability of the occurrence (non-occurrence) of other, i.e

$$P(A \cap B) = P(A) - P - (B)$$

14. If A and B are independent events, then

$$P(A \cup B) = 1 - P(\overline{A})\, P(\overline{B})$$

15. $P(\overline{A} \cap \overline{B}) = 1 - P(A \cup B)$
16. $P(\overline{A} \cup \overline{B}) = 1 - P(A \cap B)$
17. $P(A) = P(A \cap B) + P(A \cap \overline{B})$
18. $P(B) = P(A \cap B) + P(B \cap \overline{A})$

Conditional Probability

The probability of occurrence of an event A, given that B has already occurred is called conditional probability of occurrence of A, i.e.

$$P(A/B) = \frac{P(A \cap B)}{P(B)}$$

Baye's Theorem

Let E_j be mutually exclusive events such that.

$P(E_j) > 0$ for $j = 1, 2, \ldots n$ and $S = \bigcup_{j=1}^{n} E_j$.

Let A be an event with $P(A) > 0$.

Then for $j = 1, 2 \ldots\ldots n$

$$P(E_j/A) = \frac{P(E_j)P(A/E_j)}{\sum_{i=1}^{n} P(E_i)P(A/E_i)}$$

- Probability of at most r successes in n trials

$$= \sum_{r=0}^{n} {}^{n}C_r p^r q^{n-r}$$

- Probability of at least r successes in n trials

$$= \sum_{n=r}^{n} {}^{n}C_r p^r q^{n-r}$$

- Probability of having first success at the nth trial = pq^{r-1}

chapter 42

TRIGONOMETRY

The word 'Trigonometry' is derived from the greek words – 'tri' means 'three', 'gonia' means 'an angle' and 'metron' means measure. Thus 'trigonometry' means 'three angle measure'.

ANGLE

An angle is the amount of revolution made by a straight line about one of its extremities in a plane from one position to another.

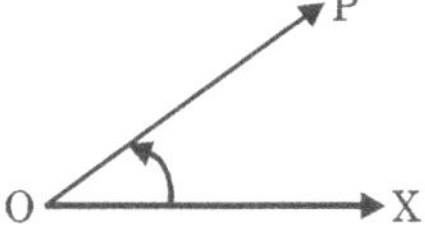

Positive angle.

If revolving line revolves in the anti-clockwise direction from its initial position, then angle described is called positive angle.

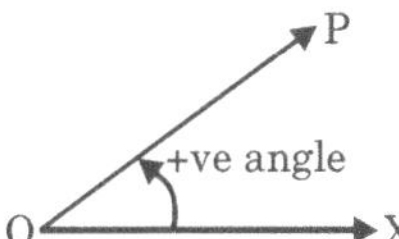

Negative angle.

If revolving line revolves in clockwise direction from its initial position, then angle described is called negative angle.

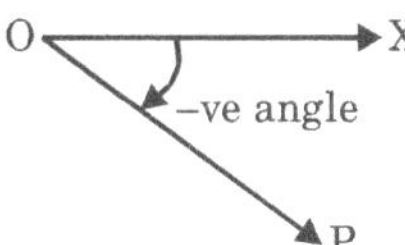

SYSTEMS FOR MEASURING ANGLES

There are three systems for measuring angles in trigonometry.

1. **Cexagesimal system or British system or English system.** In this case a right angle is divided into 90 equal parts. Each part is called a degree.

   The unit of measurement in this system is called a degree.

   1 right angle = 90° (90 degree)

   1 degree = 60' (60 minutes)

   1 minute = 60" (60 seconds)

2. **Centesimal system or French systems.** A right angle is divided into 100 equal. Each part is called a grade.

   The unit of measurement is called a grade.

   1 right angle = 100g (100 grade)

   1 grade = 100' (100 minutes)

   1 minute = 100" (100 seconds)

3. **Radian measure or Circular measure.** In this system, the unit of measurement is radian.

   Radian : The angle subtended at the centre of circle by an arc whose length is equal to the radius of the circle.

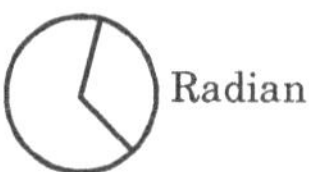

$$1 \text{ right angle} = \frac{\pi^c}{2} \left(\frac{\pi}{2} \text{ radians}\right)$$

Relation between Degree and Radian.

$$2\pi \text{ radians} = 360°$$

$$\pi \text{ radian} = 180°$$

$$\therefore \quad 1 \text{ radian} = \frac{180}{\pi} = 57°.16' \quad \left(\because \quad \pi = \frac{22}{7}\right)$$

$$1° = \frac{\pi^c}{180} = 0.01746 \text{ radian (approximately)}$$

Degrees	30	45	60	90	180	270	360
Radians	$\frac{\pi}{6}$	$\frac{\pi}{4}$	$\frac{\pi}{3}$	$\frac{\pi}{2}$	π	$\frac{3\pi}{2}$	2π

TRIGONOMETRIC RATIO'S

1. In a right angled triangle

$$\sin\theta = \frac{\text{Opposite side}}{\text{Hypotenuse}} = \frac{MP}{OP}$$

$$\cos\theta = \frac{\text{Adjacent side}}{\text{Hypotenuse}} = \frac{OM}{OP}$$

$$\tan\theta = \frac{\text{Opposite side}}{\text{Adjacent side}} = \frac{MP}{OM}$$

$$\cot\theta = \frac{\text{Adjacent side}}{\text{Opposite side}} = \frac{OM}{MP}$$

$$\sec\theta = \frac{\text{Hypotenuse}}{\text{Adjacent side}} = \frac{OP}{OM}$$

$$\cot\theta = \frac{\text{Hypotenuse}}{\text{Opposite side}} = \frac{OM}{MP}$$

2. $$\sin\theta = \frac{1}{\text{cosec}\,\theta}$$

$$\Rightarrow \quad \text{cosec}\,\theta = \frac{1}{\sin\theta}$$

$$\Rightarrow \quad \sin\theta\ \text{cosec}\,\theta = 1$$

3. $$\cos\theta = \frac{1}{\sec\theta}$$

$$\Rightarrow \quad \sec\theta = \frac{1}{\cos\theta}$$

$$\Rightarrow \quad \sec\theta\cos\theta = 1$$

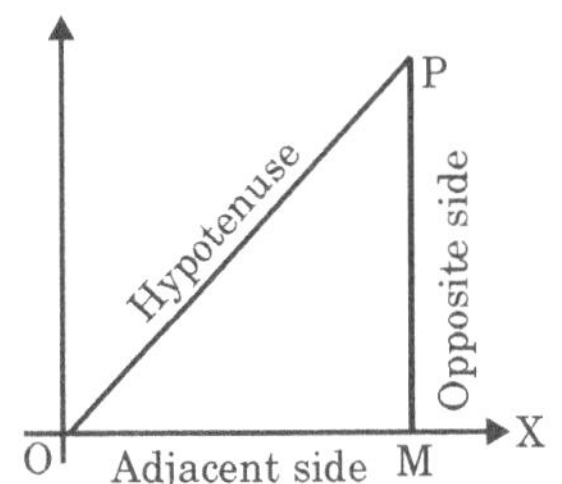

4. $$\tan\theta = \frac{1}{\cot\theta}$$

$$\Rightarrow \quad \cot\theta = \frac{1}{\tan\theta}$$

$$\Rightarrow \quad \tan\theta.\cot\theta = 1$$

5. $\tan\theta = \dfrac{\sin\theta}{\cos\theta}$

6. $\cot\theta = \dfrac{\cos\theta}{\sin\theta}$

SIGNS OF TRIGONOMETRIC FUNCTIONS

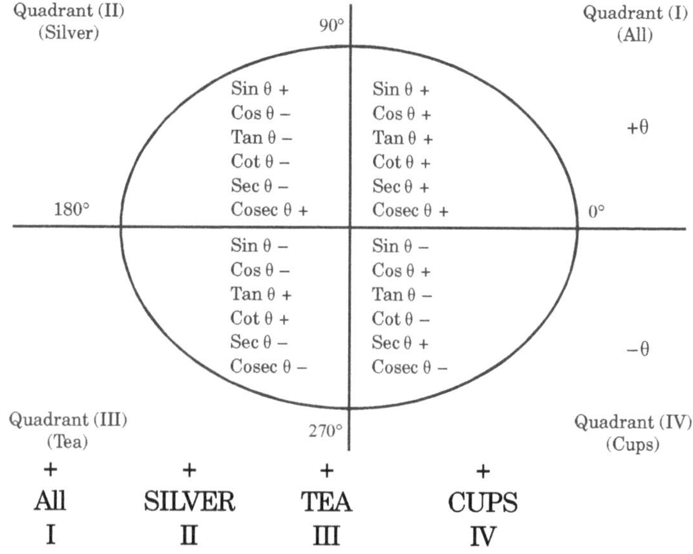

+	+	+	+
All	SILVER	TEA	CUPS
I	II	III	IV

1. In the first quadrant ($0° < \theta < 90°$), all trigonometric ratios are positive.
2. In the second quadrant ($90° < \theta < 180°$), sin and cosec are positive and the rest of all are negative.
3. In the third quadrant ($180° < \theta < 270°$), tan and cot are positive and the rest of all are negative.
4. In the fourth quadrant ($270° < \theta < 360°$ or $0°$), sec and cos positive and the rest of all are negative.

TRIGONOMETRIC RATIO'S

1. **Allied Angles :**

Two angles are called allied when their sum or difference is a multiple of 90°.

Thus θ and $-\theta$; θ and $90° - \theta$; θ and $90° + \theta$; θ and $180° - \theta$; θ and $180° + \theta$; θ and $270° - \theta$; θ and $270° + \theta$; θ and $360° - ....$ etc. are allied angles; it is assumed that θ is measured in degrees.

(*i*) If allied angle is $90° \pm \theta$ or $270° \pm \theta$, trigonometric ratio is changed as follows :

(*a*) sin is changed into cosine, and cosine is changed into sin.

(*b*) tan is changed into cot, and cot is changed into tan.

(*c*) sec is changed into cosec, and cosec is changed into sec.

(*ii*) If allied angle is $-\theta$ or $180° \pm \theta$ or $360 \pm \theta$, trigonometric ratio is not changed in form, i.e.

(*a*) sin remain sin; cos remains cos.

(*b*) tan remains tan; cot remains cot.

(*c*) sec remains sec; cosec remains cosec.

(*iii*) $\sin(-\theta) = -\sin\theta$; $\cos(-\theta) = \cos\theta$

$\tan(-\theta) = -\tan\theta$; $\cot(-\theta) = -\cot\theta$

$\sec(-\theta) = \sec\theta$; $\text{cosec}(-\theta) = -\text{cosec}\,\theta$

Illustration :

$$\sin(-45°) = -\sin 45° = -\frac{1}{\sqrt{2}}$$

$$\cos(-45°) = \cos 45° = \frac{1}{\sqrt{2}}$$

2. Complementary Angles :

Two angles are called complementary when their sum is 90°. Each angle is the complement of the other; thus θ and $90° - \theta$ are complementary angles.

$\sin(90° - \theta) = \cos\theta$; $\cos(90° - \theta) = \sin\theta$

$\tan(90° - \theta) = \cot\theta$; $\cot(90° - \theta) = \tan\theta$

$\sec(90° - \theta) = \operatorname{cosec}\theta$; $\operatorname{cosec}(90° - \theta) = \sec\theta$

Illustration :

$$\sin 60° = \sin(90° - 30°) = \cos 30° = \frac{\sqrt{3}}{2}$$

$$\cos 30° = \cos(90° - 60°) = \sin 60° = \frac{\sqrt{3}}{2}$$

3. $\sin(90° + \theta) = \cos\theta$; $\cos(90° + \theta) = -\sin\theta$

$\tan(90° + \theta) = -\cot\theta$; $\cot(90° + \theta) = -\tan\theta$

$\sec(90° + \theta) = -\operatorname{cosec}\theta$; $\operatorname{cosec}(90° + \theta) = \sec\theta$

Illustration :

$$\sin 120° = \sin(90° + 30°) = \cos 60° = \frac{\sqrt{3}}{2}$$

$$\cos 120° = \cos(90° + 30°) = -\sin 30° = -\frac{1}{2}$$

4. **Supplementary Angle :**

Two angles are called supplementary when their sum is 180°. Each angle is the supplement of the other. Thus θ and $(180° - \theta)$ are supplementary angles.

$\sin(180° - \theta) = \sin\theta$; $\cos(180° - \theta) = -\cos\theta$

$\tan(180° - \theta) = -\tan\theta$; $\cot(180° - \theta) = -\cot\theta$

$\sec(180° - \theta) = -\sec\theta$; $\operatorname{cosec}(90° - \theta) = \operatorname{cosec}\theta$

Illustration :

$$\sin 120° = \sin (180° - 60°) = \sin 60° = \frac{\sqrt{3}}{2}$$

$$\cos 150° = \cos (180° - 30°) = -\cos 30° = -\frac{\sqrt{3}}{2}$$

5. $\sin (180° + \theta) = -\sin \theta$; $\cos (180° + \theta) = -\cos \theta$

$\tan (180° + \theta) = \tan \theta$; $\cot (180° + \theta) = \cot \theta$

$\sec (180° + \theta) = -\sec \theta$; $\text{cosec}\, (180° + \theta) = -\text{cosec}\, \theta$

Illustration :

$$\sin 210° = \sin (180° + 30°) = -\sin 30° = -\frac{1}{2}$$

$$\cos 240° = \cos (180° + 60°) = -\cos 60° = -\frac{1}{2}$$

6. $\sin (270° - \theta) = -\cos \theta$; $\cos (270° - \theta) = -\sin \theta$

$\tan (270° - \theta) = \cot \theta$; $\cot (270° - \theta) = \tan \theta$

$\sec (270° - \theta) = -\text{cosec}\, \theta$; $\text{cosec}\, (270° - \theta) = -\sec \theta$

Illustration :

$$\sin 210° = \sin (270° - 60°) = -\cos 60° = -\frac{1}{2}$$

$$\cos 240° = \cos (270° - 30°) = -\sin 30° = -\frac{1}{2}$$

7. $\sin (270° + \theta) = -\cos \theta$; $\cos (270° + \theta) = \sin \theta$

$\tan (270° + \theta) = -\cot \theta$; $\cot (270° + \theta) = -\tan \theta$

$\sec (270° + \theta) = \text{cosec}\, \theta$; $\text{cosec}\, (270° + \theta) = -\sec \theta$

Illustration :

$$\sin 300° = \sin (270° + 30°) = -\cos 30° = -\frac{\sqrt{3}}{2}$$

$$\cos 330° = \cos (270° + 60°) = -\sin 60° = \frac{\sqrt{3}}{2}$$

8. $\sin(360° - \theta) = -\sin\theta$; $\cos(360° - \theta) = \cos\theta$

$\tan(360° - \theta) = -\tan\theta$; $\cot(360° - \theta) = -\cot\theta$

$\sec(360° - \theta) = \sec\theta$; $\text{cosec}\,(360° - \theta) = -\text{cosec}\,\theta$

Illustration :

$$\sin 300° = \sin(360° - 60°) = -\sin 60° = -\frac{\sqrt{3}}{2}$$

$$\cos 330° = \cos(360° - 30°) = \cos 30° = \frac{\sqrt{3}}{2}$$

9. $\sin(360° + \theta) = \sin\theta$; $\cos(360° + \theta) = \cos\theta$

$\tan(360° + \theta) = \tan\theta$; $\cot(360° + \theta) = \cot\theta$

$\sec(360° + \theta) = \sec\theta$; $\text{cosec}\,(360° + \theta) = \text{cosec}\,\theta$

Illustration :

$$\sin 390° = \sin(360° + 30°) = \sin 30° = \frac{1}{2}$$

$$\cos 420° = \cos(360° + 60°) = \cos 60° = \frac{1}{2}$$

10. $\sin(n.360° - \theta) = -\sin\theta$; $\cos(n.360° - \theta) = \cos\theta$

$\tan(n.360° - \theta) = -\tan\theta$; $\cot(n.360° - \theta) = -\cot\theta$

$\sec(n.360° - \theta) = \sec\theta$; $\text{cosec}\,(n.360° - \theta) = -\text{cosec}\,\theta$

Illustration :

$$\sin 660° = \sin(2\times 360° - 60°) = -\sin 60° = -\frac{\sqrt{3}}{2}$$

$$\cos 690° = \cos(2\times 360° - 30°) = \cos 30° = \frac{\sqrt{3}}{2}$$

11. $\sin(n.360° + \theta) = \sin\theta$; $\cos(n.360° - \theta) = \cos\theta$

$\tan(n.360° + \theta) = \tan\theta$; $\cot(n.360° - \theta) = \cot\theta$

$\sec(n.360° + \theta) = \sec\theta$; $\text{cosec}\,(n.360° + \theta) = \text{cosec}\,\theta$

Illustration :

$$\sin 750° = \sin(2\times 360° + 30°) = \sin 30° = \frac{1}{2}$$

$$\cos 780° = \cos(2\times 360° + 60°) = \cos 60° = \frac{1}{2}$$

VALUES OF TRIGONOMETRIC RATIO FOR DIFFERENT ANGLES

Angle	0°	30°	45°	60°	90°	180°	270°	360°
sin	0	$\frac{1}{2}$	$\frac{1}{\sqrt{2}}$	$\frac{\sqrt{3}}{2}$	1	0	–1	0
cos	1	$\frac{\sqrt{3}}{2}$	$\frac{1}{\sqrt{2}}$	$\frac{1}{2}$	0	–1	0	1

Angle	0°	30°	45°	60°	90°
sin	0	$\frac{1}{2}$	$\frac{1}{\sqrt{2}}$	$\frac{\sqrt{3}}{2}$	1
cos	1	$\frac{\sqrt{3}}{2}$	$\frac{1}{\sqrt{2}}$	$\frac{1}{2}$	0
tan	0	$\frac{1}{\sqrt{3}}$	1	$\sqrt{3}$	∞
cot	∞	$\sqrt{3}$	1	$\frac{1}{\sqrt{3}}$	0
cosec	∞	2	$\sqrt{2}$	$\frac{2}{\sqrt{3}}$	1
sec	1	$\frac{2}{\sqrt{3}}$	$\sqrt{2}$	2	∞

Trigonometric Relations

1. (*i*) $\sin^2\theta + \cos^2\theta = 1$

$\sin^2\theta = 1 - \cos^2\theta$

$\cos^2\theta = 1 - \sin^2\theta$

(*ii*) $\sec^2\theta - \tan^2\theta = 1$

$\sec^2\theta = 1 + \tan^2\theta$

$\tan^2\theta = \sec^2\theta - 1$

(*iii*) $\text{cosec}^2\theta - \cot^2\theta = 1$

$\text{cosec}^2\theta = 1 + \cot^2\theta$

$\cot^2\theta = \text{cosec}^2\theta - 1$

2. Addition and Subtraction formulae.

(*i*) $\sin(A \pm B) = \sin A \cos B \pm \cos A \sin B$

(*ii*) $\cos(A \pm B) = \cos A \cos B \pm \sin A \sin B$

(*iii*) $\tan(A + B) = \dfrac{\tan A + \tan B}{1 - \tan A \tan B}$

(*iv*) $\tan(A - B) = \dfrac{\tan A - \tan B}{1 - \tan A \tan B}$

Cor 1: $\tan(45° - \theta) = \dfrac{1 + \tan\theta}{1 - \tan\theta}$

Cor 2: $\tan(45° + \theta) = \dfrac{1 - \tan\theta}{1 + \tan\theta}$

(*v*) $\cot(A + B) = \dfrac{\cot A \cot B - 1}{\cot A + \cot B}$

(*vi*) $\cot(A - B) = \dfrac{\cot A \cot B + 1}{\cot A - \cot B}$

3. $\sin 2A = 2 \sin A \cos A = \dfrac{2 \tan A}{1 + \tan^2 A}$

Cor: $\sin A = 2 \sin \dfrac{A}{2} \cos \dfrac{A}{2} = \dfrac{2 \tan \dfrac{A}{2}}{1 + \tan^2 \dfrac{A}{2}}$

4. $\cos 2A = \cos^2 A - \sin^2 A$

$= 1 - 2 \sin^2 A$

$= 2 \cos^2 A - 1$

$= \dfrac{1 - \tan^2 A}{1 + \tan^2 A}$

Cor : $\cos A = \cos^2\frac{A}{2} - \sin^2\frac{A}{2}$

$$= 2\cos^2\frac{A}{2} - 1$$

$$= 1 - 2\sin^2\frac{A}{2}$$

$$= \frac{1-\tan^2\frac{A}{2}}{1+\tan^2\frac{A}{2}}$$

5. (*i*) $\sin A = \sqrt{\frac{1-\cos 2A}{2}}$

(*ii*) $\cos A = \sqrt{\frac{1+\cos 2A}{2}}$

(*iii*) $\tan A = \sqrt{\frac{1-\cos 2A}{1+\cos 2A}}$

6. (*i*) $\sin(A+B)\sin(A-B) = \sin^2 A - \sin^2 B$

(*ii*) $\cos(A+B)\cos(A-B) = \cos^2 A - \sin^2 B = \cos^2 B - \sin^2 A$

7. $\tan 2A = \frac{2\tan A}{1-\tan^2 A}$

Cor : $\tan A = \frac{2\tan\frac{A}{2}}{1-\tan^2\frac{A}{2}}$

8. (*i*) $\sin 3A = 3\sin A - 4\sin^3 A$

(*ii*) $\cos 3A = 4\cos^3 A - 3\cos A$

(*iii*) $\tan 3A = \frac{3\tan A - \tan^3 A}{1-3\tan^2 A}$

(*iv*) $\cot 3A = \frac{\cot^3 A - 3\cot A}{3\cot^2 A - 1} = \frac{3\cot A - \cot^3 A}{1-3\cot^2 A}$

9. (*i*) $\sin C + \sin D = 2 \sin \frac{C+D}{2} \cos \frac{C-D}{2}$

(*ii*) $\sin C - \sin D = 2 \cos \frac{C+D}{2} \sin \frac{C-D}{2}$

(*iii*) $\cos C + \cos D = 2\cos \frac{C+D}{2} \cos \frac{C-D}{2}$

(*iv*) $\cos C - \cos D = -2 \sin \frac{C+D}{2} \sin \frac{C-D}{2}$

$= 2 \sin \frac{C+D}{2} \sin \frac{D-C}{2}$

10. (*i*) $2 \sin A \cos B = \sin (A+B) + \sin (A-B)$

(*ii*) $2 \cos A \sin B = \sin (A+B) - \sin (A-B)$

(*iii*) $2 \cos A \cos B = \cos (A+B) + \cos (A-B)$

(*iv*) $2 \sin A \sin B = \cos (A-B) - \cos (A+B)$

11. (*i*) $\sin 15° = \frac{\sqrt{3}-1}{2\sqrt{2}}$

(*ii*) $\cos 15° = \frac{\sqrt{3}+1}{2\sqrt{2}}$

(*iii*) $\tan 15° = 2 - \sqrt{3}$

(*iv*) $\cot 15° = 2 + \sqrt{3}$

(*v*) $\operatorname{cosec} 15° = \sqrt{6} + \sqrt{2}$

(*vi*) $\sec 15° = \sqrt{6} - \sqrt{2}$

(*vii*) $\sin 22\frac{1°}{2} = \cos 67\frac{1°}{2} = \sqrt{\frac{\sqrt{2}-1}{2\sqrt{2}}}$

(*viii*) $\cos 22\frac{1°}{2} = \sin 67\frac{1°}{2} = \sqrt{\frac{\sqrt{2}+1}{2\sqrt{2}}}$

(*ix*) $\tan 22\frac{1°}{2} = \cot 67\frac{1°}{2} = \sqrt{\frac{\sqrt{2}-1}{\sqrt{2}+1}} = \sqrt{2} - 1$

Values of Certain Angles

Angle	18°	36°	54°	72°
sin	$\frac{\sqrt{5}-1}{4}$	$\frac{\sqrt{10-2\sqrt{5}}}{4}$	$\frac{\sqrt{5}+1}{4}$	$\frac{\sqrt{10+2\sqrt{5}}}{4}$
cos	$\frac{\sqrt{10+2\sqrt{5}}}{4}$	$\frac{\sqrt{5}+1}{4}$	$\frac{\sqrt{10-2\sqrt{5}}}{4}$	$\frac{\sqrt{5}-1}{4}$

12. If $A + B + C = \pi$, then

$$\sin A + \sin B + \sin C = 4 \cos\frac{A}{2} \cos\frac{B}{2} \cos\frac{C}{2}$$

$$\cos A + \cos B + \cos C = 1 + 4 \sin\frac{A}{2} \sin\frac{B}{2} \sin\frac{C}{2}$$

$$\tan A + \tan B + \tan C = \tan A \tan B \tan C$$

$$\tan\frac{A}{2} \tan\frac{B}{2} + \tan\frac{B}{2} \tan\frac{C}{2} + \tan\frac{C}{2} \tan\frac{A}{2} = 1$$

$$\cot\frac{A}{2} + \cot\frac{B}{2} + \cot\frac{C}{2} = \cot\frac{A}{2} \cot\frac{B}{2} \cot\frac{C}{2}$$

$$\sin 2A + \sin 2B + \sin 2C = 4 \sin A \sin B \sin C$$

$$\cos 2A + \cos 2B + \cos 2C = -1 - 4 \cos A \cos B \cos C$$

$$\cot A \cot B + \cot B \cot C + \cot C \cot A = 1$$

$$\sin^2 A + \sin^2 B + \sin^2 C = 2(1 + \cos A \cos B \cos C)$$

$$\cos^2 A + \cos^2 B + \cos^2 C = 1 - 2 \cos A \cos B \cos C$$

13. General solution of some trigonometric equations:

$\sin\theta = 0 \Rightarrow \theta = n\pi$

$\cos\theta = 0 \Rightarrow \theta = n\pi + \frac{\pi}{2}$

$\tan\theta = 0 \Rightarrow \theta = n\pi$

$\sin\theta = \pm 1 \Rightarrow \theta = 2n\pi \pm \frac{\pi}{2}$

$\cos\theta = 1 \Rightarrow \theta = 2n\pi$

$\cos\theta = -1 \Rightarrow \theta = 2n\pi + \pi$

$\tan\theta = \pm 1 \Rightarrow \theta = n\pi \pm \dfrac{\pi}{4}$

$\sin\theta = k, -1 \le k \le 1 \Rightarrow \theta = n\pi + (-1)^n \sin^{-1}k$

$\cos\theta = k, -1 \le k \le 1 \Rightarrow \theta = 2n\pi \pm \cos^{-1}k$

$\tan\theta = k, -\infty < k < \infty \Rightarrow \theta = n\pi + \tan^{-1}k$

$\sin\theta = \sin\beta \Rightarrow \theta = n\pi + (-1)^n \beta$

$\cos\theta = \cos\beta \Rightarrow \theta = 2n\pi \pm \beta$

$\tan\theta = \tan\beta \Rightarrow \theta = n\pi + \beta$

$\sin^2\theta = \sin^2\beta \Rightarrow \theta = n\pi \pm \beta$

$\cos^2\theta = \cos^2\beta \Rightarrow \theta = n\pi \pm \beta$

$\tan^2\theta = \tan^2\beta \Rightarrow \theta = n\pi \pm \beta$

14. *Some important inverse trigonometric functions:*

$$\sin^{-1}x = \text{cosec}^{-1}\frac{1}{x} \text{ or } \text{cosec}^{-1}x = \sin^{-1}\frac{1}{x}$$

$$\cos^{-1}x = \sec^{-1}\frac{1}{x} \text{ or } \sec^{-1}x = \cos^{-1}\frac{1}{x}$$

$$\tan^{-1}x = \begin{cases} \cot^{-1}\dfrac{1}{x}, & x > 0 \\ \cot^{-1}\dfrac{1}{x} - \pi, & x < 0 \end{cases}$$

$$\cot^{-1}x = \begin{cases} \tan^{-1}\dfrac{1}{x}, & x > 0 \\ \tan^{-1}\dfrac{1}{x} + \pi, & x < 0 \end{cases}$$

$$\sin^{-1}x = \cos^{-1}\sqrt{1-x^2} = \tan^{-1}\frac{x}{\sqrt{1-x^2}}$$

$$\cos^{-1}x = \sin^{-1}\sqrt{1-x^2} = \tan^{-1}\frac{\sqrt{1-x^2}}{x}$$

$$\tan^{-1}x = \sin^{-1}\frac{x}{\sqrt{1+x^2}} = \cos^{-1}\frac{1}{\sqrt{1+x^2}}$$

$$\sin^{-1}x + \cos^{-1}x = \frac{\pi}{2}, \quad -1 \le x \le 1$$

$$\tan^{-1}x + \cot^{-1}x = \frac{\pi}{2}, \quad -\infty < x < \infty$$

$$\sec^{-1}x + \operatorname{cosec}^{-1}x = \frac{\pi}{2}, \quad x \le -1 \text{ or } x \ge 1$$

$$\sin^{-1}(-x) = -\sin^{-1}x$$

$$\cos^{-1}(-x) = \pi - \cos^{-1}x$$

$$\tan^{-1}(-x) = -\tan^{-1}x$$

$$\cot^{-1}(-x) = \pi - \cot^{-1}x$$

$$2\sin^{-1}x = \begin{cases} \sin^{-1}\left(2x\sqrt{1-x^2}\right), & |x| \le \frac{1}{\sqrt{2}} \\ \pi - \sin^{-1}\left(2x\sqrt{1-x^2}\right), & \frac{1}{\sqrt{2}} < x \le 1 \\ -\pi - \sin^{-1}\left(2x\sqrt{1-x^2}\right), & -1 \le x < -\frac{1}{\sqrt{2}} \end{cases}$$

$$2\cos^{-1}x = \begin{cases} \cos^{-1}\left(2x^2-1\right), & 0 \le x \le 1 \\ 2\pi - \cos^{-1}\left(2x^2-1\right)), & -1 \le x \le 0 \end{cases}$$

$$2\tan^{-1}x = \begin{cases} \tan^{-1}\left(\frac{2x}{1-x^2}\right) - \pi, & -1 < x < 1 \\ \pi + \tan^{-1}\left(\frac{2x}{1-x^2}\right), & x > 1 \\ \tan^{-1}\left(\frac{2x}{1-x^2}\right) - \pi, & x < -1 \\ \frac{\pi}{2} & x = 1 \\ -\frac{\pi}{2} & x = -1 \end{cases}$$

$$3\sin^{-1}x = \begin{cases} \sin^{-1}\left(3x-4x^3\right),, & -\frac{1}{2} \le x \le \frac{1}{2} \\ \pi - \sin^{-1}\left(3x-4x^3\right), & \frac{1}{2} < x \le 1 \\ -\pi - \sin^{-1}\left(3x-4x^3\right), & -1 \le x < -\frac{1}{2} \end{cases}$$

$$3\cos^{-1}x = \begin{cases} \cos^{-1}\left(4x^3 - 3x\right) & \frac{1}{2} \le x \le 1 \\ 2\pi - \cos^{-1}\left(4x^3 - 3x\right), & -\frac{1}{2} \le x \le \frac{1}{2} \\ 2\pi + \cos^{-1}\left(4x^3 - 3x\right), & -1 \le x \le -\frac{1}{2} \end{cases}$$

$$3\tan^{-1}x = \begin{cases} \tan^{-1}\left(\dfrac{3x - x^3}{1 - 3x^2}\right), & \dfrac{-1}{\sqrt{3}} < x < \dfrac{1}{\sqrt{3}} \\ \pi + \tan^{-1}\left(\dfrac{3x - x^3}{1 - 3x^2}\right), & x > \dfrac{1}{\sqrt{3}} \\ -\pi + \tan^{-1}\left(\dfrac{3x - x^3}{1 - 3x^2}\right), & x < -\dfrac{1}{\sqrt{3}} \end{cases}$$

$\sin^{-1}x + \sin^{-1}y$

$$= \begin{cases} \sin^{-1}\left(x\sqrt{1-y^2} + y\sqrt{1-x^2}\right), & xy > 0, x^2 + y^2 \le 1 \\ \pi - \sin^{-1}\left(x\sqrt{1-y^2} + y\sqrt{1-x^2}\right), & x > 0, y > 0, x^2 + y^2 > 1 \\ -\pi - \sin^{-1}\left(x\sqrt{1-y^2} - y\sqrt{1-x^2}\right), & x < 0, y < 0, x^2 + y^2 > 1 \end{cases}$$

$\sin^{-1}x - \sin^{-1}y$

$$= \begin{cases} \sin^{-1}\left(x\sqrt{1-y^2} - y\sqrt{1-x^2}\right), & xy < 0, x^2 + y^2 \le 1 \\ \pi - \sin^{-1}\left(x\sqrt{1-y^2} - y\sqrt{1-x^2}\right), & x > 0, y < 0, x^2 + y^2 > 1 \\ -\pi - \sin^{-1}\left(x\sqrt{1-y^2} - y\sqrt{1-x^2}\right), & x < 0, y > 0, x^2 + y^2 > 1 \end{cases}$$

$\cos^{-1}x + \cos^{-1}y$

$$= \begin{cases} \cos^{-1}\left(xy - \sqrt{1-x^2}\sqrt{1-y^2}\right), & |x|, |y| \le 1, x + y \ge 0 \\ 2\pi - \cos^{-1}\left(xy - \sqrt{1-x^2}\sqrt{1-y^2}\right), & |x|, |y| \le 1, x + y \le 0 \end{cases}$$

$\cos^{-1}x - \cos^{-1}y$

$$= \begin{cases} \cos^{-1}\left(xy + \sqrt{1-x^2}\sqrt{1-y^2}\right., & |x|, |y| \le 1, \quad x \le y \\ -\cos^{-1}\left(xy + \sqrt{1-x^2}\sqrt{1-y^2}\right., & |x|, |y| \le 1, \quad x \ge y \end{cases}$$

$$\tan^{-1}x + \tan^{-1}y = \begin{cases} \tan^{-1}\left(\dfrac{x+y}{1-xy}\right), & xy < 1 \\ \pi + \tan^{-1}\left(\dfrac{x+y}{1-xy}\right), & xy > 1,\ x > 0 \\ \tan^{-1}\left(\dfrac{x+y}{1-xy}\right) - \pi, & xy > 1, x < 0 \\ \dfrac{\pi}{2} & xy = 1, x > 0 \\ -\dfrac{\pi}{2} & xy = 1, x < 0 \end{cases}$$

$$\tan^{-1}x - \tan^{-1}y = \begin{cases} \tan^{-1}\left(\dfrac{x-y}{1+xy}\right), & xy > -1 \\ \pi + \tan^{-1}\left(\dfrac{x-y}{1+xy}\right), & xy < -1,\ x > 0 \\ \tan^{-1}\left(\dfrac{x-y}{1+xy}\right) - \pi, & xy < -1,\ x < 0 \\ \dfrac{\pi}{2}, & xy = -1,\ x > 0 \\ -\dfrac{\pi}{2}, & xy = -1,\ x < 0 \end{cases}$$

$$\tan^{-1}x + \tan^{-1}y + \tan^{-1}z = \tan^{-1}\left(\frac{x+y+z-xyz}{1-xy-yz-zx}\right)$$

$$\sin^{-1}x + \sin^{-1}y + \sin^{-1}z$$

$$= \begin{cases} \dfrac{\pi}{2} \Rightarrow x^2 + y^2 + z^2 + 2xyz = 1 \\ \pi \Rightarrow x\sqrt{1-x^2} + y\sqrt{1-y^2} + z\sqrt{1-z^2} = 2xyz \\ \dfrac{3\pi}{2} \Rightarrow xy + yz + zx = 3 \end{cases}$$

$$\cos^{-1}x + \cos^{-1}y + \cos^{-1}z = \begin{cases} \pi \Rightarrow x^2 + y^2 + z^2 + 2xyz = 1 \\ 3\pi \Rightarrow xy + yz + zx = 3 \end{cases}$$

$$\tan^{-1}x + \tan^{-1}y + \tan^{-1}z = \begin{cases} \frac{\pi}{2} \Rightarrow xy + yz + zx = 1 \\ \pi \Rightarrow x + y + z = xyz \end{cases}$$

$$\sin^{-1}x + \sin^{-1}y = \theta \Rightarrow \cos^{-1}x + \cos^{-1}y = \pi - \theta$$

$$\cos^{-1}x + \cos^{-1}y = \theta \Rightarrow \sin^{-1}x + \sin^{-1}y = \pi - \theta$$

$$\tan^{-1}x + \tan^{-1}y = \frac{\pi}{2} \Rightarrow xy = 1$$

$$\cot^{-1}x + \cot^{-1}y = \frac{\pi}{2} \Rightarrow xy = 1$$

15. Properties and Solutions of Triangles

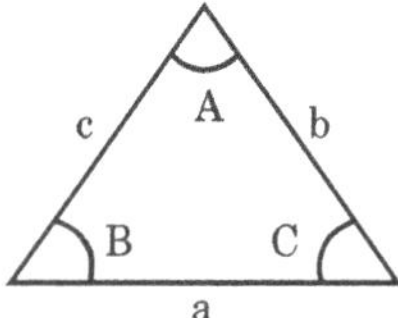

(*i*) Sine Rule :

$$\frac{a}{\sin A} = \frac{b}{\sin B} = \frac{c}{\sin C}$$

(*ii*) Cosine Rule :

$$\cos A = \frac{b^2 + c^2 - a^2}{2bc}$$

$$\cos B = \frac{c^2 + a^2 - b^2}{2ca}$$

$$\cos C = \frac{a^2 + b^2 - c^2}{2ab}$$

(*iii*) Projection Rule :

$$a = b\cos C + c\cos B$$

$$b = a\cos C + c\cos A$$

$$c = a\cos B + b\cos A$$

(*iv*) Tangent Rule :

$$\tan\left(\frac{A-B}{2}\right) = \left(\frac{a-b}{a+b}\right) \cot \frac{C}{2}$$

$$\tan\left(\frac{B-C}{2}\right) = \left(\frac{b-c}{b+c}\right) \cot \frac{A}{2}$$

$$\tan\left(\frac{C-A}{2}\right) = \left(\frac{c-a}{c+a}\right) \cot \frac{B}{2}$$

(*v*) **Half Angle Formula :**

If a + b + c = 2s, then

$$\sin\frac{A}{2} = \sqrt{\frac{(s-b)(s-c)}{bc}}, \cos\frac{A}{2} = \sqrt{\frac{s(s-a)}{bc}},$$

$$\tan\frac{A}{2} = \sqrt{\frac{(s-b)(s-c)}{s(s-a)}}$$

$$\sin\frac{B}{2} = \sqrt{\frac{(s-c)(s-a)}{ca}}, \cos\frac{B}{2} = \sqrt{\frac{s(s-b)}{ca}},$$

$$\tan\frac{B}{2} = \sqrt{\frac{(s-c)(s-a)}{s(s-b)}}$$

$$\sin\frac{C}{2} = \sqrt{\frac{(s-a)(s-b)}{ab}}, \cos\frac{C}{2} = \sqrt{\frac{s(s-c)}{ab}},$$

$$\tan\frac{C}{2} = \sqrt{\frac{(s-a)(s-b)}{s(s-c)}}$$

(*vi*) **Area of a Triangle :**

If Δ represents area of triangle ABC, then

$$\Delta = \frac{1}{2}\ ab \sin C = \frac{1}{2} bc \sin A = \frac{1}{2}\ ca \sin B$$

$$= \sqrt{s\ (s\ -a)(s-b)(s-c)} = \frac{abc}{4R} = rs$$

where, R = radius of circumcircle of triangle ΔABC

r = radius of the circle inscribed in triangle ABC.

(*vii*) **Circumcircle and Incircle of Triangle :**

$$R = \frac{a}{2\sin A} = \frac{b}{2\sin B} = \frac{c}{2\sin C} = \frac{abc}{4\Delta}$$

$$r = \frac{\Delta}{s} = (s-a)\tan\frac{A}{2} = (s-b)\tan\frac{B}{2} = (s-c)\tan\frac{C}{2}$$

$$r = 4R\sin\frac{A}{2}\sin\frac{B}{2}\sin\frac{C}{2}$$

$$r = \frac{a\sin\frac{B}{2}\sin\frac{C}{2}}{\cos\frac{A}{2}} = \frac{b\sin\frac{C}{2}\sin\frac{A}{2}}{\cos\frac{B}{2}} = \frac{c\sin\frac{A}{2}\sin\frac{B}{2}}{\cos\frac{C}{2}}$$

(*viii*) **Escribed Circle :**

The circle touching BC and two sides AB and AC produced of a triangle ABC is called escribed circle opposite angle A. Its radius is denoted by r_1.

Similarly, r_2 and r_3 denote radii of the escribed circle opposite angles B and C, respectively. They are ex-radii of triangle ABC.

$$r_1 = \frac{\Delta}{s-a} = s\tan\frac{A}{2} = \frac{a\cos\frac{B}{2}\cos\frac{C}{2}}{\cos\frac{A}{2}}$$

$$= 4R\sin\frac{A}{2}\cos\frac{B}{2}\cos\frac{C}{2}$$

$$r_2 = \frac{\Delta}{s-b} = s\tan\frac{B}{2} = \frac{b\cos\frac{A}{2}\cos\frac{C}{2}}{\cos\frac{B}{2}}$$

$$= 4R\cos\frac{A}{2}\sin\frac{B}{2}\cos\frac{C}{2}$$

$$r_3 = \frac{\Delta}{s-c} = s\tan\frac{C}{2} = \frac{c\cos\frac{A}{2}\cos\frac{B}{2}}{\cos\frac{C}{2}}$$

$$= 4R\cos\frac{A}{2}\cos\frac{B}{2}\sin\frac{C}{2}$$

$$r_1 + r_2 + r_3 = 4R + r$$

$$r_1 r_2 + r_2 r_3 + r_3 r_1 = s^2$$

(*ix*) **Cyclic Quadrilateral :**

It is quadrilateral whose vertices lie on a circle.

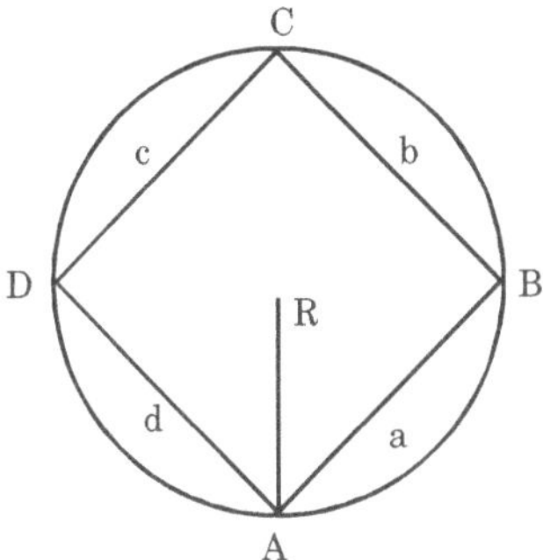

Area of cyclic quadrilateral ABCD

$$= \sqrt{(s-a)(s-b)(s-c)(s-d)}$$

where, a, b, c, d are sides of quadrilateral

$$2s = a + b + c + d$$

Circumradius of cyclic quadrilateral

$$R = \frac{1}{4}\sqrt{\frac{(ab+cd)(ad+bc)(ac+bd)}{(s-a)(s-b)(s-c)(s-d)}}$$

Angles $\cos A = \dfrac{a^2 + d^2 - b^2 - c^2}{2(ad+bc)}$, similarly other angles.

Regular Polygon :

It is a polygon whose all sides and all angles are equal.

- In a regular polygon, centroid, circumcentre and incentre are same.
- If a polygon has 'n' sides, sum of internal angles in $(n-2)\pi$ and each angle is $(n-2)\dfrac{\pi}{n}$.

- Area of regular polygon $= \frac{nl^2}{4} \cot \frac{\pi}{n} = \frac{nR^2}{2} \sin \frac{2\pi}{n} = nr^2 \tan \frac{\pi}{n}$

where,

l = length of side

n = number of sides of polygon

R = radius of circumscribing circle

r = radius of incircle of the polygon

$$R = \frac{1}{2 \sin \frac{\pi}{n}} = \frac{l}{2} \cos \frac{\pi}{n}$$

chapter

43

HEIGHTS AND DISTANCE

ANGLE OF ELEVATION

$\angle XOP$, i.e. the angle which the line joining object and eye makes with the horizontal through the eye is called *angle of elevation* (or altitude) of P as seen from O.

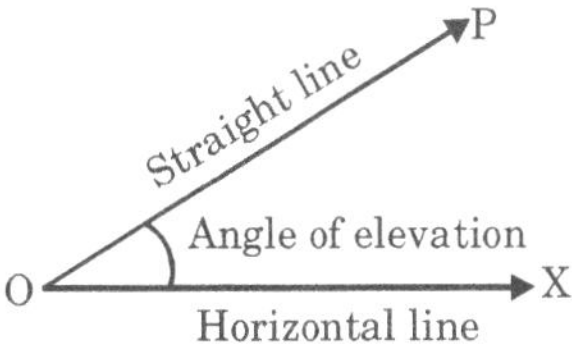

ANGLE OF DEPRESSION.

$\angle XOP$, i.e. the angle which the line joining the object and the eye makes with the horizontal through the eye is called angle of depression of "P" as seen from O.

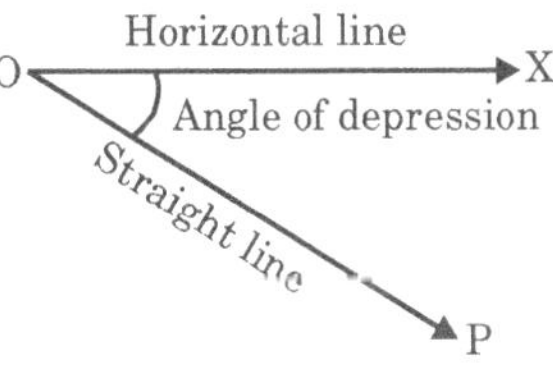

HEIGHT OF THE TOWER.

Let angle of elevation measured from the points A and B on a horizontal line from the floor of the tower are 'a' and 'b'.

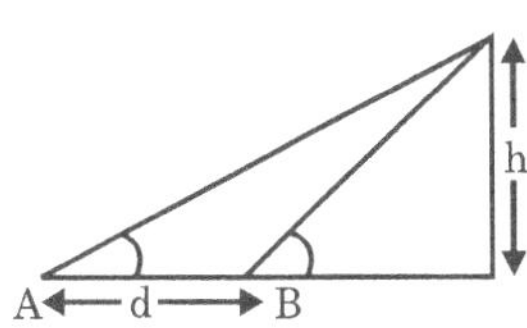

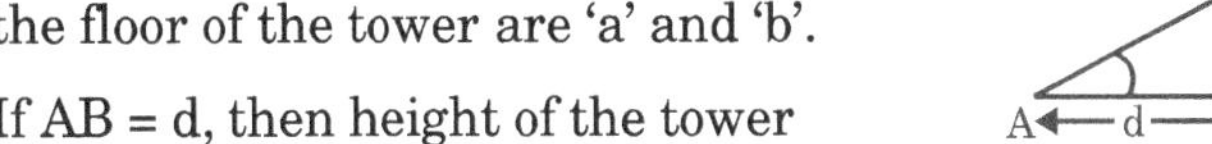

If AB = d, then height of the tower

$$h = \frac{d \tan \alpha \tan \beta}{\tan \beta - \tan \alpha}$$

or $$h = \frac{d \sin \alpha \sin \beta}{\sin (\beta - \alpha)}$$

CONCEPTS AND FORMULAE

1. Angle of Elevation and Depression.

The angle between horizontal line drawn through the observer's eye and the line joining eye to any object is called

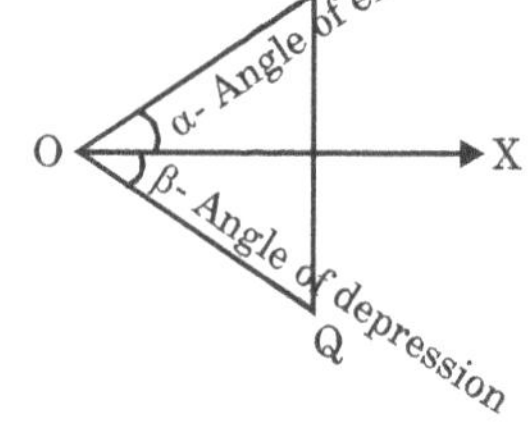

(*i*) angle of elevation of the object when it is at a higher level than the eye.

(*ii*) angle of depression of the object when it is at a lower level than the eye.

(*a*) The angle of elevation of the top of a tower, standing on a horizontal plane, from a point A is α. After walking a distance 'd' towards the foot of the tower, let the angle of elevation is found to be β. Then height of the tower

$$h = \frac{d \sin \beta \sin \alpha}{\sin (\beta - \alpha)}$$

or

$$h = \frac{d}{\cot\alpha - \cot\beta}$$

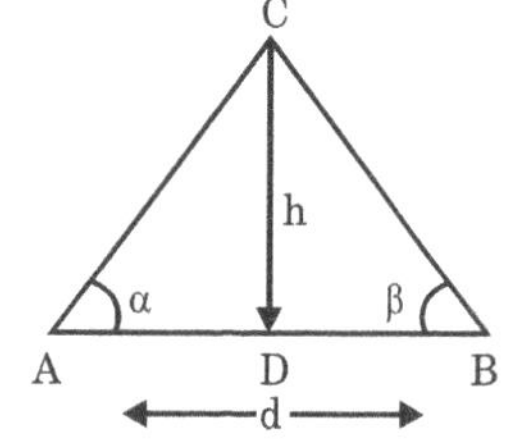

(*b*) If points of observation A and B lie on either side of tower, then height of the tower

$$h = \frac{d \sin \alpha \sin \beta}{\sin (\alpha + \beta)}$$

or

$$h = \frac{d}{\cot \alpha + \cot \beta}$$

2. If angle of elevation of the top of a tower from the bottom and top of a building of height 'd' are β and α respectively, then height of the tower

$$h = \frac{d \sin \beta \cos\alpha}{\sin (\beta - \alpha)}$$

or

$$h = \frac{d \cot\alpha}{\cot\alpha - \cot\beta}$$

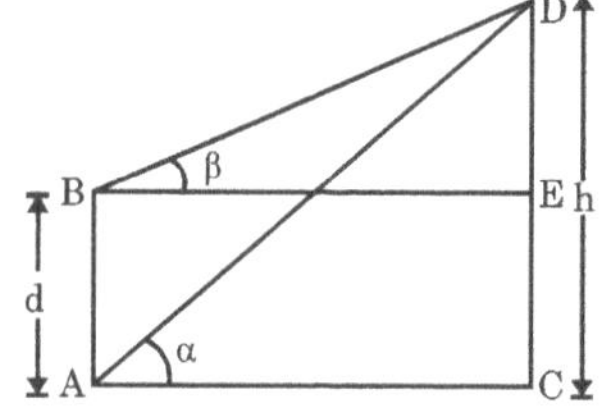

3. Let angle of elevation of a cloud from a height 'd' above the level of water in a lake is 'α' and the angle of depression of its image in the lake is 'β', then height of the cloud from the water level

$$h = \frac{d \sin(\beta + \alpha)}{\sin(\beta - \alpha)}$$

or

$$h = \frac{d(\tan\beta + \tan\alpha)}{\tan\beta - \tan\alpha}$$

or

$$h = d\left[\frac{\cot\alpha + \cot\beta}{\cot\alpha - \cot\beta}\right]$$

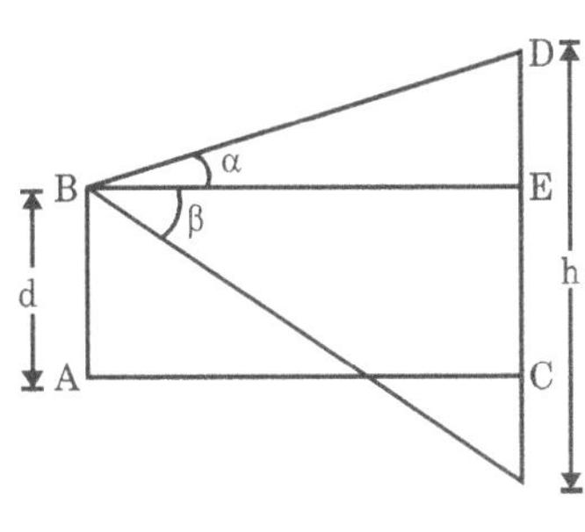

4. A balloon is observed simultaneously from the three points A,B,C on a straight road directly beneath it. The angular elevation at B is twice that at A and the angular elevation at C is thrice that at A. If AB = a and BC = b, then height of the ballon in terms of a and b is

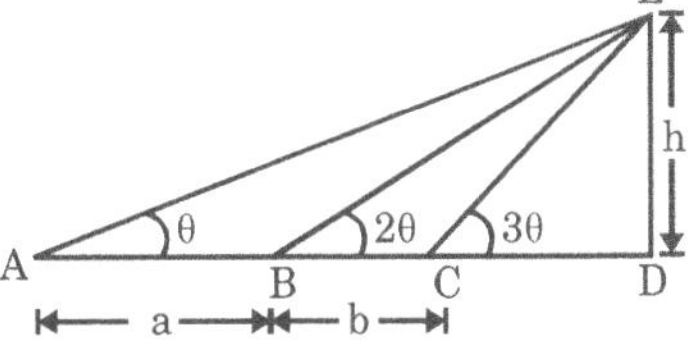

$$h = \frac{a}{2b}\sqrt{(3b - a)(a + b)}$$

5. A flag staff stands on the top of a tower of height h. If tower and flag staff subtend equal angles at a distance 'd' from the foot of the tower, then height the flag-staff is

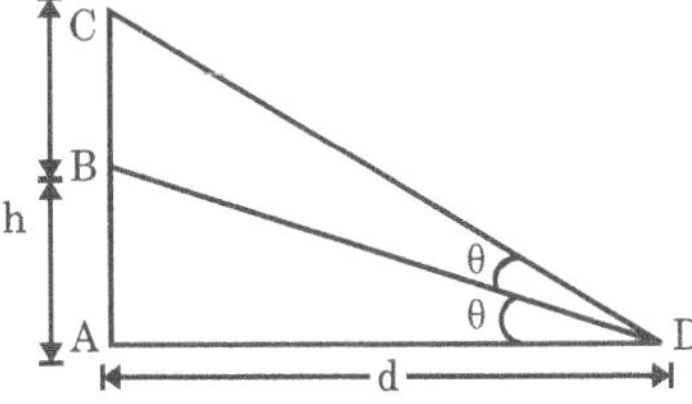

$$h\left[\frac{d^2 + h^2}{d^2 - h^2}\right]$$

chapter

44

GEOMETRY

'Thales', who introduced the study of Geometry in Greece, established an important truth concerning similar triangles.

Point. z

Point is a circle whose radius is zero. It is just a dot (.) mark on a piece of paper. It has no length, breadth and thickness.

Points are denoted by capital letters A,B,C,P,Q,R etc.

Line.

A line has a length, but neither breadth nor thickness. It extends indefinitely in both directions. Lines are denoted by

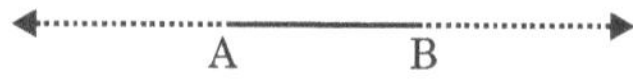

Line segment.

A line segment is limited by two end points. It is a part of a straight line between two points A and B. It is denoted by AB. A and B are end points.

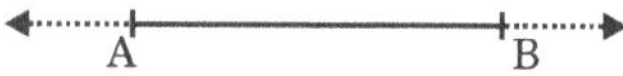

Congruent Segment.

Segment having equal lengths are called congruent segments.

Ray.

The part of a line starting from A in the direction of AB is called the ray $\overrightarrow{AB}$, where A is its initial point.

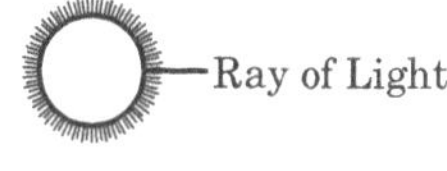

Properties

1. An indefinite number of rays can be drawn having a given points as their initial point.

2. There is only one ray having a given point as its initial point and passing through another given point.
3. An angle is the union of two different rays having the same initial point.

Collinear Points.

Three or more points lying on the same line are called collinear points.

A B C

1. If A, B and C are three collinear points and AB + BC = AC, then B lies between A and C.
2. If A, B and C are collinear and if AB = BC, then B is said to be mid-point of AC.

PLANE

A plane is a flat surface extending indefinitely in all directions.

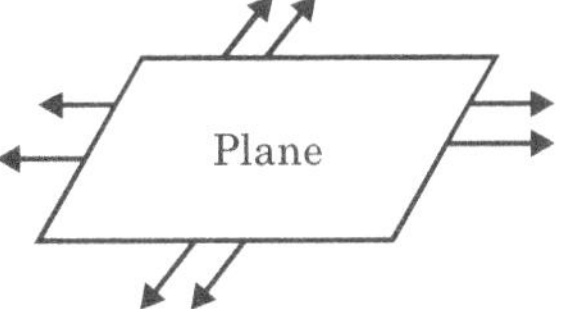

Properties.

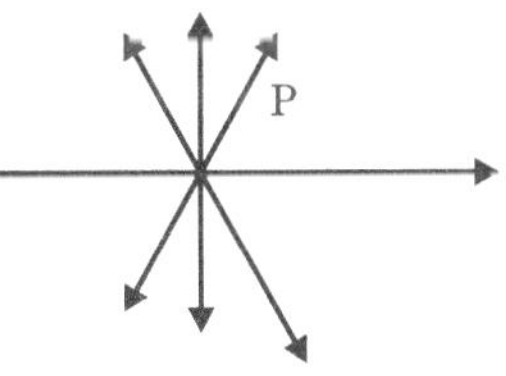

1. A plane is a set of points. It is an infinite set of points.
2. An unlimited number of lines can be drawn passing through a given point (P) in a plane.
3. Only one line can be drawn through two different points in a plane. The line wholly lies in the plane containing the two points.

A B

4. Two different lines in a plane having a common point are called intersecting lines. Two intersecting lines in plane have only one common point.

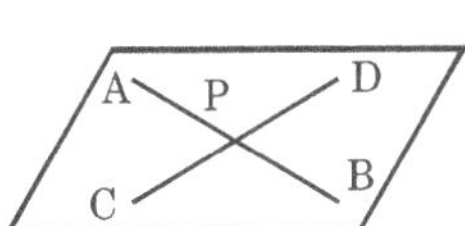

Co-planar points.

Three or more points belonging to the same plane are called co-planar points.

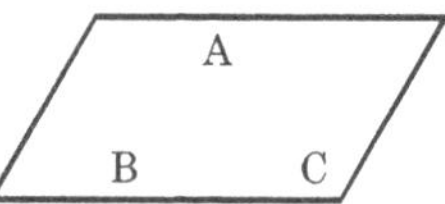

Co-planar line.

Three or more lines which belongs to the same plane are called co-planar lines.

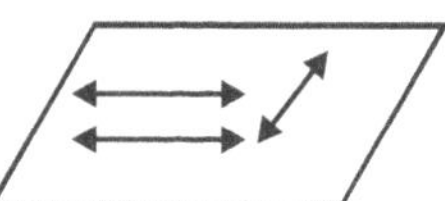

Concurrent line.

If three or more lines pass through the same point, they are called "concurrent lines" and the point through which they pass is called point of concurrence.

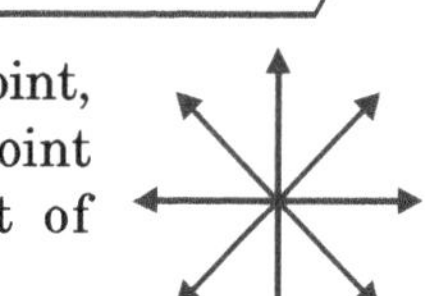

ANGLE

If two rays are drawn in different directions from a common initial point, they are said to form an angle. The common point is called an angle.

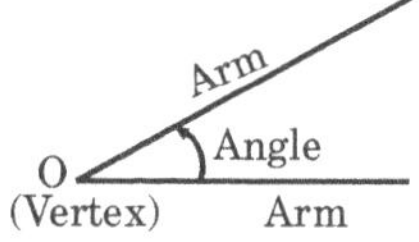

Types of Angles.

1. **Acute angle :** An acute angle has a measure less than 90°.

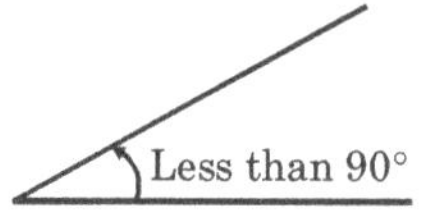

2. **Right angle :** An angle whose measure is 90° is called a right angle.

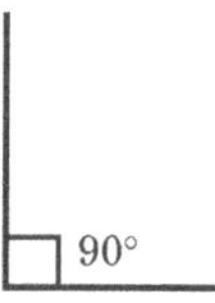

3. **Obtuse angle :** An angle whose measure is more than 90° is called the obtuse angle.

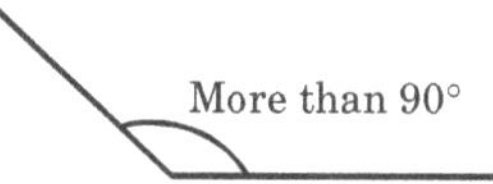

4. **Straight line :** An angle whose measure is 180° is called a straight angle. It is between two opposite rays.

Angle on a point is 360°.

5. **Complementary angles** : Two angles are said to be complementary angles if their sum is equal to 90°.
6. **Supplementary angles** : Two angles are said to be supplementary angles if their sum is equal to 180°.
7. **Reflex angle** : An angle whose measure is between 180° and 360° is called a reflex angle.

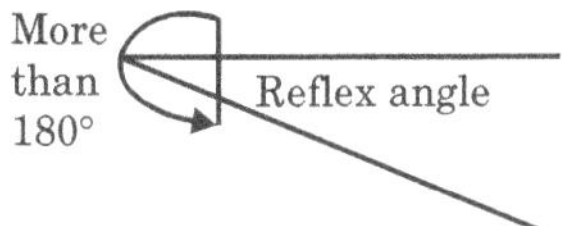

8. **Adjacent angle** : When the angles have a common arm and a common vertex, they are called adjacent angles.

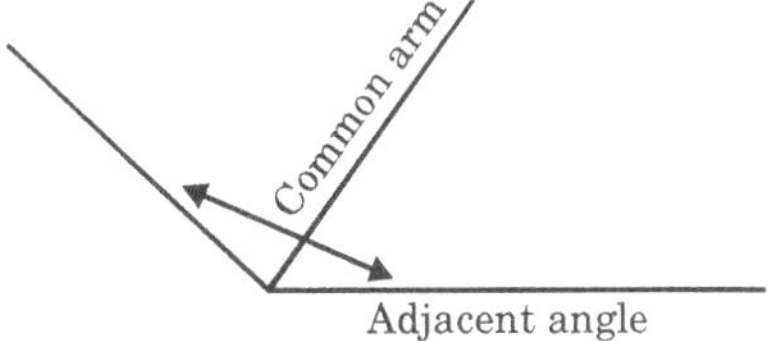

9. **Parallel lines** : Two or more straight lines are said to tbe parallel to each other if they are in the same plane and do not meet when produced on either sides.

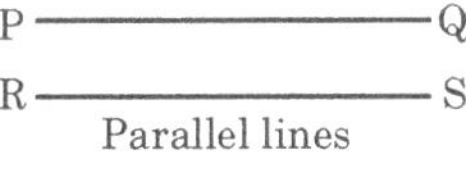

Note : $m_1 = m_2$ (m_1 and m_2 are slopes of the lines)

10. **Perpendicular lines** : If the angle between the two lines is 90°, then those lines are called perpendicular lines.

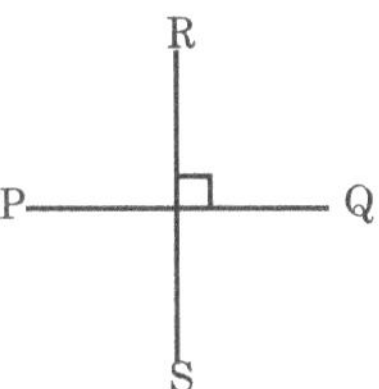

Note : $m_1 m_2 = -1$ (m_1 and m_2 are slopes of the lines)

11. **Transversal** : A straight line which cuts two or more given straight lines is called a transversal.

e.g. xy is a transversal. The angels formed are distinguished by different names.

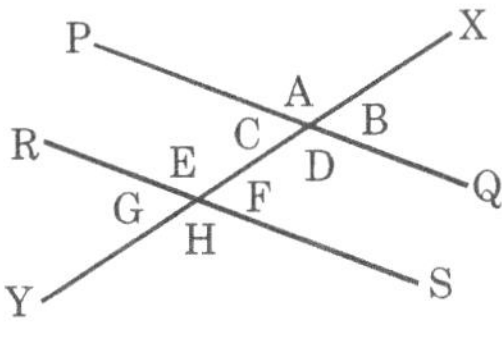

(*i*) ∠B and ∠F are corresponding angles (similarly placed) so also ∠D and ∠H; ∠A and ∠E, ∠C and ∠G.

(*ii*) ∠C and ∠F are alternate angles (placed on opposite sides of xy) so also ∠D and ∠E.

(*iii*) ∠A, ∠B, ∠G and ∠H are exterior angles.

(*iv*) ∠C, ∠D, ∠E and ∠F are interior angles; of these ∠D. ∠F, ∠C and ∠E are pairs of co-interior angles.

12. In the figure

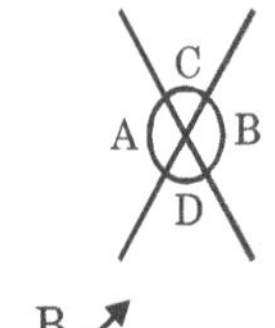

∠A = ∠B and ∠C = ∠D

Linear pair :

If the sum of two adjacent angles is 180°, then they are said to be a linear pair.

∠AOB + ∠COB = 180°

TRIANGLES

A figure that has three sides and three angles is called a triangle and is denoted by the Greek letter Δ (delta).

TYPES OF TRIANGLES

1. Scalene triangle : A triangle is called a scalene triangle if lengths of its sides are not equal to one another.

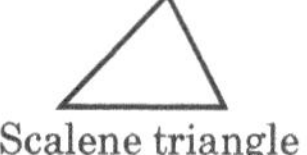
Scalene triangle

2. Isosceles triangle : A triangle is called an isosceles triangle if lengths of any two of the three sides of the triangle are equal.

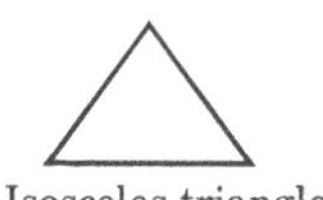
Isosceles triangle

3. Equilateral triangle : A triangle is called an equilateral triangle if lengths of the three sides of the triangle are equal. Each angle of an equilateral triangle 60°.

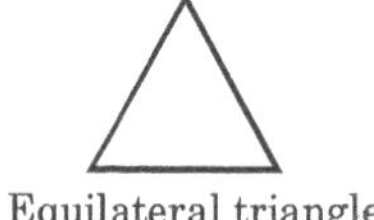
Equilateral triangle

4. Acute angled triangle : A triangle is called actue angled triangle if one of its angles is an acute angle (< 90°).

Acute angled triangle

5. Obtuse angled triangle : A triangle is called an obtuse angled triangle if one of its angles is an obtuse angle (>90°).

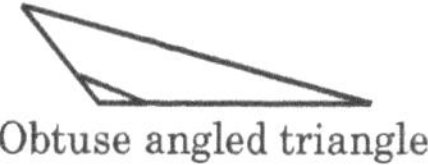
Obtuse angled triangle

6. **Right angled triangle :** A triangle is called a right angled triangle if one of its angles is a right angle (90°). The side opposite to the right angle in a right-angled triangle is called its 'Hypotenuse'.

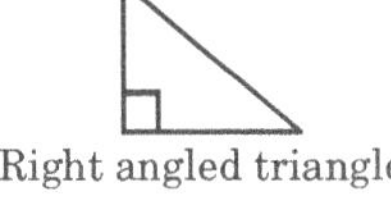
Right angled triangle

If lengths of the two sides containing the right angle in a right angled triangle are equal, then it is called 'right angled isosceles triangle'.

7. **Similar triangles :** Two triangles are similar if angles of one are equal to the corresponding angles of the other and corresponding sides are in the same ratio.

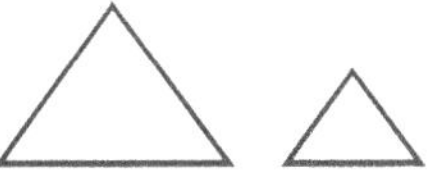

Remember :

(*i*) Area of the right angled triangle = $\frac{1}{2} \times \text{base} \times \text{height}$.

(*ii*) Area of the scalene triangle = $\sqrt{s(s-a)(s-b)(s-c)}$

where a, b and c are sides of the triangle, and

$$s = \frac{a+b+c}{2}$$

(*iii*) Area of the equilateral triangle = $\frac{\sqrt{3}}{4}a^2$

where, a = side of the triangle.

(*iv*) If altitude of an equilateral triangle is h, then

$$\text{area of the equilateral triangle} = \frac{h^2}{\sqrt{3}}.$$

(*v*) Altitude of an equilateral triangle is $\frac{\sqrt{3}}{2}$ times its side.

(*vi*) In an isosceles right triangle, hypotenuse is $\sqrt{2}$ times it side.

(*vii*) Ratio of the sides opposite to angles 30°, 60° and 90° respectively in a triangle is $1 : \sqrt{3} : 2$.

(*viii*) Ratio of the sides opposite to angles 45°, 45° and 90° respectively in a triangle is $1 : 1 : \sqrt{2}$.

Trisection.

The point which divided AB in the ratio of 1 : 2 or 2 : 1 is called point of trisection.

Centroid of a Triangle.

The point of concurrence of the medians of a triangle is called centroid of the triangle. It is usually denoted by G. It divide every median in the ratio 2: 1.

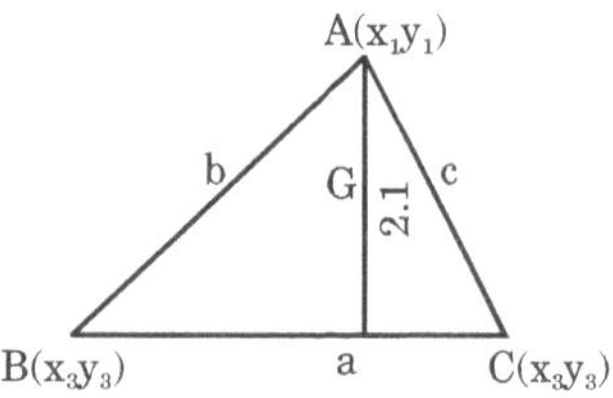

If $A(x_1,y_1)$ $B(x_2,y_2)$ and $C(x_3,y_3)$ are vertices of a triangle, then

$$\text{Centroid (G)} = \left(\frac{x_1+x_2+x_3}{3}, \frac{y_1+y_2+y_3}{3}\right)$$

Incentre.

Point of occurrence of the internal bisector of the angles of a triangle is called incentre of the triangle.

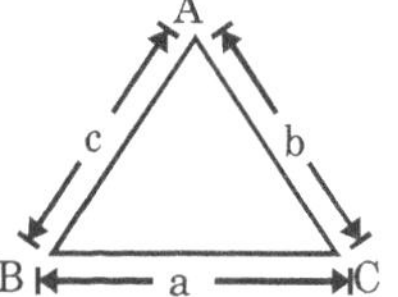

In the figure,

1. Incentre, $I = \left(\frac{ax_1+bx_2+cx_3}{a+b+c}, \frac{ay_1+by_2+cy_3}{a+b+c}\right)$

2. Excentre opposite to A is

$$I_1 = \left(\frac{-ax_1+bx_2+cx_3}{-a+b+c}, \frac{-ay_1+by_2+cy_3}{-a+b+c}\right)$$

3. Excentre opposite to B is

$$I_2 = \left(\frac{ax_1-bx_2+cx_3}{a-b+c}, \frac{ay_1-by_2+cy_3}{a-b+c}\right)$$

4. Excentre opposite to C is

$$I_3 = \left(\frac{ax_1+bx_2-cx_3}{a+b-c}, \frac{ay_1+by_2-cy_3}{a+b-c}\right)$$

5. Let points $A(x_1, y_1)$, $B(x_2, y_2)$ and $C(x_3, y_3)$ are vertices of a triangle. Area of the Δ ABC

$$= \frac{1}{2}\left|\sum x_1(y_2 - y_3)\right|$$

$$= \frac{1}{2}\left|x_1(y_2 - y_3) + x_2(y_3 - y_1) + x_3(y_1 - y_2)\right|$$

$$= \frac{1}{2}\begin{vmatrix} x_1 - x_2 & y_1 - y_2 \\ x_1 - x_3 & y_1 - y_3 \end{vmatrix} \text{ square units.}$$

$A(x_1\ y_1)$

$B(x_2\ y_2)$ $C(x_3\ y_3)$

6. Area of the triangle formed by (0,0), (x_1,y_1) and (x_2,y_2)

$$= \frac{1}{2}\left|x_1y_2 - x_2y_1\right|$$

7. Area of the quadrialteral formed by (x_1, y_1), (x_2, y_2), (x_3, y_3) and(x_4, y_4)

$$= \frac{1}{2}\begin{vmatrix} x_1 - x_3 & y_1 - y_3 \\ x_2 - x_4 & y_2 - y_4 \end{vmatrix}$$

8. Condition of the three points to be collinear is

$$\Delta ABC = 0.$$

9. If in the triangle ABC, G is the centroid, then

$$\Delta GAB = \Delta GBC = \Delta GAC = \frac{1}{3}\Delta ABC$$

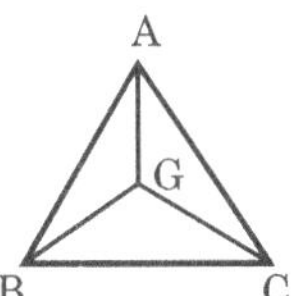

10. If in the Δ ABC, D, E, F are the mid points of the sides, then

$$\Delta AEF = \Delta BFD = \Delta CED = \Delta DEF = \frac{1}{4}ABC$$

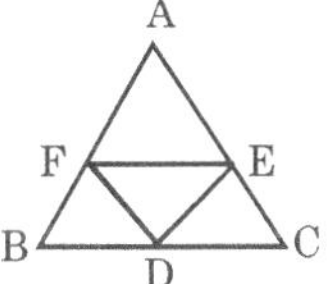

ORTHO CENTRE OF A TRIANGLE

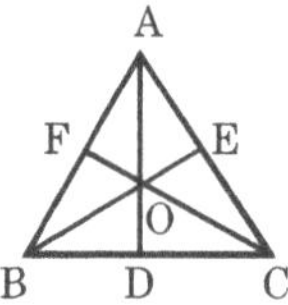

The perpendicular drawn from vertex A to the opposite side is called altitude of a triangle, and the point of intersection of altitudes of a triangle is called ortho centre. It is denoted by 'O'.

Properties

1. The orthocentre of an acute triangle lies inside the triangle.
2. The orthocentre of a right triangle is the vertex containing the right angle.
3. The orthocentre of an obtuse triangle lies in the exterior of the triangle.

CIRCUMCENTRE

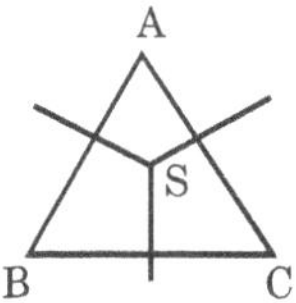

The point of intersection of the perpendicular bisectors of the sides is called circumcentre. It is denoted by 'S'.

Properties

1. Circumcentre of a triangle is equidistance from vertices of a triangle

   i.e. $SA = SB = SC$

2. Equation of the perpendicular bisector of line joining the points (x_1,y_1) and (x_2,y_2) is

$$(x_1 - x_2)\,x + (y_1 - y_2)\,y = \frac{\left[(x_1^2 + y_1^2) - \left(x_2^2 + y_2^2\right)\right]}{2}$$

3. Circumcentre, incentre. orthocentre and centroid of an isosceles triangle are collinear and for an equilateral triangle they are coincident.
4. The midpoint of hypotenuse of a right angled triangle will be equidistant from three of its vertices.

Median

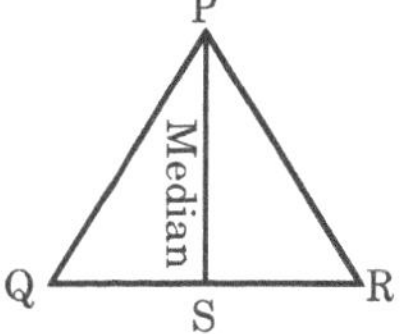

In triangle, the straight line joining the midpoint of any side to the opposite vertex is called median of the triangle.

PS is median to the side QR of ΔPQR.

Altitude.

If in a triangle, a straight line is drawn from one angular point, perpendicular to the opposite side; then straight line is called altitude (or) height with respective to that side.

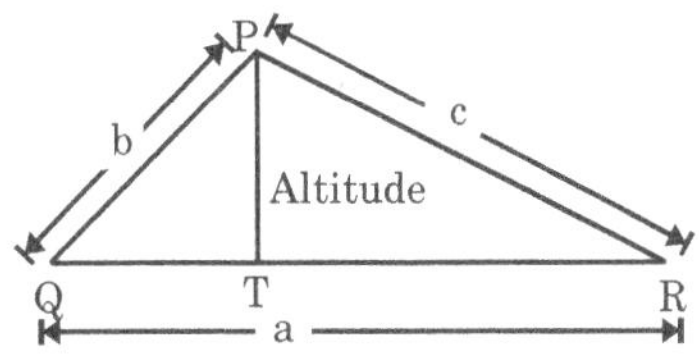

PT is an altitude of the ΔPQR.

Perimeter.

Sum of the sides of a figures is its perimeter and half the sum of the sides is called its semi-perimeter.

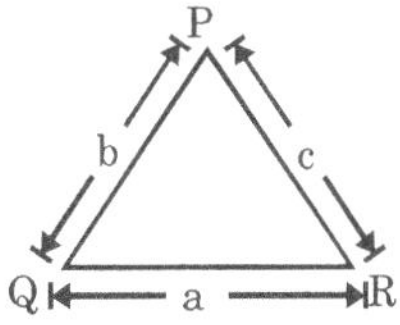

Thus $(PQ + QR + RP)$ is the perimeter of ΔPQR.

$\therefore$ Perimeter $(2S) = a + b + c$

$\therefore$ Semi-perimeter $(S) = \dfrac{a+b+c}{2}$

Properties

1. Centroid of a triangle divides the median in the ratio 2 : 1 from its vertex.
2. A triangle is isosceles if any two of its sides or medians are equal.

APPOLONIOUS THEOREM

Sum of the squares of a triangle is equal to twice the square of half of the third side plus twice the square of the median which bisects the third side.

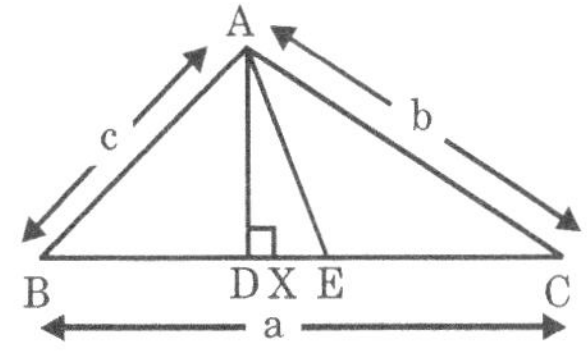

In ΔABC, AE is median on BC and $AD \perp BC$.

$$\therefore \quad AB^2 + AC^2 = 2(AE^2 + BE^2).$$

PYTHAGORAS THEOREM

In a right angled triangle, square described on hypotenuse is equal to sum of the squares described on the other two sides. Converse of this is also true.

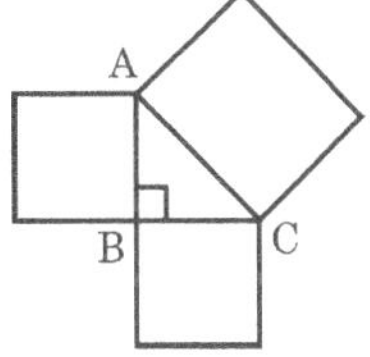

From the figure, $AC^2 = AB^2 + BC^2$.

QUADRILATERALS

A quadrilateral is a plane figure bounded by four straight lines. PQRS is a quard. PR and QS the straight lines joining the opposite angular points are called diagonals of the quadrilateral.

If diagonal of a quadrilateral be 'd', perpendicular distances from opposite vertices of the diagonal be h_1, and h_2, then its area is $\frac{1}{2}(h_1 + h_2)d$

TYPES OF QUADRILATERALS

1. **Square.**
   Square is a rectangle in which
   (*i*) adjacent sides are equal.
   (*ii*) four sides are equal.
   (*iii*) each angle is right angle.
   (*iv*) diagonals are equal.
   (*v*) diagonals bisect each other perpendicularly.
   (*vi*) each diagonal bisects the angleshrough which it passes.

   If side of a square is 'a', then

   Perimeter = $4 \times a = 4a$

   Area = $a \times a = a^2$

   Diagonal = $\sqrt{2a}$

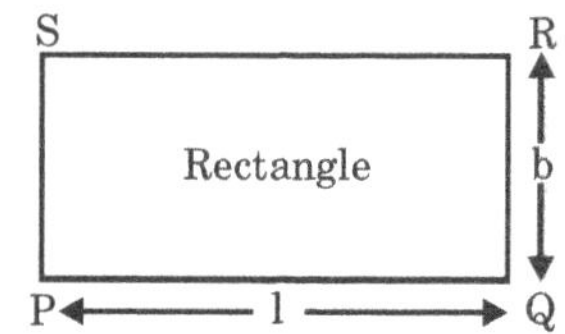

2. **Rectangle.**
   Rectangle is a parallelogram whose
   (*i*) each angle is a right angle.
   (*ii*) opposite sides are equal.
   (*iii*) diagonals are equal.
   (*iv*) diagonals bisect each other.

   Let length of a rectangle be *l*, and breadth be b, then

   Perimeter = 2(length + breadth) = $2(l + b)$

   Area (A) = length × breadth = $l \times b$.

   Diagonal = $\sqrt{l^2 + b^2}$.

3. **Parallelogram.**

Parallelogram is a quadrangle which has

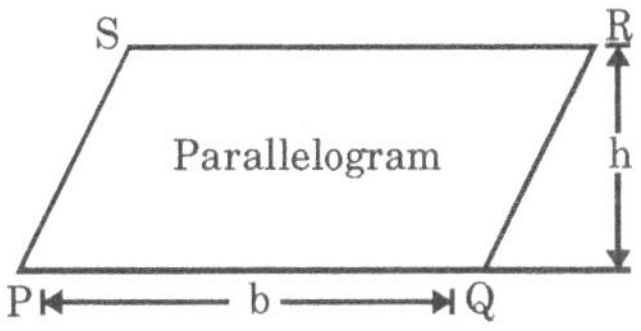

(*i*) two pairs of opposite sides parallel.

(*ii*) opposite sides are parallel and equal.

(*iii*) opposite angles are equal.

(*iv*) two angles that are formed with each side are supplementary.

(*v*) diagonals bisect each other.

Let base be 'b' and height be 'h', then

$$\text{Area} = bh.$$

Fouth vertex of a parallelogram where three consecutive vertices (x_1, y_1), (x_2, y_2), (x_3, y_3) is

$$(x_1 + x_3 - x_2), (y_1 + y_3 - y_2)$$

4. **Rhombus.**

Rhombus is a parallelogram which has

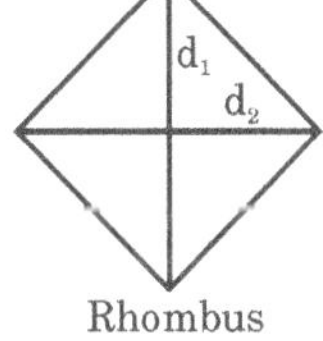

Rhombus

(*i*) two adjacent sides equal

(*ii*) four sides are equal.

(*iii*) opposite angles are equal.

(*iv*) diagonals bisect each other perpendicularly.

(*v*) two angles that are formed with each side are supplementary.

(*vi*) each diagonal bisects the angles through which its passes.

Let d_1, d_2 be the diagonals of the rhombus, then

$$\text{Area of rhombus} = \frac{1}{2} d_1 \, d_1$$

5. **Trapezium.**

It is a quadrilateral which has a pair of opposite sides parallel but the other two sides are non-parallel.

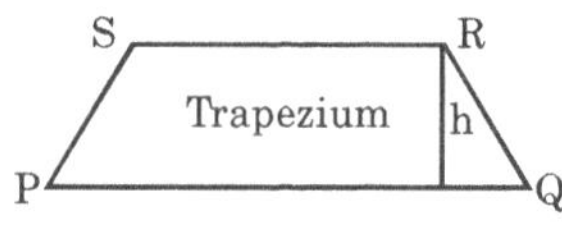

A pair of opposite sides are parallel.

Let a, b be the parallel sides and h be the distance between them, then

$$\text{Area} = \frac{1}{2}(a + b)\,h$$

6. **Quadrilaterals.**

Area of the quadrilateral formed by the points

$A(x_1, y_1), B(x_2, y_2), C(x_3, y_3)$ and $D(x_4, y_4)$ is

$$\frac{1}{2}\begin{vmatrix} x_1 - x_3 & x_2 - x_4 \\ y_1 - y_3 & y_2 - y_4 \end{vmatrix}$$

Note: Absolute value of the determinant should be taken as the area.

REMEMBER
(*i*) Sum of the three angles of a triangle are together equal to 180°.
(*ii*) Sum of the four angles of a quadrilateral are together equal to 360°.
(*iii*) The diagonal of a square is $\sqrt{2}$ times its side.
(*iv*) In a square, the ratio of a side and its diagonals is $1 : \sqrt{2}$.
(*v*) In a rhombus, sum of the squares of its diagonals is equal to the sum of the squres of its sides.

MIDPOINT THEOREM

The line segment joining mid points of two sides of a triangle is parallel to the third side and equal to half of it.

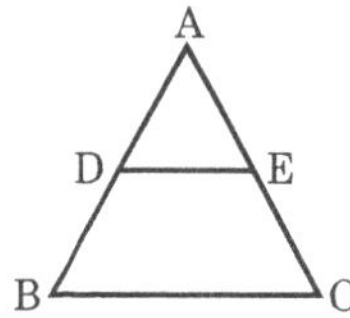

$$DE \,||\, BC \text{ and } DE = \frac{1}{2}BC$$

CIRCLE

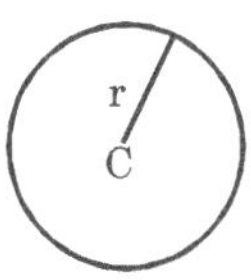

The locus of a moving point which moves in a plane so that its distance from a fixed point is constant, is called circle.

The fixed point is called *centre* and the constant distance is called the radius.

Formulae

1. If centre of a circle is (0, 0) and radius is r, then equation of the circle is

$$(x - 0)^2 + (y - 0)^2 = r^2$$

$$\Rightarrow \quad x^2 + y^2 = r^2$$

2. If centre of a circle is (h,k) and radius is r, then

$$(x - h)^2 + (y - k)^2 = r^2$$

3. If r is the radius, then

$$\text{circumference} = 2\pi r$$

and $$\text{area} = \pi r^2$$

4. If C is the centre of a circle of radius r and P is a point in its plane such that

   OP < r, then P is in the interior of the circle.

   OP = r, the P is on the circle.

   OP > r, the P is in exterior of the circle.

CONGRUENT CIRCLES

Two circels of equal radii are congruent circles.

SEMI-CIRCLE

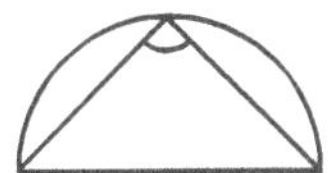

Each diameter divides the circle into segments.

Referring figure,

$$\text{circumference} = \pi r + 2r$$

and $$\text{area} = \frac{1}{2}\pi r^2$$

Angle of semi circle is a right angle.

SECTOR

A sector is a figure enclosed by two radii and the area lying between them.

Referring figure,

$$\text{area of the sector} = \frac{\theta}{360^\circ} \times \pi r^2$$

$$= \frac{1}{2}(\text{arc} \times r)$$

$$= \frac{1}{2} \times l \times r$$

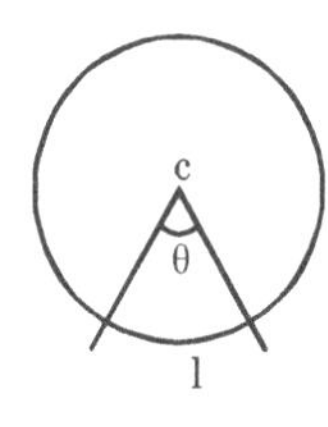

$$\text{length of the arc} = \frac{\theta}{360^\circ} \times 2\pi r$$

RADIUS

The distance between centre of the circle and any point on the circle is called its radius.

A circle has an unlimited number of radii.

CHORD

The line segment joining and two points of the circle is called a chord.

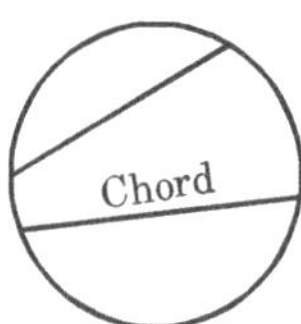

DIAMETER

A chord that passes through the centre of a circle is called its diameter, (or) diameter is the largest chord in a circle.

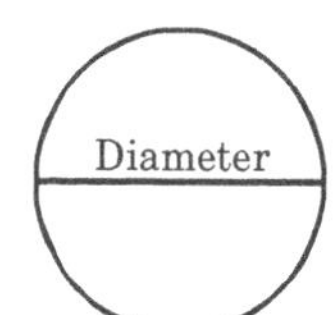

A circle has an unlimited number of diameters.

$$\text{Diameter} = 2 \times \text{radius}$$

ARC

The part of a circle that is cut off by a chord is called an arc of the circle.

SEGMENT OF A CIRCLE

A region bounded by an arc and a chord is called segment of a circle.

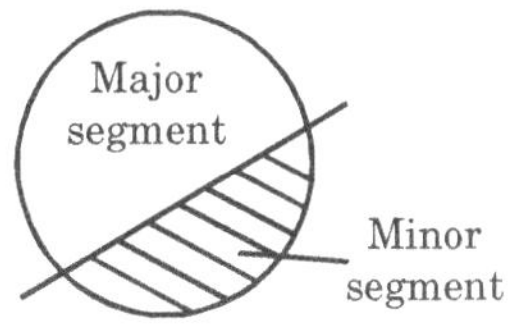

CIRCUMFERENCE OF A CIRCLE

Length of the circle is called circumference of the circle.

POINT OF TANGENCY

The point which is common to the line and the circle, is called point of tangency.

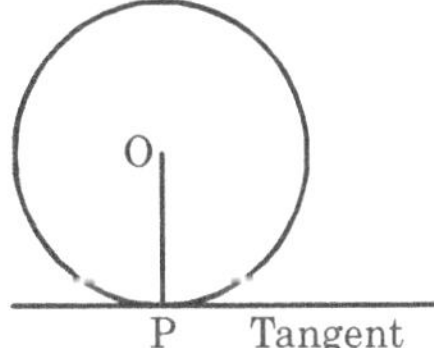

POINT OF CONTACT

The tangent at any point of a circle is perpendicular to the radius drawn to the point of contact.

The perpendicular to a tangent at its a point of contact passes through the centre.

SECANT

A line which has two points in common with the circle is called its secant.

REMEMBER
1. The number of circles drawn through three non-collinear points in a plane is one.
2. A parallelogram inscribed in a circle is a rectangle.

THEOREMS

Theorem 1.
Parallelograms on the same base and between same parallels are equal in area.

Cor. A parallelogram and a rectangle on the same base and between same parallels are equal in area and have the same heights or altitude.

Theorem 2.
Area of triangle is half that of a parallelogram if they are on the same base and between same parallels.

Theorem 3.
Triangles on the same base (or equal bases) and equal altitudes are equal in area.

Theorem 4.
Triangles on the same base and with equal areas lie between the same parallels.

A median of a triangle divides the triangle into two triangles of equal area (1:1).

Theorem 5 (Basic proportionality Theorem).
If a line is drawn parallel to one side of a triangle, then it will divide the other two sides in the same ratio.

Cor. A line parallel to one side of a triangle divides the other two sides externally proportionally.

Converse of the theorem : If a line divides two sides of a triangle in the same ratio, then it will be parallel to the third side.

In a triangle, the bisector of the vertical angle divides the base in the ratio of other two sides.

Theorem 6 (AAA similarity).
If three angles of one triangle are respectively equal to the three angles of another triangle, then the two triangles are similar.

Cor. If two pairs of corresponding angles are equal, then the two triangles are similar.

Cor. If a line is parallel to one side of a triangle and intersect the other two sides, then a triangle is formed which is similar to the given triangle (AAA - Angle, Angle, Angle)

Theorem 7 (SSS similarity).

If the corresponding sides of two triangles are in the same ratio, then the triangles are similar (SSS = Side, Side, Side)

Theorem 8 (SAS similarity).

If two sides of a triangle are proportional to the two sides of another triangle and the included angles are equal, then the two triangles are similar (SAS = Side, Angle, Side).

Theorem 9.

If a perpendicular is drawn from the vertex of the right angle of the right angled triangle to the hypotenuse, then triangles formed on each side of the perpendicular are similar to the given triangle and to each other.

Theorem 10.

The ratio of areas of two similar triangles is equal to the ratio of the squares on the corresponding sides.

Corresponding altitudes of similar triangle are in same ratio as the corresponding sides.

Theorem 11 (Pythagorus theorem).

In a triangle, square of the hypotenuse is equal to the sum of the squares of the other two sides.

Converse of the theorem : If square of one side of a triangle is equal to the sum of the squares of the other two sides, then these two sides contain a right angle.

In ΔABC, $\angle B < 90^\circ$ and AD ^ B. C.

$$\therefore \quad b^2 = a^2 + c^2 - 2ax$$

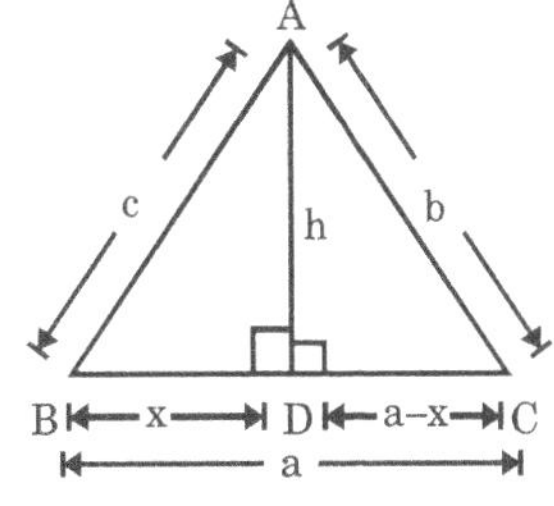

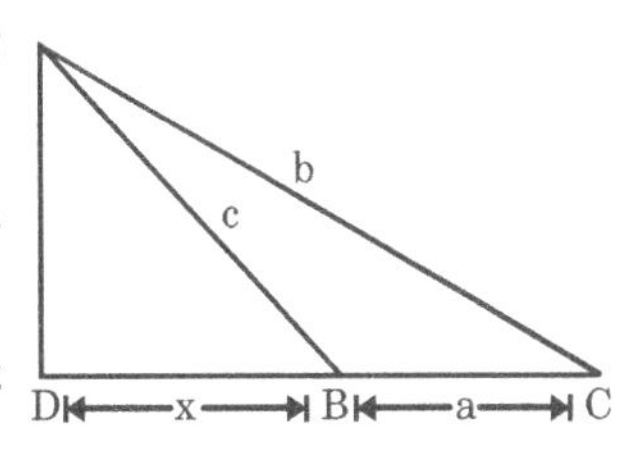

In ABC, $\angle B > 90^\circ$ and AD $\perp$BC produced

$$\therefore \quad b^2 = a^2 + c^2 + 2ax$$

REGULAR HEXAGON.

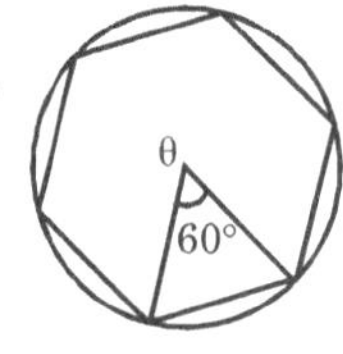

A simple closed figure bounded by six sides and all its angles and sides are equal is called *regular hexagon.*

The angle subtended by a regular hexagon at the centre of circumscribed circle is 60°.

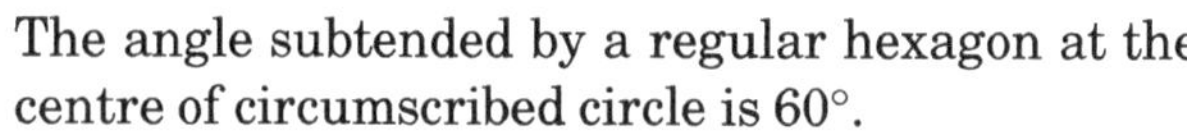

$$\text{Area of regular hexagon} = \frac{3\sqrt{3}}{2}a^2 \text{ or } \frac{6\sqrt{3}}{4}a^2$$

where, a = side of the regular hexagon.

REGULAR OCTAGON.

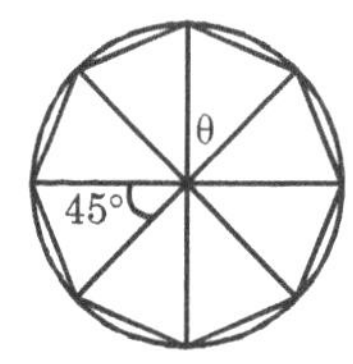

The angle subtend by a regular octagon at the centre of circumscribed circle is 45°.

$$\text{Area of the regular octagon} = 2\left(1+\sqrt{2}\right)a^2$$

where a = side of the regular octagon.

REGULAR POLYGON.

Let 'n' be the number of sides. Then

sum of interior angles of a convex polygon of n sides

$$= (2n - 4) \text{ right angles.}$$

$$\text{each interior angles} = \frac{(2n-4)}{n} \text{ right angles.}$$

$$\text{each exterior angle} = \left(\frac{360}{n}\right)^n$$

$$\text{Number of sides} = \frac{360°}{\text{Exterior angle}}$$

SIMILAR POLYGONS.

Two polygons are said to be similar to each other, if

1. their corresponding angles are equal and
2. lengths of their corresponding sides are proportional.

    (*i*) The symbol '~' stands for 'is similar to'. Remember that always two congruent polygons are similar, but two similar polygons are not necessarily congruent.

(*ii*) Congruent polygonal regions have the same areas, but if figures have the same area, they need not be congruent.

(*iii*) To every polygonal region, there corresponds a unique positive real number called its area.

(*iv*) All regular polygons are cyclic.

(*v*) *Number of measurement required to construct the following figures.*

(*a*) Quadrilateral-Five

(*b*) Trapezium-Four

(*c*) Parallelogram - Three

(*d*) Rhombus - Two

(*e*) Rectangle - Two

(*f*) Square - One

(*g*) Triangle - Three (one of them should be a side)

(*h*) Isosceles Triangle - Two (one of them should be a side)

(*i*) Right Angled Triangle - Two (since one of them is a right angle)

(*j*) Equilateral Triangle - One (a side)

chapter

45

ANALYTICAL GEOMETRY

STRAIGHT LINE

Rectangular Axis

Let x′ o x, y′ o y be two fixed straight lines whose positive direction of is shown by the arrow and which meet at right angles in o (origin). Then

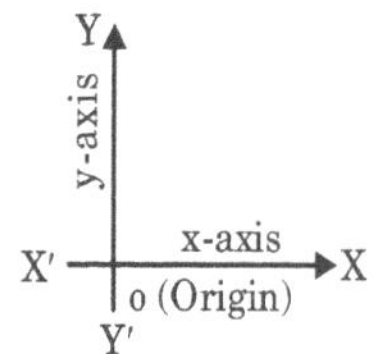

1. x′ o x is called axis of x or the x-axis.
2. y′ o y is called axis of y or the y-axis.

Co-ordinates

Let P be a point in the plane of the rectangular axis. From P draw PM perpendicular on the x-axis. Then

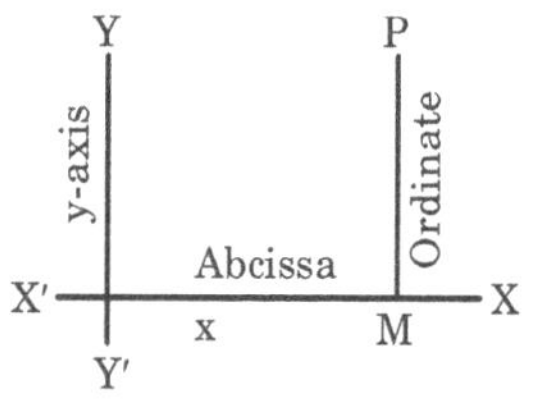

1. length OM is called *abscissa of P* and is denoted by x.
2. length MP is called *ordinate of P* and is denoted by y.
3. the two togehter taken in this order are called *co-ordinates* of P and are denoted by (x, y).

   where, x is x co-ordinate and y is y co-ordinate.
4. point of intersection of the co-ordinate axis is called *origin.*

RULES FOR SIGNS OF CO-ORDINATES

1. x or abcissa is +ve if it is measured to the right of the origin and -ve if measure to the left of the origin.
2. y or ordinate is +ve if it is measured above the x-axis and –ve if measured below the x-axis.

QUADRANTS.

The x-axis and y-axis divide the co-ordinate plane into four parts, each part is called a quadrant.

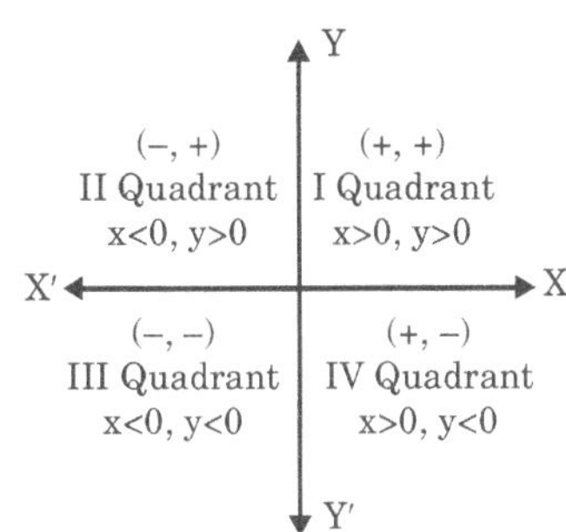

The axis x′ o x and y′ o y divide the plane into four quadrants.

1. x o y is called first quadrant.
2. y o x′ is called the second quadrant.
3. x′ o y′ is called the third quadrant
4. y′ o x is called the fourth quadrant.

DISTANCE FORMULA

1. Distance between two points (x_1, y_1) and (x_2, y_2) is

$$\sqrt{(x_2 - x_1)^2 + (y_2 - y_1)^2}$$

2. Distance of a point P (x_1, y_1) from the origin O(0, 0) is

$$\sqrt{(x_1 - 0)^2 + (y_1 - 0)^2}, \text{ i.e. } \sqrt{x_1^2 + y_1^2}$$

3. If point C divides the line segment AB in the ratio m : n internally and A (x_1, y_1), B (x_2, y_2), then co-ordinates of C are given by $\left(\frac{mx_2 + nx_1}{m+n}, \frac{my_2 + ny_1}{m+n}\right)$.

4. If the point C divides the line segment AB in the ratio m : n externally, then C is given by $\left(\frac{mx_2 - nx_1}{m-n}, \frac{my_2 - ny_1}{m-n}\right)$.

Harmonic Conjugate of Point.

The P (α, β) divides the line joining A (x_1, y_1) and B (x_2, y_2) in the ratio $(\alpha - x_1) : (\alpha - x_2)$ or $(\beta - x_1) : (\beta - x_2)$.

$P(\alpha, \beta)$

$A(x_1, y_1)$ $B(x_2, y_2)$

Mid Point.

Mid point of the line joining the points (x_1, y_1) and (x_2, y_2) is $\left(\frac{x_1 + x_2}{2}, \frac{y_1 + y_2}{2}\right)$

EQUATION OF THE STRAIGHT LINES.

Step 1 : Let P(x, y) be any point on the line.

Step 2 : Using the facts given about the line, find a relation between x and y and known constants. This is the required equation of the line.

PROPERTIES OF STARIGHT LINES

1. The first-degree equation $ax + by + c = 0$, $x, y \in R$ represents a staight line.
2. Equation of the x-axis is $y = 0$
3. Equation of the straight line parallel to the x-axis and at a distance b from it is
$$y = b$$
Also equation of the line parallel to x-axis and passing through (x_1, y_1) is
$$y = y_1$$
4. Equation of the y-axis is $x = 0$
5. Equation of the straight line parallel to the y-axis and at a distance 'a' from it, is
$$x = a$$
Also equation of the line parallel to y-axis and passing through (x_1, y_1) is
$$x = x_1$$

Two Point form.

1. Equation of the line joining (x_1, y_1) and (x_2, y_2) is
$$\frac{y - y_1}{y_2 - y_1} = \frac{x - x_1}{x_2 - x_1}$$
or
$$(y_1 - y_2)x - (x_1 - x_2)y = (y_1 - y_2)x_1 - (x_1 - x_2)y_1$$

Equation of the line passing through (α, β) and perpendicular to line joining (x_1, y_1) and (x_2, y_2) is

$$(x_1 - x_2)x + (y_1 - y_2)y = (x_1 - x_2)\,\alpha + (y_1 - y_2)\,\beta$$

(α, β)

(x_1, y_1) (x_2, y_2)

2. Equation of the line passing through (x_1, y_1) and is parallel to $ax + by + c = 0$ is

$$a\,(x - x_1) + b(y - y_1) = 0$$

3. Equation of the line passing through (x_1, y_1) and is perpendicular to $ax + by + c = 0$ is

$$b(x - x_1) - a(y - y_1) = 0$$

4. Equation of the straight line passing through the origin and makingan angle θ with the positive direction of the x-axis is

$$y = mx$$

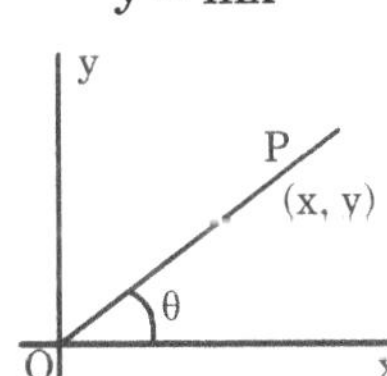

5. Equation of the straight line which cuts off a given intercept 'c' on the y-axis and is inclined at a given angle 'θ' to x-axis is

$$y = mx + c$$

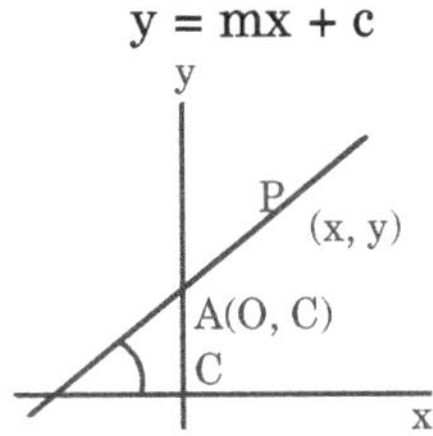

6. Equation of the straight line which cuts off given intercepts a and b from x and y axis respectively is

$$\frac{x}{a}+\frac{y}{b}=1$$

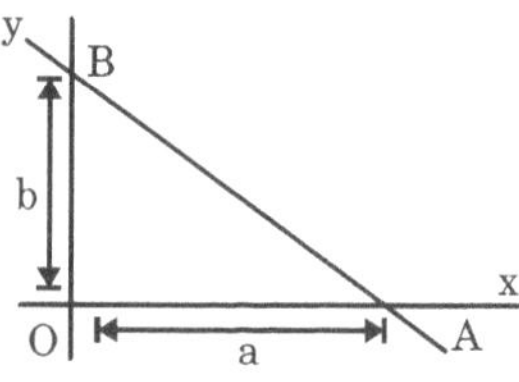

Note : The line meets the axes at the points (a, 0) and (0.b).

7. Equation of a straight line in terms of 'p', length of the perpendicular from the origin upon it, and α the angle which this perpendicular makes with the x-axis is

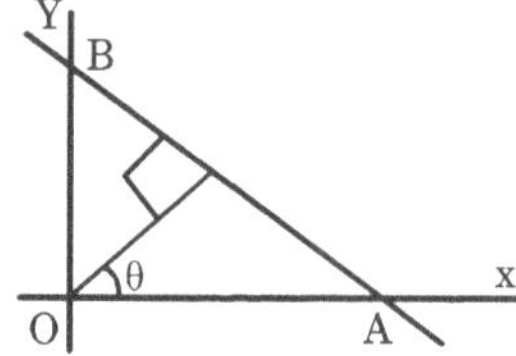

$$x \cos \theta + y \sin \theta = p$$

Point Slope form.

The equation of a line passing through the point (x_1, y_1) and having the slope m is

$$y - y_1 = m(x - x_1).$$

1. If the point $(x_1 y_1)$ divides the line segment AB between the axis in the rato m : n, then equation of the line is

$$\frac{mx}{x_1}+\frac{ny}{y_1}=m+n$$

2. If the point (x_1, y_1) bisects the line segment between axis, then equation of line is

$$\frac{x}{x_1}+\frac{y}{y_1}=2 \qquad ...(m : n = 1 : 1)$$

Intercepts made by the line ax + by + c on co-ordinate axis is

x-intercept $= -\frac{c}{a}$

y-intercept $= -\frac{c}{b}$

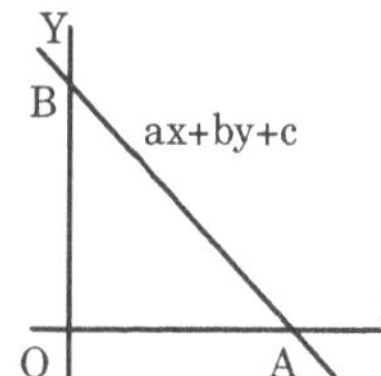

3. Area of the triangle formed by ax + by + c = 0 with co-ordinate axis

$$= \frac{1}{2} |(OA)(OB)|$$

$$= \frac{1}{2}\left(\frac{-c}{a}\right)\left(\frac{-c}{b}\right) = \frac{1}{2}\left|\frac{c^2}{ab}\right|$$

4. If $P(x_1, y_1)$ and $Q(x_2, y_2)$ are two points on a line, then

$$\text{slope of the line} = \frac{y_2 - y_1}{x_2 - x_1}, \; x_1 \neq x_2$$

$$= \frac{\text{difference of y-cordinates}}{\text{difference of x-cordinates}}$$

5. **General form of the equation of a line :** Equation ax + by + c = 0 is called general equation of the first degree in x and y.

6. Slope of the line ax + by + c = 0 is $-\frac{a}{b}$.

$$\therefore \quad \text{Slope} = -\frac{\text{x-coefficient}}{\text{y-coefficient}}$$

Conditions of Parallelisim.

1. Lines $y = m_1x + c_1$ and $y = m_2x + c_2$ will be parallel if

$$m_1 = m_2$$

i.e. Slope of one line = Slope of the other.

2. Lines $a_1x + b_1y + c_1 = 0$ and $a_2x + b_2y + c_2 = 0$ will be parallel if

$$\frac{a_1}{b_1} = \frac{a_2}{b_2}$$

Conditions of Perpendicularity.

1. Lines $y = m_1x + c$ and $y = m_2x + c$ will be perpendicular if $\quad m_1m_2 = -1$

or $\quad m_2 = -\frac{1}{m_1}$

2. Lines $a_1x + b_1y + c_1 = 0$ and $a_2x + b_2y + c_2 = 0$ may be a perpendicular if
$$a_1a_2 + b_1b_2 = 0$$
i.e. product of the co-efficients of x
+ product of the coefficients of y = 0.

3. Equation of a line passing through the point of intersection of the lines $a_1x + b_1y + c_1 = 0$ and $a_2x + b_2y + c_2 = 0$ is
$$(a_1x + b_1y + c_1) + k\,(a_2x + b_2y + c_2) = 0$$
where k is a parameter.

4. Equation of the straight lines which pass through a given point (x_1, y_1) and make a given angle α with the given straight line $y = mx + c$ are
$$y - y_1 = \frac{m \pm \tan\alpha}{1 \mp m\tan\alpha}(x - x_1)$$

5. The angle θ between two lines $y = m_1x + c_1$ and $y = m_2x + c_2$ is given by
$$\tan\theta = \pm\frac{m_1 - m_2}{1 + m_1m_2}$$

6. Point of intersection of the two given lines $a_1x + b_1y + c_1 = 0$ and $a_2x + b_2y + c_2 = 0$ is given by
$$\left(\frac{b_1c_2 - b_2c_1}{a_1b_2 - a_2b_1}, \frac{c_1a_2 - c_2a_1}{a_1b_2 - a_2b_1}\right)$$

7. Length of the perpendicular from the point (x_1, y_1) to the line $ax + by + c = 0$ is given by
$$p = \frac{|ax_1 + by_1 + c|}{\sqrt{a^2 + b^2}}$$

8. Distance between two parallel lines $ax + by + c = 0$ and $ax + by + c' = 0$ is given by
$$d = \frac{|c' - c|}{\sqrt{a^2 + b^2}}$$

9. Equation of the bisector of the angles between the lines $a_1x + b_1y + c_1 = 0$ and $a_2x + b_2y + c_2 = 0$ are given by

$$\frac{a_1x + b_1y + c_1}{\sqrt{a_1^2 + b_1^2}} = \pm \frac{a_2x + b_2y + c_2}{\sqrt{a_2^2 + b_2^2}}$$

10. Equation of a line parallel and perpendicular to a given line $ax + by + c = 0$ is given by

$$ax + by + \lambda = 0, \quad \text{Parallel line}$$

$$ax - by + \lambda = 0, \quad \text{Perpendicular line}$$

Coordinate of a New point in new Co-ordinate System

1. If origin is shifted to point (h,k) without rotation of axis, then co-ordinate of new point is obtained by replacing.

$$x' = x + h$$

$$y' = y + k$$

2. If axis of system are rotated by angle θ in anticlockwise, then co-ordinate of new point is obtained by replacing.

$$x' = x \cos\theta + y \sin\theta$$

$$y' = -x \sin\theta + y \cos\theta$$

3. If origin is shifted to point (h,k) and system is also rotated by an angle θ in anti-clock wise, then co-ordinate of new point $P'(x', y')$ is obtained by replacing

$$x' = h + \cos\theta + y \sin\theta$$

$$y' = k - x \sin\theta + y \cos\theta$$

4. **Area of a triangle**

There area of ΔABC with vertices $A(x_1, y_1)$, $B(x_2, y_2)$ and $C(x_3, y_3)$ is given by

$$\Delta = \frac{1}{2}\begin{vmatrix} x_1 & y_1 & 1 \\ x_2 & y_2 & 1 \\ x_3 & y_3 & 1 \end{vmatrix}$$

5. Area of a polygon

Area of a polygon of n-sides with vertices $A_1(x_1, y_1)$, $A_2(x_2, y_2)$ .... $A_n(x_n, y_n)$

$$= \frac{1}{2}\left[\begin{vmatrix} x_1 & y_1 \\ x_2 & y_2 \end{vmatrix} + \begin{vmatrix} x_2 & y_2 \\ x_3 & y_3 \end{vmatrix} + ... \begin{vmatrix} x_{n-1} & y_{n-1} \\ x_n & y_n \end{vmatrix} + \begin{vmatrix} x_n & y_n \\ x_1 & y_1 \end{vmatrix}\right]$$

6. Condition for collinearity of three points is

$$\begin{vmatrix} x_1 & y_1 & 1 \\ x_2 & y_2 & 1 \\ x_3 & y_3 & 1 \end{vmatrix} = 0.$$

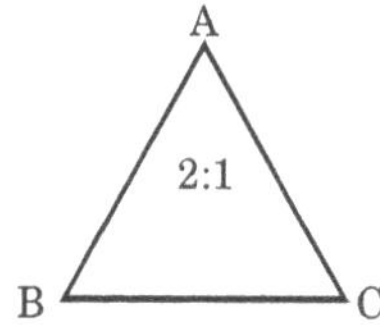

Centroid of a triangle.

Centroid of a triangle whose vertices are given as $A(x_1, y_1)$, $B(x_2, y_2)$ and $C(x_3, y_3)$ is

$$G = \left(\frac{x_1 + x_2 + x_3}{3}, \frac{y_1 + y_2 + y_3}{3}\right)$$

PAIR OF STRAIGHT LINES

1. An equation of the form $ax^2 + 2hxy + by^2 = 0$ is called homogeneous equation of second degree. It represents a pair of straight lines both passing through the origin.
2. The lines are real and distinct if $h^2 > ab$
3. The lines are real and coincident if $h^2 = ab$
4. The lines are imaginary if $h^2 < ab$
5. The lines are perpendicular if $a + b = 0$
6. $ax^2 + 2hxy + by^2 = 0 \Rightarrow (y - m_1x)(y - m_2x) = 0$

$$\therefore \quad m_1 + m_2 = -\frac{2h}{b} \text{ and } m_1m_2 = \frac{a}{b}$$

7. Angle between pair of straight lines is

$$\tan\theta = \pm\frac{2\sqrt{h^2 - ab}}{a + b}$$

8. Equation of the bisectors of the angles between pair of lines is

$$\frac{x^2 - y^2}{a - b} = \frac{xy}{h}$$

9. General equation of second degree in x and y,

$ax^2 + 2hxy + by^2 + 2gx + 2fy + c = 0$ will represent a pair of straight lines if and only if

$$\Delta = \begin{vmatrix} a & h & g \\ h & b & f \\ g & f & c \end{vmatrix} = 0 \text{ and } h^2 - ab \geq 0$$

10. Two pair of straight lines are parallel if $\frac{a}{h} = \frac{h}{b} = \frac{g}{f}$

and distance between these two lines is $d = 2\sqrt{\frac{g^2 - ac}{a(a+b)}}$

11. Equation of the bisectors of the angles between pair of straight lines is

$$\frac{(x - x')^2 - (y - y')^2}{a - b} = \frac{(x - x')(y - y')}{h},$$

where (x', y') is point of intersection of the lines.

12. Point of intersection of the two pair of straight lines is

$$\left(\frac{bg - hf}{h^2 - ab}, \frac{af - gh}{h^2 - ab}\right)$$

13. Equation of the pair of lines through (α, β) and perpendicular to the pair of lines $ax^2 + 2hxy + by^2 = 0$ is

$$b(x - \alpha)^2 - 2h(x - \alpha)(y - \beta) + a(y - \beta)^2 = 0$$

CIRCLES

1. If C is a given fixed point and r is a given non negative constant, then locus of the point 'P' which moves such that OP = r is called a circle. C is called centre of the circle and r is called radius of the circle.

   If r = 0, then above locus contains exactly one point; the centre of the circle. Hence we call the circle in this case, a point circle.

2. If C (α, β) is the centre and r is the radius, then equation of the circle is given by

$$(x - \alpha)^2 + (y - \beta)^2 = r^2$$

When C is (0, 0), then equation of circle is

$$x^2 + y^2 = r^2$$

3. The general second degree equation

$$ax^2 + 2hxy + by^2 + 2gx + 2fy + c = 0$$

represents a circle if $a = b \neq 0$, and $h = 0$

When the equation $g^2 + f^2 - ac \geq 0$, represents a circle, then centre is $\left(\frac{-g}{a}, \frac{f}{a}\right)$ and radius is $\frac{\sqrt{g^2 + f^2 - ac}}{|a|}$.

4. The standard general equation of the circle may be taken to be

$$x^2 + y^2 + 2gx + 2fy + c = 0$$

When equation of the circle is written in this form, then centre is (–g, –f) and the radius is $\sqrt{g^2 + f^2 - c}$.

5. *Chord of the circle :* The line segment joining two points A and B on a circle is called chord of the circle.

Secant of the circle. The line $\vec{AB}$ is called secant of the circle.

Diameter of the circle : If a chord passes through the centre, it is called 'diametre of the circle'.

The length of every diameter of a circle is twice its radius. *Semi circle :* Every diametre of the circle cuts the circle into two equal parts, each of which is called a semi circle. Each diameter makes a right angle at any point on the circle.

6. If (x_1, y_1) and B (x_2, y_2) are the ends of a diametre $\overline{AB}$ of a circle, then its equation is given by

$$(x - x_1)(x - x_2) + (y - y_1)(y - y_2) = 0$$

7. Given three non collinear points A, B and C. There exists a unique circle that passes through them. It is actually the circumcircle of ΔABC. Therefore perpendicular bisector of each chord of the circle passes through the centre of the circle.

8. Parametric equations of the circle with centre $c(\alpha, \beta)$ and radius r are given by

$$x = \alpha + r \cos \theta \; ; \; y = \beta + r \sin \theta; \; 0 \le \theta \le 2\pi.$$

Hence every point on this circle may be represented in the form $(\alpha + r \cos \theta, \beta + r \sin\theta)$ for some $0 \le \theta < 2\pi$; point of this form is called θ point on the circle.

9. If centre is (0, 0) for a circle whose radius is r, any point on the circle may be taken in the form $(r \cos \theta, r \sin \theta)$, $0 \le \theta \le 2\pi$.

10. *Notations :* If S = 0 denotes equation $x^2 + y^2 + 2gx + 2fy + c = 0$ and (x_i, y_i) and (x_j, y_j) are any points, then we write S_i and S_{ij} for

$$xx_i + yy_i + g(x + x_i) + f(y + y_i) + c,$$

and $\quad x_ix_j + y_iy_j + g(x_i + x_j) + f(y_i + y_j) + c$ respectively.

11. Given any point $P(x_1, y_1)$ and a circle with centre C and radius r, then number $CP^2 - r^2$ is called power of P with respect to that circle.

12. Power of a point $P(x_1, y_1)$ with respect to the circle S = 0 is equal to $\quad S_{11} = x_1^2 + y_1^2 + 2gx_1 + 2fy_1 + c$.

13. A given point $P(x_1, y_1)$ lies

(*i*) inside the circle S = 0 if $S_{11} < 0$

(*ii*) outside the circle S = 0 if $S_{11} > 0$

(*iii*) on the circle S = 0 if $S_{11} = 0$.

14. *Tangent of the circle :* A straight line having exactly one point in common with a given circle is called tangent of that circle.

15. A given line $lx + my + n = 0$ is a tangent to S = 0 if and only if perpendicular distance of the centre to the line is equal to radius of the circle,

i.e. $$g^2 + f^2 - c = r^2 = \left|\frac{lg + mf - n}{\sqrt{l^2 + m^2}}\right|^2 = d^2$$

16. (*i*) If a point lies inside the circle S = 0, then no tangent of S = 0 which passes through P.

(*ii*) If point P lies on the circle S = 0, then only one tangent of S = 0 which passes through P.

(*iii*) If P is a point lying outside the circle S = 0, then there are exactly two tangents of S = 0 which passes through P.

17. (*i*) Given a line and a circle, if we denote the perpendicular distance of the centre to the line by 'd' and radius by 'r', then line cuts the circle in two points if and only if $r^2 > d^2$ and length of the chord so formed is $2\sqrt{r^2 - d^2}$.

(*ii*) Given line do not cut the circle when $r^2 < d^2$ and becomes a tangent when $r^2 = d^2$.

18. (*i*) Tangent of S = 0, which have a given slope 'm' can be expressed by the formula

$$y + f = m(x + g) \pm r\sqrt{1 + m^2}$$

where r is radius of S = 0.

(*ii*) Tangents of $x^2 + y^2 = r^2$ with slope m are given by

$$y = mx \pm r\sqrt{1 + m^2}$$

19. Slopes of the two tangents to S = 0 through an external point $P(x_1, y_1)$ are given by

$$m = \frac{(x_1 + g)(y_1 + f) \pm r\sqrt{S_{11}}}{(x_1 + g)^2 - r^2}$$

20. When $P(x_1, y_1)$ is an external point to S = 0, and a tangent is drawn through P to touch the circle at T, then length PT is called the length of the tangent from P to the circle and this length can be comuted by the formula

$$PT = \sqrt{S_{11}}$$

21. If tangents to S = 0 through an extenral point $P(x_1,y_1)$ touch the circle at T_1 and T_2 and $\angle T_1PT_2 = \theta$, then

$$\tan\left(\frac{\theta}{2}\right) = \frac{r}{\sqrt{S_{11}}}$$

or $$\theta = \tan^{-1}\left(\frac{r}{\sqrt{S_{11}}}\right)$$

22. If C is centre of the circle $S = 0$, then

$$\text{area of } \Delta PCT_1 = \frac{1}{2} r\sqrt{S_{11}}$$

and area of the quadrilateral $PT_1\,CT_2 = r\sqrt{S_{11}}$

Also, $\quad \text{area of } \Delta PT_1T_2 = \left|\dfrac{r(S_{11})^{3/2}}{S_{11} + r^2}\right|$

Here T_1, T_2 are points of contact of tangents through P.

23. (*i*) Length of the chord cut by $S = 0$ on the x-axis is $2\sqrt{g^2 - c}$.
Hence circle touches the x-axis if and only if

$$g^2 = c \text{ and } |f| = \text{radius.}$$

(*ii*) Length of the chord cut by $S = 0$ on the y-axis is $2\sqrt{f^2 - c}$.
Hence circle touches the y-axis if an only if

$$f^2 = c \text{ and } |g| = \text{radius.}$$

24. Equation of the secant line that cuts $S = 0$ in $A(x_1, y_1)$ and $B\,(x_2, y_2)$ is

$$S_1 + S_2 = S_{12}$$

25. Equation of the tangent line that touches $S = 0$ at $P(x_1, y_1)$ is

$$S_1 = 0$$

26. Equation of the second line that pass through θ, ϕ on the circle $S = 0$ is

$$(x + g) \cos\left(\frac{\theta + \phi}{2}\right) + (y + f) \sin\left(\frac{\theta + \phi}{2}\right) = r \cos\left(\frac{\theta + \phi}{2}\right)$$

27. Equation of the tangent at θ on $S = 0$ is

$$(x + g) \cos\theta + (y + f) \sin\theta = r$$

28. A given line $lx + my + n = 0$ is normal to $S = 0$ if and only if it passes through the centre, i.e.

$$lg + mf = n.$$

29. If P (x_1,y_1) is an external point to S = 0 and tangents to S = 0 through P touches it at T_1 and T_2, second line through T_1 and T_2, is called chord of constant of S = 0 with respect to P. It's equation is given by $S_1 = 0$.
30. If a line is perpendicular to the radius of a circle at its end point on the circle, then the line is a tangent to the circle.
31. If a line is tangent to a circle, then it is perpendicular to the radius at the point of contact.

    Cor. Perpendicular to a tangent at its point of contact passes through the centre of the circle.
32. If two circles touch externally, then circles are on either side of the tangent.

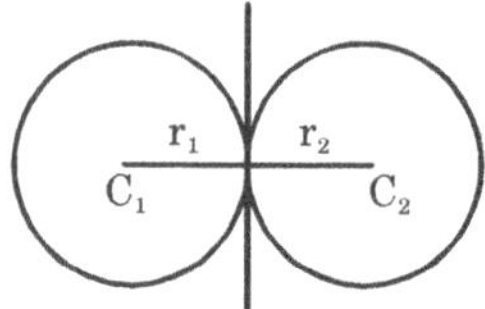

If two circles touch externally, then distance between their centres is equal to sum of their radii,

i.e. $$C_1C_2 = r_1 + r_2$$

33. If two circles touch internally, then circles are on same side of the tangent.

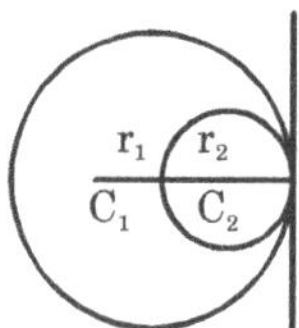

If two circles touch internally, then distance between their centres is equal to the difference of their radii,

i.e. $$C_1C_2 = r_1 - r_2$$

34. If a line touches two circles at two different points and also that both the circles are one the same side of the line, then the line is called a direct common tangent.

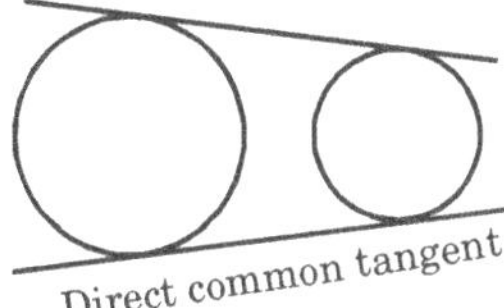

35. If a line touches two circles at different points and also that the circles are on either side of the line, then the line is called a transverse common tangent.

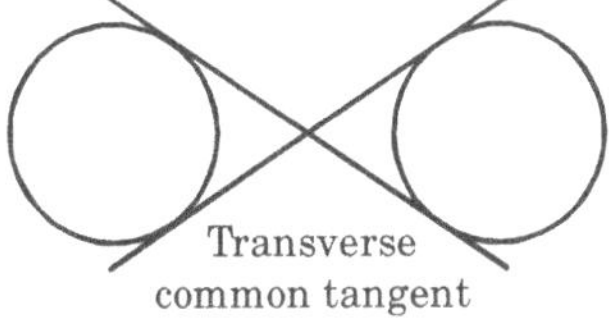

36. If two circles intersect, then the number of common tangents that can be drawn is two.
37. If two circles touch internally, then the number of common tangents that can be drawn is one.
38. If two circles touch externally, then the number of common tangents that can be drawn in three.
39. For non-intersecting circles, two direct and two transverse common tangents can be drawn.
40. If two circles touch, then their lines of centres passes through the point of contact.
41. If a line touches a circle and from the point of contact, a chord is drawn, then the angles between tangent and the chord are equal to the angels in the alternate segment.

Converse of Theorem

If an angle between chord of a circle and a straight line drawn through one end of the chord, is equal to an angle in the alternate segments of the circle, then straight line is a tangent to the circle at the end of the chord.

REMEMBER

1. Length of two tangents from an external point to a circle are equal.
2. Length of the direct common tangent = $\sqrt{d^2 - (R - r)^2}$

   where, R and r are radii of two circles.
3. Length of the transverse common tangent = $\sqrt{d^2 - (R + r)^2}$.
4. Tangents drawn at the extreme points of a diameter of a circle are parallel.
5. If two circles touches externally, then distance between their centres is sum of their radii (R + r).
6. If two circles touches internally, then distance between their centres is difference of their radii (R – r).

chapter

46

COMPLEX NUMBERS

A number of the form a + ib where a, b ∈ R, the set of real numbers, and $i = \sqrt{-1}$, is called a complex number.

If z = a+ ib, then real part of z is denoted by Re(z) = a and imaginary part of z is denoted by Im (z) = b.

If a = 0, z is purely imaginary and if b = 0, z is purely real.

ALGEBRAIC OPERATIONS

Let, $z_1 = a + ib$, $z_2 = c + id$

1. **Equality:**

$$z_1 = z_2 \quad \text{if } Re(z_1) = Re(z_2) \Rightarrow a = c$$

and

$$Im(z_1) = Im(z_2) \Rightarrow b = d$$

2. **Addition:**

$$z_1 + z_2 = (a+c) + i(b+d)$$

3. **Subtraction:**

$$z_1 - z_2 = (a-c) + i(b-d)$$

4. **Multiplication:**

$$z_1.z_2 = (ac - bd) + i(ad + bc)$$

5. **Division:**

$$\frac{z_1}{z_2} = \frac{ac+bd}{c^2+d^2} + i\frac{bc-d}{c^2+d^2}$$

Conjugate of a Complex Number

Conjugate of a complex number z = a + ib is defined as $\bar{z} = a - ib$

Properties

1. $\overline{(\bar{z})} = z$

2. $z = \begin{cases} \bar{z} \text{ if and only if } z \text{ is purely real} \\ -\bar{z} \text{ if and only if } z \text{ is purely imaginary} \end{cases}$

3. $z + \bar{z} = 2\,\text{Re}\,(z),\ z - \bar{z} = 2i\,\text{Im}\,(z)$

4. $\overline{z_1 + z_2} = \overline{z_1} + \overline{z_2}$

5. $\overline{z_1 - z_2} = \overline{z_1} - \overline{z_2}$

6. $\overline{z_1 . z_2} = \overline{z_1} \cdot \overline{z_2}$

7. $\overline{\left(\dfrac{z_1}{z_2}\right)} = \dfrac{\bar{z}_1}{\bar{z}_2}$

MODULUS OF A COMPLEX NUMBER

Let z = a + ib be a complex number, then modulus of z is denoted by

$$|z| = \sqrt{a^2 + b^2}$$

Properties

1. $|z| \geq 0$ and $|z| = 0$ if and only if $z = 0$, i.e. $a = 0$, $b = 0$
2. $|z| = |\bar{z}| = |-z| = |-\bar{z}|$
3. $z\bar{z} = |z|^2$
4. $-|z| \leq \text{Re}\,(z) \leq |z|$ and $-|z| \leq I_m\,(z) \leq |z|$
5. $|z^n| = |z|^n$
6. $|z_1 z_2| = |z_1| . |z_2|$
7. $\left|\dfrac{z_1}{z_2}\right| = \dfrac{|z_1|}{|z_2|}$
8. $|z_1 + z_2| \leq |z_1| \pm |z_2|$
9. $|z_1 - z_2| \geq |z_1| - |z_2|$
10. $|z_1 + z_2|^2 + |z_1 - z_2|^2 = 2\,(|z_1|^2 + |z_2|^2)$

ARGUMENT OF A COMPLEX NUMBER

Argument or amplitude is denoted by

$$\arg(z) = q = \tan^{-1}\left(\frac{b}{a}\right)$$

Properties

1. $\arg(z_1 z_2) = \arg(z_1) + \arg(z_2)$
2. $\arg\left(\frac{z_1}{z_2}\right) = \arg(z_1) - \arg(z_2)$
3. $\arg\left(\frac{z}{\bar{z}}\right) = 2\arg(z)$
4. $\arg(z^n) = n\arg(z)$
5. If $\arg\left(\frac{z_1}{z_2}\right) = \theta$, then $\arg\left(\frac{z_2}{z_1}\right) = 2k\pi - \theta, k \in I$
6. $\arg(\bar{z}) = -\arg(z) = \arg\left(\frac{1}{z}\right)$
7. $\arg(z\bar{z}) = \arg(|z|^2)$

Polar form of Complex Number

If $z = x + iy$, then

$x = r\cos\theta$ and $y = r\sin\theta$

where, $z = r(\cos\theta + i\sin\theta)$ is called polar form.

$\cos\theta = \frac{x}{\sqrt{x^2+y^2}}$ and $\sin\theta = \frac{y}{\sqrt{x^2+y^2}}$

Modulus, $|z| = r = \sqrt{x^2+y^2}$

Argument, $\theta = \tan^{-1}(y/x)$

Basic Polar Forms

$i = 0 + i.1 = \cos\frac{\pi}{2} + i\sin\frac{\pi}{2}$

$i^2 = -1 + i.0 = \cos\pi + i\sin\pi$

$i^3 = 0 + i(-1) = \cos\left(-\frac{\pi}{2}\right) + i\sin\left(-\frac{\pi}{2}\right)$

$i^4 = 1 + i.0 = \cos 0 + i\sin 0$

Eulerian Representation of a Complex Number

$$e^{i\theta} = \cos\theta + i\sin\theta, \ \left|e^{i\theta}\right| = 1$$

$$z = x + iy = r(\cos\theta + i\sin\theta) = re^{i\theta}$$

where $|z| = r$, and $\arg(z) = \theta$

$$\cos\theta = \ \sin\theta = \frac{e^{i\theta} - e^{-i\theta}}{2}$$

De' Moivre's Theorem

- If $z = r(\cos\theta + i\sin\theta)^n$, then

$$z^{1/n} = r^{1/n}\left[\cos\left(\frac{2\pi k + \theta}{n}\right) + i\sin\left(\frac{2k\pi + \theta}{n}\right)\right]$$

where, $k = 0, 1 \ldots\ldots. n - 1$

- $(\cos\theta + i\sin\theta)^n = \cos(n\theta) + i\sin(n\theta)$
- $(\cos\theta + i\sin\theta)^{-n} = \cos(n\theta) - i\sin(n\theta)$
- $\dfrac{1}{\cos\theta + i\sin\theta} = (\cos\theta + i\sin\theta)^{-1} = \cos\theta - i\sin\theta$
- $(\cos\theta_1 + \sin\theta_1)(\cos\theta_2 + i\sin\theta_2) \ldots\ldots (\cos\theta_n + i\sin\theta_n)$
$$= \cos(\theta_1 + \theta_2 + \ldots..\theta_n) + i\sin(\theta_1 + \theta_2 + \ldots..\theta_n)$$

ROOTS OF UNITY

Cube Roots of Unity

$$z = 1^{1/3}$$

$$\Rightarrow \quad z^3 - 1 = 0$$

i.e. $z = 1, \dfrac{-1 + i\sqrt{3}}{2}, \dfrac{-1 - i\sqrt{3}}{2}$ are cube roots of unity.

REMEMBER
1. If $\omega = \dfrac{-1+i\sqrt{3}}{2}$, then $\omega^2 = \dfrac{-1-i\sqrt{3}}{2}$
2. $1 + \omega + \omega^2 = 0$
3. $\omega^3 = 1$
4. $\omega^{3n} = 1,\ \omega^{3n+1} = \omega,\ \omega^{3n+2} = \omega^2$

n^{th} Roots of Unity

$z = 1^{1/n} = (\cos 0 + i \sin 0)^{1/n}$

$$= \cos\left(\frac{2\pi k}{n}\right) + i \sin\left(\frac{2\pi k}{n}\right),$$

$$= e^{i\frac{2\pi k}{n}}, \text{ where } k = 0, 1.....n-1$$

$$= 1,\ e^{\left(\frac{2\pi k}{n}\right)}, e^{\left(\frac{4\pi k}{n}\right)}, ...\ e^{\left(\frac{2\pi(n-1)}{n}\right)}$$

$$= 1, \omega, \omega^2 ..... \omega^{n-1}, \text{ where } \omega = e^{\left(\frac{i2\pi}{n}\right)}$$

$1 + \omega + \omega^2 + ...\omega^{n-1} = 0$

$1 \cdot \omega \cdot \omega^2 \cdot\ ....\omega^{n-1} = (-1)^{n-1}$

GEOMETRICAL PROPERTIES OF COMPLEX NUMBER

1. If z_1 and z_2 are two complex numbers, then complex number

   $z = \dfrac{nz_1 + mz_2}{m+n}$ divides the join of z_1 and z_2 in the ratio m : n

2. Distance between two complex numbers z_1 and z_2 is $|z_1 - z_2|$
3. Equation of the line in parametric form joining z_1 and z_2 is given by

   $z = tz_1 + (1 - t)z_2$, where t is a real parameter.

4. Equation of the line in non-parametric form joining z_1 and z_2 is given by

$$\frac{z-z_1}{z_2-z_1}=\frac{\bar{z}-\bar{z}_1}{\bar{z}_2-\bar{z}_1} \text{ or } \begin{vmatrix} z & \bar{z} & 1 \\ z_1 & \bar{z}_1 & 1 \\ z_2 & \bar{z}_2 & 1 \end{vmatrix}=0$$

5. General equation of a straight line is

$\bar{a}z + a\bar{z} + b = 0$, where b is a real number.

6. Three points z_1, z_2 and z_3 are collinear if

$$\begin{vmatrix} z_1 & \bar{z}_1 & 1 \\ z_2 & \bar{z}_2 & 1 \\ z_3 & \bar{z}_3 & 1 \end{vmatrix}=0$$

7. Equation of circle having centre z_0 and radius r is

$$|z-z_0| = r \text{ or } z\bar{z}-z_0\bar{z}+z_0\bar{z}_0-r^2=0$$

8. General equation of the circle is

$$z\bar{z}+a\bar{z}+\bar{a}z+b=0,$$

where b is a real number.

Centre of this circle is $-a$ and its radius is $\sqrt{a\bar{a}-b}$.

9. Equation of the circle described on the line segment joining z_1 and z_2 as diameter is

$$(z-z_1)\left(\bar{z}-\bar{z}_2\right)+(z-z_2)\left(\bar{z}-\bar{z}_1\right)=0$$

10. If z_1, z_2 and z_3 are vertices of an equilateral triangle and z_0 be the circumcentre, then

$$z_1^2+z_2^2+z_3^2 = 3z_0^2$$

11. If z_1, z_2, z_3 are vertices of a triangle, then triangle is equilateral if

$$(z_1-z_2)^2+(z_2-z_3)^2+(z_3-z_1)^2=0$$

12. Equation $|z-z_1|^2 + |z-z_2|^2 = k$, where k is real number represent a circle with centre at $\frac{1}{2}(z_1+z_2)$ and radius $\frac{1}{2}\sqrt{2k-|z_1-z_2|^2}$, provided

$$k \geq \frac{1}{2}|z_1-z_2|^2.$$

chapter

47

CONIC SECTION

A conic section is the locus of a point which moves in a plane such that its distance from a fixed point bears a constant ratio to its distance from a fixed line. The fixed point is called *focus* and fixed line is called *directrix* of the conic. The constant ratio is called *eccentricity of the conic* and is denoted by the letter 'e'

$$\text{Conic} = \begin{cases} \text{ellipse when } e < 1 \\ \text{parabola when } e = 1 \\ \text{hyperbola when } e > 1 \end{cases}$$

PARABOLA

It is locus of a point which moves such that its distance from a fixed point (called focus) is equal to its distance from fixed line (called directrix).

$y^2 = 4ax$ is the standard form of the equation of the parabola.

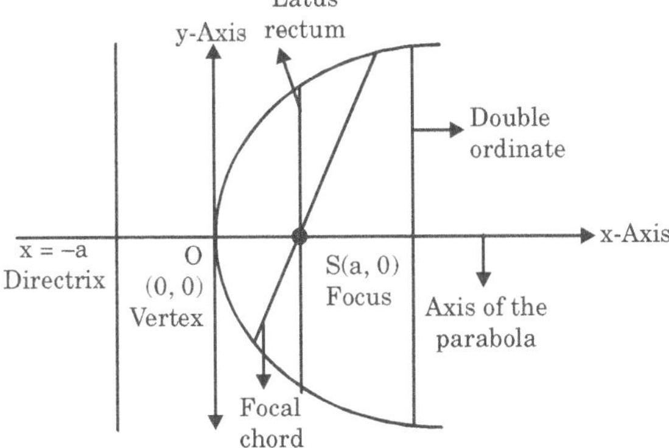

Terms used to describe a parabola :

Vertex : The point O (0,0) is called vertex of the parabola. Tangent to the parabola at the vertex is $x = 0$.

Axis : The line joining vertex 'O' and the focus S(a, 0) is called axis of the parabola and therefore its equation is $y = 0$.

Double ordinate : Any chord of the parabola perpendicular to its axis is called double ordinate.

Focal Chord : Any chord of the parabola passing through its focus is called focal chord.

Latus rectum : Focal chord of the parabola perpendicular to its axis is called its latus rectum, and therefore length of this latus rectum is 4a.

Co-normal points : Points on a parabola, normals at which are concurrent, are called co-normal points of the parabola.

Diameter : A line which bisects a system of parallel chords of a parabola is called diameter of the parabola.

Some standards results for the parabola $y^2 = 4ax$:

1. Parametric equations of the parabola or co-ordinates of any point on it are

$$x = at^2,\ y = 2at.$$

2. Tangent to the parabola at (x', y') is

$$yy' = 2a\,(x + x')$$

and that at $(at^2, 2at)$ is $ty = x + at^2.$

3. Condition that the line $y = mx + c$ is a tangent to the parabola is $c = a/m$

and equation of any tangent to it (not parallel to the y-axis) is

$$y = mx + \frac{a}{m}.$$

4. Chord of contact of (x', y') with respect to the parabola is

$$yy' = 2a\,(x + x')$$

5. Chord with mid-point (x', y') of the parabola is $T = s'$,

where $T \equiv yy' - 2a\,(x + x')$ and $S' \equiv y'^2 - 4\,ax'$.

6. Equation of the pair of tangents from (x′ y′) to the parabola is

$$T^2 = SS'.$$

7. Normal at $(at^2, 2at)$ to the parabola is $y = -tx + 2at + at^3$.

If m is slope of this normal, then its equation is

$$y = mx - 2am - am^3,$$

which is the normal to the parabola at $(am^2, -2\,am)$.

Ellipse and Hyperbola

An ellipse (hyperbola) is locus of a point which moves such that its distance from a fixed point (the focus) is always 'e' times its distance from a fixed line (the directrix), where e < 1(>1) is the eccentricity of the ellipse (hyperbola).

For e >1, equation of the ellipse (hyperbola) in standard form is

$$\frac{x^2}{a^2} + \frac{y^2}{b^2} = 1, \left(\frac{x^2}{a^2} - \frac{y^2}{b^2} = 1\right)$$

Ellipse

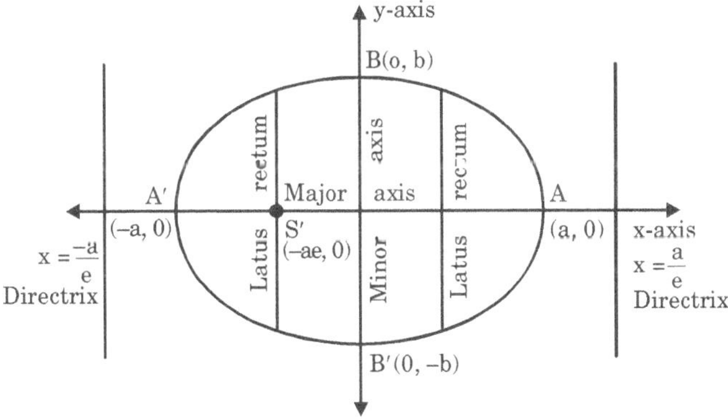

Hyperbola

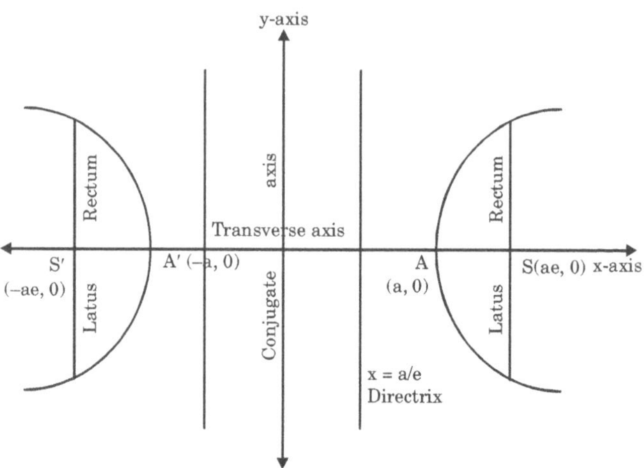

Terms used to describe an ellipse (a hyperbola):

Centre : The point C (0,0) is called centre of the ellipse (hyperbola).

Principal axis : The lines A′A and B′B are called principal axes. A′A is called major (transverse) axis and its length is 2a.

B′B is called minor (conjugate) axis and its length is 2b.

Vertices : The points A(a, 0), A′(–a, 0), B(0, b) and B′ (0,– b) are called four vertices of the ellipse (hyperbola).

Lactus rectum : A line through the focus S of the ellipse (hyperbola) and perpendicular to its major (transverse) axis, is called its latus rectum. Its equation is $x = \pm\, ae$ and its length is $\frac{2b^2}{a}$.

Focus : The ellipse (hyperbola) has two foci, S (ae, 0) and S′(–a e, 0) and also two directrices, $x = a/e$ and $x = -a/e$ respectively.

Some standard results for an ellipse (hyperbola) :

1. Parametric equations of an ellipse (hyperbola) or coordinates of any point on the ellipse (hyperbola) are

   $$x = a\cos\theta,\ y = b\sin\theta\ (x = a\sec\theta,\ y = b\tan\theta).$$

   The point is denoted ‘θ’.

2. Equation of the tangent at the above point 'θ' is

$$\frac{x}{a}\cos\theta+\frac{y}{b}\sin\theta=1\quad\left(\frac{x}{a}\sec\theta-\frac{y}{b}\tan\theta=1\right)$$

3. Equation of the normal at the same point 'θ' is

$$\frac{ax}{\cos\theta}-\frac{by}{\sin\theta}=a^2-b^2\left(\frac{ax}{\sec\theta}+\frac{by}{\tan\theta}=a^2+b^2\right).$$

4. Equation of tangent at the point p(x′, y′) and equation of chord of contact of (x′, y′) with respect to ellipse (hyperbola) is

$$\frac{xx'}{a^2}+\frac{yy'}{b^2}=1\left(\frac{xx'}{a^2}-\frac{yy'}{b^2}=1\right)$$

5. Condition that the line $y = mx + c$ touches the ellipse (hyperbola) is

$$c^2 = a^2m^2 + b^2\,(c^2 = a^2m^2 - b^2)$$

And equation of ellipse (hyperbola) is

$$y = mx \pm \sqrt{a^2m^2+b^2}\ \ (y = mx \pm \sqrt{a^2m^2-b^2})$$

6. Equation of the chord of the ellipse (hyperbola) whose mid-point is (x′, y′) is

$$T = S'$$

where, $T \equiv \frac{xx'}{a^2}+\frac{yy'}{b^2}-1 \quad \left(T\equiv\frac{xx'}{a^2}-\frac{yy'}{b^2}-1\right)$

$$S' \equiv \frac{x'^2}{a^2}+\frac{y'^2}{b^2}-1 \quad \left(S'\equiv\frac{x'^2}{a^2}-\frac{y'^2}{b^2}-1\right)$$

7. Equations of the pair of tangents from a point (x′, y′) to the ellipse (hyperbola) is

$$T^2 = SS'$$

where, $S \equiv \frac{x^2}{a^2}+\frac{y^2}{b^2}-1 \left(S\equiv\frac{x^2}{a^2}-\frac{y^2}{b^2}-1\right)$

chapter

48

VECTOR ALGEBRA

SCALAR QUANTITY

It is a quantity which has only magnitude and no direction.

VECTOR QUANTITY

It is a quantity which has magnitude as well as direction.

Unit Vector

It is a vector whose magnitude is unity.

$$\hat{a} = \frac{\vec{a}}{|\vec{a}|}$$

Zero or Null Vector

It is a vector whose magnitude is zero.

Collinear or Parallel Vectors

Vectors which are parallel to the straight line are called *collinear vectors.*

Vectors which are not parallel to the same line are called *non-collinear vectors.*

Like and Unlike Vectors

Collinear vectors having same direction are called *like vectors* collinear vectors having opposite directions are called *unlike vectors.*

Reciprocal Vectors

A vector whose direction is that of $\vec{a}$ but modulus is $\frac{1}{|\vec{a}|}$.

$$\vec{a}^{-1} = \frac{\vec{a}}{|\vec{a}|}$$

Coplanar and Non-coplanar Vectors

Three or more vectors are called *coplanar vectors* when they are parallel to the same plane; otherwise they are called *non-coplanar vectors.*

Coinitial Vectors

These are the vectors which have the same initial point.

Negative of a Vector

A vector having same modulus as that of a given vector $\vec{a}$ and the direction opposite to that of $\vec{a}$, is called negative of $\vec{a}$ and is denoted by $-\vec{a}$.

$$\overrightarrow{AB} = \vec{a} \Rightarrow \overrightarrow{BA} = -\vec{a} = -\overrightarrow{AB}$$

Equal Vectors

Two vectors $\vec{a}$ and $\vec{b}$ are called equal when they have equal magnitude and same direction.

PROPERTIES OF VECTORS

1. $\vec{a}+\vec{b} = \vec{b}+\vec{a}$
2. $(\vec{a}+\vec{b})+\vec{c} = \vec{a}+(\vec{b}+\vec{c})$
3. $\vec{a} + (-\vec{a}) = (-\vec{a})+\vec{a} = \vec{0}$
4. $(m+n)\,\vec{a} = m\vec{a}+n\vec{a}$, where m, n are scalars
5. $m(\vec{a}+\vec{b}) = m\vec{a}+m\vec{b}$
6. $\vec{a}-\vec{b} \neq \vec{b}-\vec{a}$
7. $|\vec{a}+\vec{b}| \leq |\vec{a}| + |\vec{b}|$
8. $|\vec{a}-\vec{b}| \geq |\vec{a}| - |\vec{b}|$
9. If $\vec{a}$ and $\vec{b}$ are non-zero, non-collinear vectors, then

$$x\vec{a} + y\vec{b} = x'\vec{a}+y'\vec{b}$$

$$\Rightarrow \quad x = x', y = y'$$

10. If $\vec{a}, \vec{b}$ and $\vec{c}$ are non-zero, non-coplanar vectors, then any vector $\vec{r}$, coplanar with $\vec{a}$ and $\vec{b}$, can be expressed uniquely as a linear combination of $\vec{a}$ and $\vec{b}$, i.e. there exist unique x and y $\in R$ such that $\vec{r} = x\vec{a} + y\vec{b}$

Linear Dependent and independent Vectors

The system of n vectors $a_1, a_2.....a_n$ is called *linearly dependent*, if there exist scalars $x_1, x_2,.....x_n$ not all zero such that

$$x_1 a_1 + x_2 a_2 + ...x_n a_n = 0$$

The same vectors is called linearly independent if all scalars are zero, i.e.

$$x_1 = x_2 = ...= x_n = 0.$$

Section Formula

The position vector of a point which divides the line joining points with position vectors $\vec{a}$ and $\vec{b}$ in the ratio m : n, is

$$\frac{n\vec{a} + m\vec{b}}{m + n}, \ (m \neq -n)$$

Test of Collinearity

Three points with position vectors $\vec{a}$, $\vec{b}$ and $\vec{c}$ are collinear if and only if there exist scalars x, y and z, not all zero, such that

$$x\vec{a} + y\vec{b} + z\vec{c} = 0$$

where $x + y + z = 0$.

Test of Coplanarity

Four points with position vectors $\vec{a}$, $\vec{b}, \vec{c}$ and $\vec{d}$ are coplanar if and only if there exist scalars x, y, z and w not all zero, such that

$$x\vec{a} + y\vec{b} + z\vec{c} + w\vec{d} = 0$$

where

$$x + y + z + w = 0$$

Note:

1. If $\vec{a} = a_1\vec{i} + a_2\vec{j} + a_3\vec{k}$; $\vec{b} = b_1\vec{i} + b_2\vec{j} + b_3\vec{k}$; $\vec{c} = c_1\vec{i} + c_2\vec{j} + c_3\vec{k}$ are three linearly dependent vectors, then

$$\begin{vmatrix} a_1 & b_1 & c_1 \\ a_2 & b_2 & c_2 \\ a_1 & b_2 & c_3 \end{vmatrix} = 0$$

2. Let $\vec{a}, \vec{b}, \vec{c}$ be three non-coplanar vectors.

   Then vectors $x_1\vec{a} + y_1\vec{b} + z_1\vec{c}$, $x_2\vec{a} + y_2\vec{b} + z_2\vec{c}$ and $x_3\vec{a} + y_3\vec{b} + z_3\vec{c}$ will be coplanar if

$$\begin{vmatrix} x_1 & y_1 & z_1 \\ x_2 & y_2 & z_2 \\ x_3 & y_3 & z_3 \end{vmatrix} = 0$$

SCALAR OR DOT PRODUCT

Scalar or dot product of two vectors $\vec{a}$ and $\vec{b}$ is given by $|\vec{a}|\,|\vec{b}|\cos\theta$, where θ $(0 \le \theta \le \pi)$ is angle between vectors $\vec{a}$ and $\vec{b}$. It is denoted by placing a dot between $\vec{a}$ and $\vec{b}$, i.e.

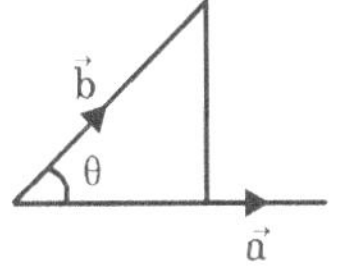

$$\vec{a}.\vec{b} = |\vec{a}|\,|\vec{b}| \cos\theta$$

Properties of Scalar or Dot Product

1. $\vec{a}.\vec{b} = \vec{b}.\vec{a}$

2. $\vec{a}.\vec{a} = |\vec{a}|^2 = a^2$

3. $\vec{a}\cdot(\vec{b}+\vec{c}) = \vec{a}.\vec{b} + \vec{a}.\vec{c}$

4. Projection of $\vec{a}$ on $\vec{b} = \dfrac{\vec{a}.\vec{b}}{|\vec{b}|}$

5. $(\vec{a}+\vec{b}).(\vec{a}-\vec{b}) = a^2 - b^2$

6. $(\vec{a}+\vec{b})^2 = \vec{a}^2 + \vec{b}^2 + 2\vec{a}.\vec{b}$

7. Two vectors $\vec{a}$ and $\vec{b}$ make an

   acute angle if $\vec{a}.\vec{b} > 0$,

   obtuse angle if $\vec{a}.\vec{b} < 0$

   and inclined at a right angle if

$$\vec{a}.\vec{b} = 0$$

8. If $\vec{i}$, $\vec{j}$ and $\vec{k}$ are three unit vectors along three mutually perpendicular lines, then

$$\vec{i}.\vec{i} = \vec{j}.\vec{j} = \vec{k}.\vec{k} = 1 \text{ and } \vec{i}.\vec{j} = \vec{j}.\vec{k} = \vec{k}.\vec{i} = 0$$

9. If $\vec{a} = a_1\vec{i} + a_2\vec{j} + a_3\vec{k}$ and $\vec{b} = b_1\vec{i} + b_2\vec{j} + b_3\vec{k}$

   then,
$$\vec{a}.\vec{b} = a_1b_1 + a_2b_2 + a_3b_3$$
$$|\vec{a}| = \sqrt{a_1^2 + a_2^2 + a_3^2}$$
$$|\vec{b}| = \sqrt{b_1^2 + b_2^2 + b_3^2}$$
$$\cos\theta = \frac{a_1b_1 + a_2b_2 + a_3b_3}{\sqrt{a_1^2 + a_2^2 + a_3^2}\sqrt{b_1^2 + b_2^2 + b_3^2}}$$

10. Components of a vector $\vec{b}$ along vector $\vec{a}$ is $\left(\dfrac{\vec{a}.\vec{b}}{|\vec{a}|}\right)\vec{a}$

11. $|\vec{i} + \vec{j} + \vec{k}| = \sqrt{3}$

12. $(a\,.\,b)^2 \le |a|^2\,|b|^2$

VECTOR OR CROSS PRODUCT

Vector product of two vectors $\vec{a}$ and $\vec{b}$, denoted by $\vec{a} \times \vec{b}$, is the vector

$$\vec{c} = |\vec{a}||\vec{b}| \sin\theta\ \vec{n},$$

where θ is the angle between $\vec{a}$ and $\vec{b}$, with $0 \le \theta \le \pi$.

$\vec{c}$ is supported by the line perpendicular to $\vec{a}$ and $\vec{b}$, and direction of $\vec{c}$ is such that $\vec{a}$, $\vec{b}$ and $\vec{c}$ form a right-handed system.

Properties of the Cross-product

1. $\vec{a} \times \vec{b} = -\vec{b} \times \vec{a}$

2. $\vec{a} \times \vec{a} = 0$

3. $\vec{a} \times (\vec{b} + \vec{c}) = \vec{a} \times \vec{b} + \vec{a} \times \vec{c}$

4. $(\vec{a} \times \vec{b})^2 = \vec{a}^2\vec{b}^2 - (\vec{a}.\vec{b})^2$

5. $\vec{i} \times \vec{i} = \vec{j} \times \vec{j} = \vec{k} \times \vec{k} = 0,$

   $\vec{i} \times \vec{j} = \vec{k},$

   $\vec{j} \times \vec{h} = \vec{i},$

   $\vec{k} \times \vec{i} = \vec{j},$

   $\vec{j} \times \vec{i} = -k,$

   $\vec{k} \;\; \vec{j} = -\vec{i},$

   $\vec{i} \times \vec{k} = -\vec{j}$

6. Two non-zero vectors $\vec{a}$ and $\vec{b}$ are collinear if and only if

$$\vec{a} \times \vec{b} = 0$$

   Angle θ between two vectors $\vec{a}$ and $\vec{b}$ is given by

$$\sin \theta = \frac{|\vec{a} \times \vec{b}|}{|\vec{a}||\vec{b}|}$$

7. If $\vec{a} = a_1\vec{i} + a_2\vec{j} + a_3\vec{k}$ and $\vec{b} = b_1\vec{i} + b_2\vec{j} + b_3\vec{k}$, then

$$\vec{a} \times \vec{b} = \begin{vmatrix} \vec{i} & \vec{j} & \vec{k} \\ a_1 & a_2 & a_3 \\ b_1 & b_2 & b_3 \end{vmatrix}$$

VECTOR TRIPLE PRODUCT

Vector triple product of three vectors $\vec{a}$, $\vec{b}$ and $\vec{c}$ is the vector $\vec{a} \times (\vec{b} \times \vec{c})$

i.e., $\vec{a} \times (\vec{b} \times \vec{c}) = (\vec{a}.\vec{c})\vec{b} - (\vec{a}.\vec{b})\vec{c}$

and $(\vec{a} \times \vec{b}) \times \vec{c} = (\vec{a}.\vec{c})\vec{b} - (\vec{b}.\vec{c})\vec{a}$

Note: $\vec{a} \times (\vec{b} \times \vec{c}) \neq (\vec{a} \times \vec{b}) \times \vec{c}$

$\vec{a} \times (\vec{b} \times \vec{c}) = (\vec{a} \times \vec{b}) \times \vec{c}$ if and only if vectors $\vec{a}$ and $\vec{c}$ are collinear.

SCALAR TRIPLE PRODUCT

Scalar triple product of three vectors $\vec{a}, \vec{b}$ and $\vec{c}$ is denoted by $[\vec{a}\ \vec{b}\ \vec{c}]$ and is defined as

$$\vec{a}.(\vec{b} \times \vec{c}) = (\vec{a} \times \vec{b}).\vec{c}.$$

Properties of Scalar Triple Product

1. $[\vec{a}\ \vec{b}\ \vec{c}] = [\vec{b}\ \vec{c}\ \vec{a}] = [\vec{c}\ \vec{a}\ \vec{b}] = -[-\vec{b}\ \vec{a}\ \vec{c}] = -[\vec{b}\ \vec{a}\ \vec{c}] = -[\vec{c}\ \vec{b}\ \vec{a}]$

2. $(\vec{a} \times \vec{b}).\ \vec{c} = (\vec{b} \times \vec{c}).\vec{a} = (\vec{c} \times \vec{a}).\vec{b}$

3. If $\vec{a} = a_1\vec{i} + a_2\vec{j} + a_3\vec{k}$; $\vec{b} = b_1\vec{i} + b_2\vec{j} + b_3\vec{k}$; $\vec{c} = c_1\vec{i} + c_2\vec{j} + c_3\vec{k}$

   then $$[\vec{a}\ \vec{b}\ \vec{c}] = \begin{vmatrix} a_1 & a_2 & a_3 \\ b_1 & b_2 & b_3 \\ c_1 & c_2 & c_3 \end{vmatrix}$$

4. Any three vectors $\vec{a}, \vec{b}$ and $\vec{c}$ are coplanar if and only

   if $$[\vec{a}\ \vec{b}\vec{c}] = 0$$

5. $[\vec{a} + \vec{b}\vec{c}\vec{d}] = [\vec{a}\vec{c}\vec{d}] + [\vec{b}\vec{c}\vec{d}] = 0$

6. Three vectors $\vec{a}, \vec{b}$ and $\vec{c}$ from a right-handed or left- handed system according as $\left[\vec{a}\,\vec{b}\,\vec{c}\right]$ > or <.

7. Four points with position vectors $\vec{a}, \vec{b}$ and $\vec{c}, \vec{d}$ will be coplanar if $\left[\vec{a}\ \vec{b}\,\vec{c}\right] = \left[\vec{d}\ \vec{b}\,\vec{c}\right] + \left[\vec{d}\,\vec{c}\,\vec{a}\right] + \left[\vec{d}\,\vec{a}\,\vec{b}\right]$

8. $\left(\vec{a} \times \vec{b}\right) . \left(\vec{c} \times \vec{d}\right) = \begin{vmatrix} \vec{a}.\vec{c} & \vec{b}.\vec{c} \\ \vec{a}.\vec{d} & \vec{b}.\vec{d} \end{vmatrix}$

9. $\left[\vec{a}\ \vec{b}\ \vec{c}\right]\ \left[\vec{u}\,\vec{v}\,\vec{w}\right] = \begin{bmatrix} \vec{a}.\vec{u} & \vec{b}.\vec{u} & \vec{c}.\vec{u} \\ \vec{a}.\vec{v} & \vec{b}.\vec{v} & \vec{c}.\vec{v} \\ \vec{a}.\vec{w} & \vec{b}.\vec{w} & \vec{c}.\vec{w} \end{bmatrix}$

10. $\left[\lambda\vec{a}\ \vec{b}\,\vec{c}\right] = \lambda\left[\vec{a}\,\vec{b}\,\vec{c}\right], \lambda \in R$

11. $\left[\vec{a} - \vec{b}\quad \vec{b} - \vec{c}\quad \vec{c} - \vec{a}\right] = 0$

12. $\left[\vec{a} + \vec{b}\quad \vec{b} + \vec{c}\quad \vec{c} + \vec{a}\right] = 2\left[\vec{a}\quad \vec{b}\quad \vec{c}\right]$

13. $\left[\vec{a} \times \vec{b}\quad \vec{b} \times \vec{c}\quad \vec{c} \times \vec{a}\right] = \left[\vec{a}\quad \vec{b}\quad \vec{c}\right]^2$

14. Unit vector perpendicular to the plane of $\vec{a}$ and $\vec{b}$ is $\frac{\vec{a} \times \vec{b}}{\left|\vec{a} \times \vec{b}\right|}$ and a vector of magnitude λ perpendicular to the plane of $\vec{a}$ and $\vec{b}$ is $\pm\frac{\lambda\left(\vec{a} \times \vec{b}\right)}{\left|\vec{a} \times \vec{b}\right|}$

GEOMETRICAL AND PHYSICAL APPLICATION

Work done

If force F acts at a point A and displaces it to the point B, then work done by force F = $\vec{F} . \overrightarrow{AB}$.

Moment

Moment of a force F applied at B about the point A is the vector $\vec{AB} \times \vec{F}$.

Area of Triangle and Parallelogram

Area of parallelogram whose adjacent sides are represented by the vectors $\overrightarrow{OA} = \vec{a}$ and $\overrightarrow{OA} = \vec{b}$, is $|\vec{a} \times \vec{b}|$. Area of triangle OAB is $\frac{1}{2}\,|\vec{a} \times \vec{b}|$.

Volume of Tetrahedron

Volume = $\frac{1}{6}\left[\vec{a}\ \ \vec{b}\ \ \vec{c}\right]$

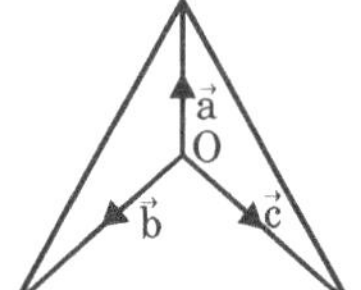

If $\vec{a}, \vec{b}, \vec{c}$ and $\vec{d}$ are position vectors of vertices of a tetrahedron, then

$$\text{Volume} = \frac{1}{6}\left[\vec{b}-\vec{a}\ \ \ \vec{c}-\vec{a}\ \ \ \vec{d}-\vec{a}\right]$$

Bisector of Angle

If $\vec{a}$ and $\vec{b}$ are unit vectors along the sides of an angle, then $\vec{a}+\vec{b}$ and $\vec{a}-\vec{b}$ are vectors along the internal and external bisectors of the angle, respectively.

Bisector of the angles between lines $\vec{r} = x\vec{a}$ and $\vec{r} = y\vec{b}$ are given by

$$\vec{r} = \lambda\left(\frac{\vec{a}}{|\vec{a}|} \pm \frac{\vec{b}}{|\vec{b}|}\right), \lambda \in R$$

Vectorial Equation of Line

Let $\vec{a}$ be the position vector of any point P, and $\vec{b}$ be a vector parallel to a given line. Then equation of the line is

$$\vec{r} = \vec{a} + t\vec{b}\text{ ; t being a parameter.}$$

Equation of Plane

Equation of a plane passing through the point with position vector $\vec{a}$ and parallel to the plane containing vector $\vec{b}$ and $\vec{c}$, is

$$\vec{r} = \vec{a} + \lambda \vec{b} + \mu \vec{c}$$

Equation of a plane through three points $\vec{a}, \vec{b}, \vec{c}$ is

$$\vec{r} = (1 - \lambda - \mu)\vec{a} + \lambda \vec{b} + \mu \vec{c}\,,\ \lambda, \mu \text{ being a parameter.}$$

Reciprocal Systems of Vectors

Let $\vec{a}, \vec{b}$ and $\vec{c}$ be a system of three non-coplanar vectors. Then the system $\vec{a}', \vec{b}'$ and $\vec{c}'$, which satisfies

$$\vec{a}.\overrightarrow{a'} = \vec{b}.\overrightarrow{b'} = \vec{c}.\vec{c}' = 1$$

and $\vec{a}.\overrightarrow{a'} = \vec{a}.\vec{c}' = \vec{b}.\vec{a}' = \vec{b}.\vec{c}' = \vec{b}.\vec{a}' = \vec{c}.\vec{b}' = 0$

is called reciprocal system to the vectors $\vec{a}$, $\vec{b}$ and $\vec{c}$.

$$\left[\vec{a}\ \ \vec{b}\ \ \vec{c}\right] = \frac{1}{\left[\vec{a}'\,\vec{b}'\,\vec{c}'\right]}$$

$$\vec{a}' = \frac{\vec{b} \times \vec{c}}{\left[\vec{a}\,\vec{b}\,\vec{c}\right]}, \quad \vec{b}' = \frac{\vec{c} \times \vec{a}}{\left[\vec{a}\,\vec{b}\,\vec{c}\right]}, \quad \vec{c}' = \frac{\vec{a} \times \vec{b}}{\left[\vec{a}\,\vec{b}\,\vec{c}\right]}$$

chapter 49

FACTORIZATION

The process of writing an expression as the product of two or more expressions is called Factorization.

Each expression occurring in the product is called *factor* of the given expression.

FACTORIZATION IN VARIOUS SITUATIONS.

Case 1 : *When each term of the given expression contains a common monomial factor.*

In this case, we take out common multiplier and use distributive law.

Example. Factorize $6a^2 - 8ab + 4a$.

Solution.

G.C.D. of $6a^2$, 8ab, 4a is 2 a.

2a is a common factor of each term.

$\therefore \quad (6a^2 - 8ab + 4a) = 2a\,(3a - 4b + 2)$.

Case 2 : *When a polynomial is a common multiplier of each term of the given expression.*

Example. Factorize $3x\,(a + 2b) - 2y\,(a + 2b)$.

Solution.

$(a + 2b)\,(3x - 2y)$

GROUPING OF TERMS.

Some times we have to make a suitable arrangement of the terms so as to have a common polynomial.

Example. Factorize $x^2 - y + xy - x$.

Solution.

$$x^2 + xy - x - y$$
$$= x(x + y) - 1(x + y)$$
$$= (x + y)(x - 1)$$

Case 3 : *When given expression is the difference of squares of two terms.*

In this case, we use the formula $(a^2 - b^2) = (a + b)(a - b)$

Factorization of Trinomials of the form $(x^2 + px + q)$.

Let us find two numbers a and b such that

$$a + b = p \quad \text{and} \quad ab = q$$

Then $x^2 + px + q = x^2 + (a + b)x + ab$

$$= x^2 + ax + bx + ab$$
$$= x(x + a) + b(x + a)$$
$$= (x + a)(x + b)$$

chapter 50

PAPER MEASURE

12 sheets	= 1 dozen
24 sheets or 2 dozens	= 1 quire
12 dozens	= 1 gross
20 quires (or) 480 sheets	= 1 ream
500 sheets	= 1 long ream
10 reams	= 1 bale.

chapter 51

BODMAS

To do the simplification, we should always carry out the operations in the order of each letter of the word 'BODMAS', where

B	brackets	[{ ( ) }]
O	of	or
D	division	$\div$
M	multiplication	$\times$
A	addition	$+$
S	subtraction	$-$

Examples.

1. $12 - 4 \times 5 + 36 \div 9 + 8$

$$= 12 - 4 \times 5 + 4 + 8$$
$$= 12 - 20 + 4 + 8$$
$$= 24 - 20$$
$$= 4.$$

2. $1 \div [1 + 1 \div \{1 + 1 \div (1 + 1 \div 2)\}]$

$$= 1 \div [1 + 1 \div \{1 + 1 \div (1 + \frac{1}{2})\}]$$
$$= 1 \div [1 + 1 \div \{1 + 1 \div \frac{3}{2}\}]$$
$$= 1 \div [1 + 1 \div \{1 + \frac{2}{3}\}]$$
$$= 1 \div [1 + 1 \div \frac{5}{3}]$$

$$= 1 \div [1 + \frac{3}{5}]$$

$$= 1 \div \frac{8}{5}$$

$$= \frac{5}{8}$$

3. $$1 + \cfrac{1}{1 + \cfrac{1}{1 + \frac{1}{3}}}$$

$$= 1 + \cfrac{1}{1 + \cfrac{1}{\frac{4}{3}}}$$

$$= 1 + \frac{1}{1 + \frac{3}{4}} = 1 + \frac{1}{\frac{7}{4}}$$

$$= 1 + \frac{4}{7} = \frac{11}{7}.$$

4. $$\frac{8.73 \times 8.73 \times 8.73 + 4.27 \times 4.27 \times 4.27}{8.73 \times 8.73 - 8.73 \times 4.27 + 4.27 \times 4.27}$$

Putting a = 8.73 and b = 4.27, the given expression becomes

$$\frac{a^3 + b^3}{a^2 - ab + b^2} = \frac{(a + b)(a^2 - ab + b^2)}{(a^2 - ab + b^2)}$$

$$= a + b$$

Substituting the values of a and b, we get

$$8.73 + 4.27 = 13.$$

chapter 52

LOGARITHMS

DEFINITION.

Let N, a being any two positive real numbers and for some real 'x' if $N = a^x$, then x is called logarithm of 'N' to the base 'a' and is written as $\log_a N = x$

(or)

Logarithm of a number to the given base is index or power to which the base should be raised to get the given number.

$$\log_a N = x$$

$$\Rightarrow \quad N = a^x$$

log is abbrevation of the word 'logarithm'.

Note : Logarithms are defined only for positive real numbers.

- $a = a^1 \Rightarrow \log_a a = 1$

  i.e. if logarithm of any number and its base are equal, then its value is '1'.

- $1 = a \Rightarrow \log_a 1 = 0$

© i.e. logarithm of '1' to any base is 'zero',

FORMULAE

- **Product Formula** : $\log_a mn = \log_a m + \log_a n$
- **Quotient Formula** : $\log_a \left(\frac{m}{n}\right) = \log_a m - \log_a n$
- **Power Formula** : $\log_a m^n = n \log_a m$

- Base change formula : $\log_b a = \log_c a . \log_b c = \dfrac{\log_c a}{\log_c b} = \dfrac{\log a}{\log b}$
- $\log_a a^m = m \log_a a = m$
- $\log_b a = \dfrac{\log a}{\log b}$ (to any base)
- $\log_b a = \dfrac{1}{\log_a b}, \quad \Rightarrow \quad \log_b a . \log_a b = 1.$
- $\log_b a^{m/n} = \dfrac{m}{n} \log_b a.$
- $\log_b a . \log_c b . \log_a c = 1.$
- $\log_b a^m = m \log_b a.$
- $\log_b a^{1/n} = \dfrac{1}{n} \log_b a.$
- $a^{\log b} = b^{\log a}$
- $\log_a m = \log_a n$

  $\Rightarrow \quad m = n.$
- $\log_a m = \log_b m$

  $\Rightarrow \quad a = b.$

TYPE OF LOGARITHMS

1. **Natural or Napier logarithms.**
   The logarithms with base 'e' (e = 2.718) are called natural logarithms.

   e.g. $\log_e x$, $\log_e 25$ etc.
2. **Common or Briggs logarithms.**
   The logarithm with base '10' are called common logarithm.

   e.g. $\log_{10} x$, $\log_{10} 75$, etc.

In a logarithmic expression when the base is not mentioned, it is taken as 10 (common logarithms)

e.g. log 5 means $\log 10^5$.

CHARACTERISTIC AND MANTISSA

Consider $\log_{10} 10 = 1$, $\log_{10} 100 = 2$, $\log_{10} 1000 = 3$

Hence logarithm of a two digit number above 10 will be 1 + m, where m will be a decimal.

Similarly, logarithm of a 3 digit number above 100 will be 2 + m, where m will be a decimal

Again, $\log_{10} 0.1 = -1$, $\log_{10} 0.01 = -2$; $\log_{10} 0.001 = -3$.

Hence logarithm of a decimal number between 1 and 0.1 will be –1 + m, where m will be a decimal.

Logarithm of a decimal between 0.1 and 0.01 will be –2 + m, where m will be a decimal.

Similarly logarithm of a decimal between 0.01 and 0.001 will be –3 + m and so on.

The integral part of a logarithm is called **characteristic** and decimal part is called **mantissa.**

PROPERTIES OF LOGARTHM

1. Characteristic of the logarithm of any number greater than 1 will be less than number of digits in the 'Integral part of the number'.
2. Characteristic of the logarithm of a number less than one is negative and is one more than the number of zeros to the right of the decimal point in the number.
3. Since a negative number can never be expressed as the power of 10, mantissa should always be kept positive. Hence, whenever characteristic is negative, minus sign is placed above the characteristic and not to its left to show that the mantissa is always positive.
4. Mantissa of the logarithm of all the numbers having same digits in the same order will be the same, irrespective of the position of the decimal point.

$$\begin{aligned}\log 3846 &= \log (3.846 \times 10^3) \\ &= \log 3.845 + 3 \log 10 \\ &= m + 8, \text{ where } m = \log 3.846\end{aligned}$$

$$\begin{aligned}
\log 3.846 &= \log(3.846 \times 10\ ) \\
&= \log 3.846 \times 0 \\
&= \text{m} \\
\log 384.6 &= \log(3.846 \times 10^2) \\
&= \log 3.846 + 2 \log 10 \\
&= \text{m} + 2 \\
\log 0.03846 &= \log(3.846 \times 10^{-2}) \\
&= \log 3.846 + (-2 \log 10) \\
&= \text{m} + (-2) \\
\log 0.0003846 &= \log(3.846 \times 10^{-4}) \\
&= \log 3.846 + (-4) \\
&= \text{m} + (-4).
\end{aligned}$$

Use of Logarithmic Tables

1. The tables used in schools are four figure tables. These enable to find mantissa for the logarithm of numbers with four significant digits. All the mantissa are given correct to four decimal places.
2. Decimal points are omitted from the table to make it less crowded.
3. Always remember to place the decimal point before the mantissa.
4. Mantissa for the logarithm of 10, 100 and 1000 are same as for 1; similarly for 20, 200, 2000; 30, 300, 3000 etc.
5. In order to find the mantissa, we ignore decimal point in the number if any and consider only significant figures.

ANTILOGARITHM.

If $\log_x a = b$, then b is the antilogarithm of a to the base x.

Finding Antilogarithm.

1. If characteristic is 1, then place decimal after two digits from the left.
2. If characteristic is 2, then place decimal after three digits from the left.

3. If characteristic is 3, then place decimal after four digits from the left.
4. If characteristic is 4, then place decimal after five digits from the left (fifth digit will be zero).
5. If characterisitc is $\bar{1}$, then place decimal point and write all the digits of the antilog.
6. If characteristic is $\bar{2}$, then place decimal point and write the zero and then write all the digits of the antilog.

www.ingramcontent.com/pod-product-compliance
Ingram Content Group UK Ltd.
Pitfield, Milton Keynes, MK11 3LW, UK
UKHW021932200726
13853UKWH00010B/445